SHOTS ON THE BRIDGE

SHOTS ON
THE BRIDGE

POLICE VIOLENCE AND COVER-UP
IN THE WAKE OF KATRINA

Ronnie Greene

BEACON PRESS
Boston

BEACON PRESS
Boston, Massachusetts
www.beacon.org

Beacon Press books
are published under the auspices of
the Unitarian Universalist Association of Congregations.

18 17 16 15   8 7 6 5 4 3 2 1

This book is printed on acid-free paper that meets the uncoated paper
ANSI/NISO specifications for permanence as revised in 1992.

Text design and composition by Kim Arney

Library of Congress Cataloging-in-Publication Data
Greene, Ronnie.
    Shots on the bridge : police violence and cover-up in the wake of Katrina /
Ronnie Greene.
        pages   cm
    Includes bibliographical references.
    ISBN 978-0-8070-3350-0 (hardback)
    ISBN 978-0-8070-3351-7 (ebook)
1. Police brutality—Louisiana—New Orleans. 2. Racial profiling in law
enforcement—Louisiana—New Orleans. 3. Minorities—Civil rights—
Louisiana—New Orleans. 4. Hurricane Katrina, 2005. I. Title.
    HV8141.G74 2015
    364.1'32—dc23
                                                            2015004201

*To the families who suffered unspeakable
loss atop the Danziger Bridge, September 4, 2005,
and in honor of their quest for justice*

. . .

*And to Abby and Emma and Beth,
my sun and my moon and my soul*

CONTENTS

ON THE BRIDGE

IT IS 9:00 A.M. ON THE FIRST Sunday after Hurricane Katrina, September 4, 2005, and azure skies greet a city buried in water, panic, and death. New Orleans Police Department officers are gathered at their makeshift nerve center, the Crystal Palace banquet hall at Chef Menteur Highway and Read Boulevard, fueled up on Vienna sausages and bracing for another day of hell. The Crystal Palace *CP* insignia is scripted in cursive atop the building façade, an elegant touch capping a structure that rises on a crest set back from the highway, apart from used auto-parts stores, fast-food chicken drive-thrus, and quick cash payout hubs. The Palace features winding staircases, crystal chandeliers, a streaming water fountain, and a ballroom grand enough to hold seven hundred people. Its "romantic atmosphere" is perfect, its proprietors say, for the loveliest of weddings. Now it is ground zero for law enforcement in a swath of eastern New Orleans flooded in despair.

Six days earlier, Hurricane Katrina thrashed lower Louisiana in the eerie early hours of Monday morning August 29, an onslaught that began with menacing winds that held the city's inhabitants in lockdown, and then biblical floods. Fifty minutes after Katrina's landfall southeast of New Orleans, a levee collapse at the Industrial Canal sent oceans of water pouring into neighborhoods through a breach two football fields in width. In twenty-three minutes, water rose to fourteen feet in height. City 911 dispatchers, fielding six-hundred emergency pleas for help in those initial twenty-three minutes, began sobbing between calls, helpless to aid the voices on the other end of the line. Adults floated toddlers in plastic buckets, searching for safe harbor. Personal boats piled up against bridges like toys flung against a wall. Survivors climbed to the top of minivans and rode where the waters took them as frantic hangers-on raced to grab a piece of the roof as a post-hurricane lifeline. A police car was buried by the waters, the red lights on its roof barely visible. "This whole place is going under water!" a storm chaser uttered as he contrived to navigate his way out of New Orleans and its failed levees.

New Orleans was profoundly unprepared for Katrina. The city had no plan in place to aid the one hundred thousand souls who stayed behind as the hurricane advanced, and as the storm swallowed homes and buried victims, the police chain of command collapsed. "There were no rules in place other than 'Wait it out and, when the winds wind down, begin your patrols,'" said Eric Hessler, a former narcotics officer who returned days later to help search for bodies. "Basically they gave you nothing. You might see a case of bottled water. Other than that, you were on your own."

Each day after Katrina's landfall, the officers of the New Orleans Police Department ventured into the city's streets with two core missions: To save the residents who, by poor judgment or misfortune, made the choice to stay in their homes as the mayor practically begged his constituents to flee Hurricane Katrina's approach. And, to accost the opportunists and window smashers who turned the hurricane's misery into a wheel-of-fortune grab from stores stocked with goods on their shelves but no one at the cash register. Officers headed into New Orleans's streets prepared for combat, occasionally passing dead bodies floating face down, and on high alert for the desperate or the deranged. Some officers toted their own AK-47s, keeping their assault rifles wedged in the front seat beside them as they navigated the streets in vast rental trucks commandeered after Katrina. Like the rest of New Orleans, many officers were prisoners of the hurricane's wake—barely connected to the outside world, sustained by shared rations, and searching for sleep in the pitch-dark nights.

In this new world, the Crystal Palace became the department's command center for a pocket of east New Orleans that instantly felt like a war zone. The Palace stood on the highest ground in that section of the city, making it a home port for police. Officers slept on its carpeted and gleaming floors, on chairs, on any space they could find each night. In the morning, they gathered underneath the chandeliers and staircases to plot their day's patrols.

This Sunday morning, the sun announcing itself overhead, the officers await their command.

One, Robert Faulcon Jr., at forty-one, is older than most, and a black former military man and son of a minister who sent his pregnant fiancée away to higher ground as he stayed behind to report for duty. Before this day, he had never fired his police firearm while on patrol. Another officer, pale skinned, black haired, had beat back a second degree murder charge three years earlier in the shooting death of a black man—and then, like his father before him, Sergeant Kenneth Bowen was a police officer by day and law school student at night. Another young white officer sent his wife and four children to Houston before Katrina's arrival, and then headed into the New Orleans streets each day with his thirty-inch personal assault rifle tucked between the two front seats. Discharged early from the marines, Officer Michael Hunter had twice been suspended by a New Orleans police force noted for leniency when investigating its own.

Over the years, the NOPD had generated a lengthy rap sheet. In the 1990s, one burly black officer, Len Davis, nicknamed Robocop in the housing projects, ran a business protecting cocaine dealers while donning the badge. He also amassed a log of abuse complaints so thick local attorneys likened it to a phone book. Most times, the department and district attorney turned the other way—until Robocop, enraged that a young black mother filed an abuse complaint against him, ordered a hit man to kill her. Robocop was a symbol of the NOPD at its most severe, but the department's wayward ways were not limited to one outlaw with a badge.

In 1995 a black female officer and her teenage accomplice took three lives in an armed holdup at a Vietnamese restaurant where she had worked security, killing a white off-duty officer and two children of the proprietors of the Kim Anh restaurant. After the melee, the officer dropped her partner off, heard the 911 call about the shooting, and returned to Kim Anh in uniform. A restaurant worker, cowering for safety in a walk-in cooler during the bloodshed, pointed at Antoinette Frank, the twenty-three-year-old officer. Hired at the NOPD despite scoring low on her psychological exam, Frank today sits on death row.

Fifteen years earlier police found one of their own, a young white officer, dead aside a ditch in the city neighborhood of Algiers, a bullet in his neck. Soon, scores of young black men were whisked into police headquarters, some at gunpoint, where they suffered strong-arm interrogation until police got what they sought: names. Within five days, four black residents were killed by police fire, including a twenty-six-year-old woman, riddled with bullets as she lay naked in her bathtub. The force said it fought fire with fire, killing those responsible for the officer's death. Then a black officer turned and unmasked the lies. The victims were unarmed. Activists launched marches at city hall, yet convicting police in their hometown of New Orleans would be no easy task. A state grand jury refused to indict officers in the so-called Algiers 7 case. A federal grand jury did return an indictment: not for the deaths but for the roughhouse treatment of witnesses that violated their civil rights. When officers were finally put on trial, it was in Dallas, not New Orleans. Three white officers went to prison.

The ghosts of Algiers 7 and Robocop haunt the city still.

New Orleans Police Department officers continue to aim their muscle, and fire their weapons, at black targets in numbers out of context even for a city with a majority black population. "If you are a black teenager and grew up in New Orleans, I guarantee you have had a bad incident with the police," an Orleans Parish judge acknowledged to the US Department of Justice. Each time a city officer fired a weapon in a seventeen-month period from 2009 to 2010, the target was black. When the community complained about the police use of force, the department most always closed ranks. The NOPD did not find that a single officer-involved shooting so much as violated departmental policy in at least six years, a 2011 Justice Department civil rights review found. "Even the most serious uses of force, such as officer-involved shootings and in-custody deaths, are investigated inadequately or not at all." Exploring abuses long after Robocop's horrors were supposed to have triggered change, the Justice Department report concluded, "NOPD's mishandling of officer-involved shooting investigations was so blatant and egregious that it appeared intentional in some respects."

Critics say the problems start at the top, at city hall. Three years before Katrina's arrival, a cable company executive with no political experience won the mayor's seat, defeating a former New Orleans police superintendent who came from Washington, DC, and had built a record of disciplining wayward officers and working with the FBI. New mayor Ray Nagin appointed an insider to run the force, a jovial commander known for befriending fellow officers. The FBI was no longer embedded within the department.

Months into this new administration the force had cheered when a judge tossed out the second degree murder charge against Kenneth

Bowen, one of the men now gathered for duty on this Sunday, the one soon to become a lawyer. Other officers huddled alongside him had developed their own logs of abuse complaints while serving a tough urban core with a murder rate at or near the top for the entire country. Like Robocop a decade before them, the officers were almost always cleared of wrongdoing. One heavy-eyed, broad-shouldered white sergeant awaiting his mission this Sunday had been the subject of seven unauthorized force and abuse complaints in a five-year stretch before Hurricane Katrina. Each time, internal police files show, the department cleared Sergeant Robert Gisevius Jr. "Exonerated," the police Public Integrity Bureau reports say. "Not sustained." Like many of his brethren, he had sent his family to safety as the killer hurricane approached. To the police brotherhood, the officers who stayed behind as Hurricane Katrina churned toward their city did so for all the right reasons: to put the safety of others above their own. They found themselves largely alone in the fight, the federal government barely visible, the state leadership ensconced in safe bunkers. "They didn't desert," said Paul Fleming Jr., a local lawyer. "They rescued people. They pulled people off of rooftops, pulled people out of their attics. . . . Some of these men were rescued themselves; one off his own rooftop. And right after that, they jump right in and they get to work. They do the best they could without adequate leadership, without adequate food, without adequate shelter, without adequate clothing, without adequate rest, without adequate supplies, and without adequate support."

This morning a mix of black and white officers stand ready at the Palace. In the days after the hurricane the Katrina police corps bonded deeply, their connection intensified by their experience of the storm, the chaos, and their survival. More than race, the men and women of the NOPD were tethered by the blue cloth of their police-issued uniforms. Five days earlier a black officer, turning out to quell looting at a Chevron gas station, took a bullet to the head as he began to pat down a group of men. The bond grows tighter. "It was just a horrible time where anything could happen," one veteran lieutenant said. Another officer said, "My self-preservation mode went *way* up."

Not every resident these officers encountered in the city's streets stayed back solely on blind faith. Some did so because they felt they had no choice but to hunker down, say their prayers, and brace for Katrina's advance.

The mother of one New Orleans family wouldn't flee the coming storm because she had just one van, but eleven family members needing a way out, all huddled in her apartment looking to her for answers. If they all could not go, Susan Bartholomew decided, they all would stay. She prayed her second-floor apartment, off the Interstate 10 service road near Walmart, would provide refuge.

In another corner of east New Orleans, two brothers of the long-established Madison family stayed behind because the younger brother, a forty-year-old with the mental development of a six-year-old, refused to leave his family dachshunds behind. The family always kept a close watch on Ronald Madison, a gentle figure who waved at passersby whether he knew them or not. Now his older brother Lance, a onetime football player who landed two NFL tryouts before settling into a job working for Federal Express at the airport, stayed back to watch over him, and the dogs, at his two-story New Orleans condo.

Katrina's wrath forced the Bartholomew and Madison families from their homes, the roiling waters chasing them to their respective rooftops, where they begged for a helicopter rescue that did not come. This Sunday, as police stand poised for duty at the Crystal Palace, the two families venture out into the morning glare. The Bartholomews and a teenage friend, James Brissette Jr., are headed toward a Winn-Dixie in search of medicine for a sick grandmother and cleaning supplies for their decrepit hotel rooms. On foot, the Madison brothers set out for their mother's home two miles away. They dream of hopping on bikes and pedaling as far from the misery as they can.

Each family will traverse the Danziger Bridge to reach their destination.

Named after a former lawyer for Governor Huey Long, the bridge stretches a mere seven-tenths of a mile and takes less than one minute to travel by car. The overpass rises just a breath and runs parallel, like a little brother, to the more expansive I-10. Going up, the eye scans billboards, looks down upon a body of water, the Industrial Canal, and over to the higher reaching I-10. The Danziger Bridge is largely forgettable, the kind of thruway residents pass hundreds or thousands of times in their lifetimes without much thought. The two families cross paths this morning without exchanging a word, stepping upon a bridge that rises from Chef Menteur Highway, the same road housing the makeshift police headquarters, a straight shot not five minutes away.

. . .

"ONE-O-EIGHT! OFFICER NEEDS ASSISTANCE!"

At the Crystal Palace, rage and fear suddenly mix like a bomb. Over the police radio, the 108 call registers. "Officer's life in danger! Shots being fired!"

Officers sprint to a behemoth Budget rental truck commandeered after the storm, pile in, and race to the Danziger Bridge, the scene of the reported shooting. They grip police issued Glocks and their own personal weaponry: AK-47s, pump-action shotguns, an M4 high-powered rifle. The truck driver, Michael Hunter, has his thirty-inch assault rifle at the ready. Kenneth Bowen sits beside him in the passenger seat, and nine other officers scramble to the cargo area in back, holding steady as the truck rumbles forth. The back doors swing open, allowing the officers in back to see the hurricane-ravaged buildings they pass, but not what's ahead. The officers barely speak, the truck's gears grinding over pavement as it speeds the 3.3 miles separating the Palace from the bridge, busting through intersections where lights don't work and spinning past Lucky's Lounge, Jack's Motel, and Dollar Store.

Steering with his right hand, the ex-marine leans out the window and fires a handgun with his left toward a pack of people he glimpses ahead, gathered at the foot of the bridge. The truck screeches to a halt, sending some in back tumbling over, and officers pour out. They say nothing. One, Anthony Villavaso II, rips nine shots from his AK-47. *Pop, pop, pop, pop, pop, pop, pop, pop, pop.* Officer Faulcon hits the ground, pumps his shotgun, then fires. He pumps again, then fires. He pumps a third time, and fires. And then a fourth pump, and fire. Police aim for backs, arms, necks, legs, feet, heads, and stomachs of two groups of people now diving over a concrete railing or scattering atop the bridge. One officer aims his pistol at the back of a slight figure sprinting away from the bridge, and pulls the trigger twice. Another points his rifle toward two men trying to race up and over the bridge for cover, and fires. The cacophony is so deafening the truck's driver has to flap his arms, using a command he learned in the marines. "Cease fire!"

When the shooting stops, seventeen-year-old James Brissette Jr. is dead, bullets riddling his nearly six-foot, 130-pound body from the heel of his foot to the top of his head. Susan Bartholomew is trying to crawl on the pavement, her right arm dangling by a thread. Her daughter's stomach is shredded by a bullet. Her husband's head is pierced by shrapnel. Her nephew Jose is shot in the neck, jaw, stomach, elbow, and hand. A paramedic arriving soon after says not to bother with him; the teen is too far gone. "Don't give up on me," Jose Holmes Jr. pleads. Ronald Madison is slumped over the pavement, the back of his white shirt turned red, with seven gunshot wounds in his back. As Madison wheezes his final breaths, federal authorities will later say, Hunter watches former supervisor Bowen storm to Madison, yell, "Is this one of them?" and stomp on his back, leaving a boot print upon the slight figure sprawled in pools of blood.

Like every one of the victims, he is black, and unarmed.

In just moments, before police gather a single piece of evidence or question a single potential witness, with blood and bodies splayed around them, the NOPD officers and brass standing atop the Danziger Bridge will decide that the people they just fired upon, two lying dead and four maimed, are criminals. A well-regarded white police lieutenant, his square jaw the visage of a tough cop, arrives at the bridge moments after the gunfire quells and takes in the scene. Lieutenant Michael Lohman sees no guns by the dead teen and wounded family on one side of the bridge. He sees no gun by the forty-year-old slumped over on the other side of the expanse. The cop's cop makes a choice. "I knew this was a bullshit story, but I went along with it," he will later admit. So did his colleagues, the men who shot at the people on the bridge and the supervisors who were supposed to ferret out the truth. In the coming days and months, police will plant a phony gun, invent witnesses, craft fictional reports, and launch a public relations campaign portraying the officers as heroes infused with bravery amid the horrors wrought by a hurricane. Behind the scenes, a racial divide is exposed within the ranks. When a group of white sergeants and lieutenant begin putting their tale on paper, they initially report that only the black officers struck the victims with bullets atop the Danziger Bridge, separating the white officers from the bloodshed. Another fiction.

For a decade the families of the victims will press for truth, pierce the police façade, and uncover the lies buried with their kin. Justice for these families will not come swiftly or kindly after the shots on the bridge.

PART I
THE KILLINGS

CHAPTER I

A FAMILY'S BOND,
A THREATENING STORM

WHEN THE BABY BOY entered the world in New Orleans, Louisiana, on the first of March in 1965, his parents, James and Fuki, knew instantly what they would name him. Ronald. He was the second son born to the couple with the given name Ronald Madison.

Ronald 1, which the earlier child was sometimes remembered as, had died at one month old from sudden infant death syndrome. Two years later, as the Madisons welcomed their next son on the first Monday in March, they honored the infant they had lost by naming the new baby Ronald Curtis Madison.

Many times over the decades the family would encounter loss, and rebirth, from a union cemented when James Madison, a lean US Army enlistee attired in a crisp military uniform, met the stunning young Fuki Tanaka while on a tour of duty in Japan. The soul mates wed in Nagoya, Japan, in 1952 and had their first child, Romell James Madison, that same year. James was next stationed in Colorado, but he and the family settled in southern Louisiana. Born in St. James Parish, an hour's drive west from New Orleans, James came home to raise his family in the Crescent City. Ten children were born to the black father and Japanese mother.

Ronald 1 was not the only child who died too young. Theodore—Teddy, the youngest—died at age seventeen in a car accident. One daughter, Barbara Madison Woodfork, suffered from leukemia and died at twenty-one after falling into a coma while in college; she left behind a police-officer husband. Another daughter, Loretta, died from polio.

Two other Madison offspring were born with birth defects that left them with the minds of children as they entered adulthood. The second Ronald Madison was one of these children, along with his younger brother, Raymond.

The surviving siblings took special care to watch over Ronald and Raymond, particularly after their father died in 2002 at age seventy-four. Even into adulthood, family members referred to them as "the boys." Ronald and Raymond lived with Fuki in the same house they grew up in, on Lafon Drive in the solidly working class Academy Park neighborhood of $100,000–$150,000 homes a little more than seven miles from the Superdome downtown.

With their father's passing and the other now-grown children raising families of their own, Ronald became man of the house. Raymond grew to tower over him in height and weight, but Ronald still fixed his younger brother's meals and delivered them to him. Ronald carefully sorted and delivered the household mail, and he paid faithful attention to Bobbi and Sushi, the family dachshunds, treating the dogs as if they were kin. "They slept in the room with him," said Romell Madison. "He took care of them, fed them, walked them. They were like younger siblings to him."

The family home is not far from Interstate 10, but a wide patch of green grass stretches about one-tenth of a mile between the main drive, Chef Menteur Highway, and the neighborhood. The subdivision is lined with one- and two-story homes, many well kept, some boarded up or choked with weeds. On summer days homeowners and workers tend to lawns. A few driveways house a car and a boat, and landscaping trucks occasionally rumble through. Next to the shrubs in front of one house on the Madisons' street, a placard reads "Thou Shalt Not Kill." Another lawn sign boasts "Academy Park Association presents the Home of the Month." The Madison home on Lafon Drive stands on a lot of 6,771 square feet, with front steps leading to a stout two-paneled dark wood door that opens into the handsome edifice. Inside these walls, Ronald Madison, an adult with the mental development of a six-year-old, spoke with a child's enthusiasm. Immersing himself in his circle of family and neighbors, Ronald walked the sidewalks shoeless in shorts, but clean-cut with neatly cropped hair and a gentle manner. When he wasn't walking his dogs up and down Lafon Drive, his thin figure was sprinting, at full speed, to a neighbor's house to lend a hand. He met "Officer Friendly" at school, and when a police officer passed by, Ronald sent up a wave and flashed a grin. "We would always tell Ronald and Raymond if they ever needed help, they could always go to a police officer," said his sister Jacquelyn Madison Brown.

His siblings never let Ronald go off to the store alone and looked out as their adult brother rode his bicycle around the neighborhood. "Don't go down too far," his brothers and sisters would warn. And off Ronald would go, his family looking after him as he pedaled with a free-spiritedness. "He would maybe just ride his bike around the block. But he would always be monitored," said Jacquelyn. "We were very protective of him."

Ronald was not able to fluidly string full sentences together, but he spoke in a way his family always understood. When Fuki served a big family dinner, Ronald would greet his brothers and sisters at the door with a hug and declare, "She cooked gumbo! She cooked gumbo!" Guns, including toy ones, were forbidden inside the Madison home. "My mom would never buy any gun-type toys or any type of weapon toys," Jacquelyn said. The family knew city police officers through friendship and marriage, but Fuki never let the officers bring their guns into the house.

Though their father spent twenty-two years in the military, retiring as a Specialist 5, "my mom was the strict one, my mom would hold a grudge on you," Romell confided. James and Fuki preached to their children the importance of church and the power of education. "They wanted everyone to be something. Everybody wanted to make our parents feel proud," the oldest son said.

One daughter, Lorna, studied chemistry and then received a master's degree in mechanical engineering. Jacquelyn received a master's degree in nursing and rose to become an administrator in the dialysis unit at Tulane Medical Center in New Orleans. Son Lance Madison received a bachelor's degree in business and finance from Southern University in Baton Rouge and went on to pursue a career in professional football.

Romell became a pharmacist and then a dentist, rising into leadership roles in the community. He was active in the New Orleans Dental Association, served on the Louisiana State Board of Dentistry, and, in 2003, was appointed president of the National Dental Association. He opened a dental practice a little more than two miles from the family home, on Chef Menteur Highway at the foot of the Danziger Bridge, the expanse running less than one mile in length and shadowed by the taller I-10.

Family members would cross the bridge to reach Romell's New Orleans office, where he treated longtime customers in a brick building with black iron grates over its windows and Democratic political placards on display. Peering down through glasses low on his nose, Dr. Madison practiced in blue dentist's garb and a mesh medical mask around his neck. His office was airy and well kept, and his roster of patients included New Orleans police officers. The sign out front was adorned with an image of parents holding their hands over the head of a child.

The Madison family looked after Ronald and, likewise, encouraged him to excel in his schooling and enjoy his life. "After my dad passed we knew he was going to be our responsibility," said Romell. Ronald attended school for children with special needs, studying until the age of twenty-four, and graduating from Danneel Pre-Vocational School in New Orleans. He never married and rarely left the family cocoon. "He was just a soft-hearted young kid," his oldest brother said. "Always wanting to help people."

By 2005, at the age of forty, Ronald loved tuning into *The Little Rascals*, *The Cosby Show*, and *Diff'rent Strokes* on TV. He connected with music and movies. On birthdays his siblings bought him his favorite DVDs, which Ronald neatly stacked in his room; his brothers and sisters knew better than to disrupt his bedroom, Ronald's personal domain. Comedies and cartoons put Ronald Madison at ease. "He didn't like scary movies," Romell said. "He would be too scared to confront anybody. He'd run away from any trouble that came about."

THAT SUMMER OF 2005 trouble loomed for southern Louisiana and hundreds of thousands of homesteaders like the Madisons. Hurricane Katrina churned toward New Orleans, and residents listened as the mayor, the governor, and the president implored everyone to flee the city before Katrina arrived Monday morning, August 29. "We are facing the storm most of us have long feared," New Orleans mayor Ray Nagin, his face somber, said in ordering an evacuation of his city of nearly half a million residents. "This is a once-in-a-lifetime event." The Madisons were convinced. Convincing Ronald was another matter. He would not leave without Bobbi and Sushi. The family initially planned to leave the dogs behind at Lance's two-story New Orleans condo, providing them with plenty of food and water and hoping the storm would quickly pass. The family's planned destination in upstate Louisiana couldn't take the pets.

The siblings pressed. Ronald stood firm. He would not leave Bobbi and Sushi to fend for themselves. No, he told his mother, brothers, and sisters. He would not go. Romell found him crying about leaving the dogs alone.

The family relented to his wishes. Ronald would stay with Bobbi and Sushi in New Orleans. Lance had planned to caravan out with the family, but he would stay back with Ronald. "I was hoping they would be okay," Romell said. "I was a little upset they didn't leave."

Lance, who would turn forty-nine days after Katrina's expected arrival, was a onetime star wide receiver. He broke his leg in college but recovered well enough to land two professional free-agent contracts, with the Oakland Raiders and Kansas City Chiefs. The 1981 Chiefs roster listed wide receiver Lance Madison among the players, but on the injured reserve list. Injuries dogged his NFL hopes—Lance played with screws in his ankle—and he was released by both teams. Out of the game, he drove commercial trucks for FedEx from the New Orleans airport, a job he held for twenty-five years. Now, he would stay with his brother and the dachshunds. Compact, still nearly in football shape more than two decades after catching his last pass for Southern University, Lance Madison exuded a serious, waste-no-time attitude. He always treated Ronald more as a son than a sibling and still called him "my little brother."

As the rest of the family, including mother Fuki and brother Raymond, escaped their hometown city near the Gulf Coast, Ronald and Lance waited inside big brother's two-story wood and brick condo. Hurricane Katrina was coming.

CHAPTER 2

A MOTHER'S LAST CHANCE

IN LATE AUGUST 2005, with Hurricane Katrina propelling toward southern Louisiana, Sherrel Johnson checked in on her son, seventeen-year-old James Brissette Jr. Her thoughts reached back to when JJ resided in her belly. "I talked to him before he was even born," she said years later. "I told him how much I loved him and, 'Oh, I can't wait for you to be born!'"

Sherrel's first two children encountered hardships that would test her strength and faith. Her firstborn, Robert, known to everyone as Yogi, had toppled down the stairs at age two and suffered permanent brain damage. As he grew older, his mind grew younger. Yogi used fewer and smaller words as he developed—"mom, baby, eat"—and he lost any sense of danger. When he was ten, Sherrel placed him in a home for developmentally disabled children. Home on weekends, Yogi savored Popeye's chicken, spins on his three-wheel bike, and watching football. He was an athlete himself, competing in the Special Olympics and once winning the fifty-yard dash. At twenty-one, Yogi graduated from special schooling, and his mother can still picture him donning his cap and gown. Yet his disability followed him through his life. "I had a thirty-five-year-old who was a two-year-old," Sherrel said. "He did not know danger. He was a baby." Then in November 2004 a brain aneurysm burst, shutting down his body and leaving him in a coma. "Tubes were running all in and out of my child," his mother lamented. He died after nine days.

Sherrel's daughter, Andrea, born after Robert, was diagnosed with cerebral palsy and underwent several rounds of surgery as a child. She walked with a walker and a limp, but was determined to surmount obstacles and developed a focused intensity. As a child, Andrea didn't play with dolls and refused to be defined by the disability. A grade school teacher

7

once suggested she enroll in a class for children with special needs. "I don't belong in here," Andrea announced. "My legs may not work, but there's nothing wrong with my mind."

James "JJ" Brissette Jr., having a different father than his siblings, arrived more than a decade after Yogi and Andrea in November 1987, and Sherrel knew he would be her last child. At thirty-seven years old, her son was delivered by C-section. "I couldn't wait for him to get here. I had the stroller, the walker, and the high chair," she said. "I did everything I could to protect my unborn child."

With James "I prayed a little extra," she said. "This was my last chance, my very last chance to do this."

Andrea was fifteen years old when JJ was born, and she pampered the new child in the house. "He was my baby," Andrea said. "I helped my mom take care of him." It was as if JJ had two moms, and both spoiled him. When he opened his first e-mail account years later, he used the name "spoiledrotten." Sherrel raised him in her home in the Eighth Ward of New Orleans, that narrow stretch of the city bordered by the Mississippi River to the south, Lake Pontchartrain to the north, and the Ninth Ward to the east.

The child could charm. Seeing his mother mopping one day, three-year-old JJ pulled out a box of Spic and Span and dumped the entire contents on the floor. "I'm here to help!" he said. Catching his mother's stern gaze, JJ retreated to his bedroom and returned with all his toys gathered in his arms. "I need to be punished," he said, handing the toys over. Sherrel and Andrea, who would later earn a master's degree in organizational management, marry a city of New Orleans police officer, and raise her own family, busted out in laughter.

Now, fourteen years later, JJ had grown almost six feet tall and stick thin, no more than 130 pounds, and wearing glasses that were goggle thick. He loved to sleep, sometimes with his glasses still on his face, and was glued to books and the Discovery Channel, though he also loved *The Simpsons*. He attended a Gospel Baptist church with his sister and mom, who worked at a nursing home. He never played with guns—his mother forbade even toy guns in the house, just as the Madison family had—and wasn't much for sports. JJ's friends called him a nerd. Still, this nerd pictured himself being delivered in a limo to his prom the next year. "He said,

'I'm going to wear one of those white coats and tall hats,'" Sherrel said. "He wanted to drive in a stretch limousine."

JJ had just started calling girls on the phone and going on dates to the movies. He told his mom he hungered for the day he would flash his first car keys, dreamed of attending culinary school, and planned to become a chef.

This day Sherrel put those glimpses to the future aside and checked again the weather report. The warnings about Katrina had become dire, with the entire city ordered to evacuate. Sherrel had heard the warnings before and knew hurricanes didn't always arrive as promised. She thought of her job at the nursing home and began packing up the house. She'd stay back, keep working, and sleep over at a family friend's house on higher ground, on Burgundy Street in the city's Lower Ninth Ward.

Daughter Andrea Celestine and her two children had already fled up-state to Baton Rouge, as her police-officer husband, Lawrence Celestine, stayed behind to report for duty. Thousands of cars choked the highways out of New Orleans. With the evacuation deadline hovering, Sherrel told JJ he should leave with his daddy. JJ rang his father and learned that his dad was already on his way out of the city.

"Daddy, you going to come back?" he asked.

"Traffic is too heavy," James Brissette Sr. replied. "We can't turn around."

Hurricane Katrina kept on track toward New Orleans. JJ and Sherrel would make do.

CHAPTER 3

ELEVEN PEOPLE, ONE VAN, A SECOND-FLOOR APARTMENT

ONE OF JJ'S FRIENDS was Jose Holmes Jr., a nineteen-year-old who was keen on the piano, deft with a left-handed layup, and at ease hanging with "the nerd." With Katrina coming, Jose turned out to the second floor apartment of his aunt, Susan Bartholomew, in the Walnut Square apartment complex, just off the I-10 service road near Walmart. Susan, thirty-eight, gathered her immediate family and the larger clan that always seemed to flock to her in stormy weather. Her apartment often served as a harbor against the hurricanes and tropical storms that drenched New Orleans.

At five feet one, Susan is slight and delicately built like everyone in her family. Her husband—forty-four-year-old Big Leonard III—stands all of five feet four. Little Leonard IV, fourteen, weighed eighty-five pounds at the time and, with his hair braided, was regularly mistaken for a girl. Lesha, the oldest daughter, was seventeen and an inch shorter than her mother, and Brandon, the baby, was eight. Raised in the Ninth Ward, Susan had attended Joseph S. Clark High School and earned money selling Christian products from the family's residence. Her husband worked for years at the city's Sewerage and Water Board.

Katrina threatened to be different, a hurricane that could flood the city and kill the stragglers. Susan knew they should all flee, but the math was against it.

That August day the group included her mother, Augustine Green, a diabetic, and her nephew Jose, plus Jose's two sisters and another nephew. The family was close. Augustine had practically raised Jose, and the teen was like a big brother to Little Leonard. The boys were constantly hooked up to the PlayStation or off drawing together.

Eleven people gathered in the apartment, but the only vehicle was Susan's van, and everyone wouldn't fit. If they couldn't flee together, Susan Bartholomew decided, they would stay together. She prayed her second-floor perch would spare the family from the hardship of a hurricane.

Her decision made, Susan delivered an edict. The children, including nephews and nieces as well as her own children Lesha, Little Leonard, and Brandon, could not venture off unless Susan or Big Leonard went with them. "None of the group was allowed to go out alone," Susan said. "No one."

The children knew to obey Susan. "She's the boss," Jose said.

CHAPTER 4

AN OFFICER,
A BABY DUE, A CHOICE

NEW ORLEANS POLICE OFFICER Robert Faulcon Jr. stood aside fiancée Stacey Scineaux, nine months pregnant with their first child, at police headquarters that summer evening in August 2005. The officer and medical assistant planned to marry after the New Year, but with both the hurricane and the baby coming, Stacey was under orders to evacuate. Faulcon kissed Stacey good-bye, then handed her the keys to his car, a roomier, newer car, than hers, and took her keys in return. Stacey and her two children from a previous marriage departed for higher, drier ground upstate in Baton Rouge. Faulcon stayed behind. "I'll see you after the storm," he said.

The officer could have gone to his boss and asked to leave town. After all, his first child was due to arrive within days. But Faulcon felt the call to duty. He hoped the storm would pass quickly enough for him to join Stacey as doctors induced labor. "I assumed that we were just going to have a little flooding, and then I was going to meet her the next day at the hospital so I could be there for the birth of my son," he later explained.

One day years later, a lawyer would ask Faulcon about that choice. "Well, why didn't you go . . . and say, 'Captain, I've got a nine-month pregnant wife. They want to induce labor. They just told her to evacuate. May I be excused to go with my wife, who needs me?'"

"Well, it was my duty to report," the officer replied.

Faulcon was seemingly wired for service. Born in Brooklyn, New York, and attending high school in North Carolina, he never stirred enough trouble for his minister father to be called to the principal's office, despite the challenges facing an African American child growing up in the South. His mother was a schoolteacher and bank teller, and his brother would, like his father, become a Baptist minister. After high school, Robert Faulcon enlisted in the US Army for four years, jumping out of airplanes for the 101st Airborne in Fort Campbell, Kentucky. After a brief stint working in a family business in Detroit, he enlisted in the US Navy. He studied to become a legalman—akin to a military paralegal—and graduated from legalman school in Newport, Rhode Island. He spent four years in this wing of the military, just as he had in the army. The service fit his profile: serious, religious, with the discipline and taut physique of a military man.

Out of the service, Faulcon turned to a career in corrections and police work, working through a series of jobs before landing as an officer with the New Orleans Police Department. He joined the Orleans Parish Sheriff's Office as a correctional officer and, later, a bailiff. Next, he signed up with the NOPD, graduating from the academy in 2001 and taking SWAT training. Faulcon was trained in firing twelve-gauge pump-action shotguns and firearms.

As a trainee, he took part in paint-ball exercises, where officers are set in simulated life-threatening situations and can shoot to "kill"—using paint, not bullets. In his first few years on the force, Faulcon attended funerals of three comrades who had taken part in the paint-ball training with him.

"With the scenarios that we went through in the academy using paint ball guns, even if you get shot, if you make a mistake, you get—you know, you're still in a safe environment," he would one day testify. "Everything is going to be all right, you're going to go home at the end of the day. But a paint ball scenario in the academy does not compare to a real-life situation where at that fraction of a second you have to decide whether you're going to live or die. I mean, the fear that you have in that split second, there's just no words to describe it."

As a patrolman, he was subject of unauthorized force complaints in 2002, 2003, and 2005, the last coming a little more than six months before the hurricane's march toward New Orleans. "Complainant claims officer struck him," NOPD files say. Another case that February alleged he verbally threatened a citizen. Each time, the department ruled these allegations were without merit, police files show. The department did suspend Faulcon for three days in 2003 for lack of truthfulness.

But he also drew praise for diligence and calm. After a suspect taunted a mail carrier at gunpoint in June 2003, twice pulling the trigger but not firing the gun, Faulcon and a sergeant tracked the criminal to his house that evening and cornered him in a bedroom. The gunman pulled out his weapon and aimed it at the officers. Faulcon and the sergeant talked him down, and the man dropped his firearm. As he was escorted outside, the gunman became violent. Faulcon helped subdue him, made the arrest, and earned a commendation. He never fired his weapon that day, or at any other time on the force. Five months earlier, supervisors had nominated Faulcon as Officer of the Month, citing his flurry of police activity and calling him "a terrific addition to this platoon, always willing to accept any assignments required of him."

Now, two years later, with the hurricane charting a path toward New Orleans and his pregnant fiancée sent out of harm's way upstate, Faulcon, age forty-one, was ready to patrol. A National Weather Service bulletin predicted devastating damage, prompting police bosses to tell the troops to seek higher ground that Sunday evening, August 28, and leading authorities to open the Louisiana Superdome as a refuge of last resort.

Faulcon and a partner, Marchant Paxton, pulled into the Comfort Suites hotel off the I-10 service road. They got the last room available.

CHAPTER 5

A CITY UNDER WATER

Survivors Cling to Life,
Police Lose Their Grip

AT TEN MINUTES AFTER five on Monday morning, August 29, 2005, Hurricane Katrina made its second landfall in southern Louisiana, its winds tearing off chunks of buildings downtown, ripping open roofs atop homes fanning out of the city, and shattering any sense of calm the storm skeptics had held onto. Its winds and rains ruptured New Orleans with the force of a tornado strike, sending slabs of aluminum and shrapnel hurtling through the air as residents cowered inside their homes.

By midmorning, hundreds of thousands of southern Louisianans were trapped inside four walls with no way out, the power dead, the waters rising in a city standing some ten feet below sea level in some sections and protected by aged, fragile levees.

Then the levees broke.

A two-hundred-yard breach from the Industrial Canal gushed oceans into the Lower Ninth Ward, the water pouring from a canal that connects the Mississippi River to Lake Pontchartrain, and separates New Orleans East from the rest of the city. "It went from nothing to as high as fourteen feet within twenty-three minutes," the deputy police superintendent reported; the force and rescue workers were trapped by winds ripping at one hundred miles per hour. By eight that morning, water was rising on both sides of the Industrial Canal. Fourteen minutes later, the National Weather Service issued a flash-flood warning, predicting up to eight feet of water. "Move to higher ground *immediately*," the experts urged. More levees broke, imperiling those who were forced to bet against nature.

By nine, the Lower Ninth Ward was engulfed in eight feet of murky, swirling water, and in some areas the waters rose higher. From the sky over New Orleans and surrounding parishes, some rooftops could not be seen at all. They had vanished, swallowed by the floodwaters.

That afternoon, as the depth of disaster was beginning to take shape for the world outside New Orleans, the city's Homeland Security director told reporters that untold numbers were dead in those waters or inside homes turned death caves. "Everybody who had a way or wanted to get out of the way of this storm was able to," the director said. "For some that didn't, it was their last night on this earth."

Nearly one hundred thousand city residents could not or would not flee New Orleans. For many, escaping to a hotel was financially out of reach, a sudden one-thousand-dollar expense to evacuate, lodge, and feed a family for days. "For the poor of neighborhoods like the Lower Ninth Ward, one of the city's lowest-lying areas, this was an impossible sum, though they had an alternative in the Superdome, the city's 'refuge of last resort,'" a federal report noted. Yet the city had no plan to evacuate the stragglers, and by the time of Katrina's landfall, the Louisiana Transportation Department had taken no concrete action. Federal officials had no plan in place.

"FEMA was unprepared for a catastrophic event of the scale of Katrina," the federal report *Hurricane Katrina: A Nation Still Unprepared* would conclude. "Preparations that were adequate in the past and that might have been sufficient had Katrina been a 'typical' hurricane proved to be grievously inadequate."

The report, issued by the US Senate's Committee on Homeland Security and Governmental Affairs, cited "a failure to heed the warnings of a looming catastrophe during the weekend preceding the storm, and a failure on the day of landfall to recognize that the worst predictions had come true."

The parish director of Homeland Security and Emergency Preparedness was among those trapped and powerless, operating from a makeshift response center with the aid of his wife and secretary. "I am in the attic, I have my child with me in my attic, I need somebody to come get me out," a typical caller pleaded. "And they are crying. Let me tell you, it got to the point where my secretary and wife couldn't answer the phones anymore," he said. "We knew that the majority of these people we are talking to now were going to die and we were the last people they were talking to. There was nothing we could do. Nothing physically possible for us to do."

Katrina obliterated three hundred thousand homes, ten times the number lost in Hurricane Andrew in 1992, the last most catastrophic storm to strike the United States.

"It was the most destructive natural disaster in American history, laying waste to 90,000 square miles of land, an area the size of the United Kingdom. In Mississippi, the storm surge obliterated coastal communities and left thousands destitute. New Orleans was overwhelmed by flooding. All told, more than 1,500 people died. Along the Gulf Coast, tens of thousands suffered without basic essentials for almost a week," said the Katrina Senate report.

The Madison brothers, the Bartholomew family, JJ Brissette, and his mother, Sherrel Johnson, and officer Robert Faulcon Jr. all now faced the daunting task of finding their way out.

THE MADISON BROTHERS: A SWIM TO SURVIVAL

Before he fell asleep on the eve of Katrina, Lance Madison parked his van under the carport behind his condo in case he, Ronald, and the dogs needed to make a hasty escape. When Ronald shook him from sleep several hours later—yelling, "Water's in the house!"—the van was submerged. Lance stepped from his second floor bedroom to encounter six to eight feet of water filling the ground floor. Water was chasing them.

Back on the second floor, Lance punched through a ventilator, climbed into the attic and, with his brother and their dogs, ascended to the rooftop. Overlooking a city buried by water, they waved toward the sky, desperate for a helicopter to swoop down and lift them to safety. None came.

Without power or phones, the brothers lost contact with the outside world. With a clear view of the devastation below, they didn't need anyone to tell them how dire conditions had become.

The brothers kept waving when, finally, Ronald began sobbing. Lance stepped toward him. "He was very frightened, scared. I tried to calm him down," Lance said later. "We prayed. And I just tried to talk to him and keep him comforted."

A day later, Tuesday, August 30, they fled the rooftop. With little food and water, the brothers agreed to make their way from Lance's wood and brick condo on Chimney Wood Lane to the dental office of their brother Romell at 4819 Chef Menteur Highway.

It took nearly five hours to traverse two miles, with Ronald and Lance wading and sometimes swimming through five feet of cloudy water and carcasses of dead animals. They journeyed through muck and a hardscrabble industrial area, passing a pizza takeout joint, a local po'boys haunt, auto shop, fire station, and strip club. Off to the right, the blue and yellow Bunny Bread sign greeted them like a cruel joke, the smiling bunny out of place. They reached their brother's dental office around noon. A big hole had been punched into the roof, the floors were covered with debris, and the office looked as if it had been broken into. But it was, relatively speaking, dry and secure. The brothers tidied it up. It was their temporary home, standing at the foot of the Danziger Bridge, and two miles from the family home on Lafon Drive.

Romell's office features an airy foyer and small patient rooms in back, offering ample space for Lance and Ronald to catch their breath and plot their next move. Vitally, it had a half-dozen five-gallon tanks of water. The brothers used the water to drink and bathe. They met other survivors at the Friendly Inn Motel just next door, and one family shared a meal with them. Like others now trapped by Katrina, they were desperate for food. The Winn-Dixie stood across the street from the dental office, and survivors were already depleting its supplies. One day Lance grabbed an armful of food from its shelves, making a note to remember how much he took (about fifty dollars' worth).

After spending two nights at the dental office, Lance prepared to return to the condo alone to rescue Bobbi and Sushi that Thursday, September 1, his forty-ninth birthday. "The water was still high, and Ronald was frightened," Lance later said. He locked the door behind him, telling his brother, "I'll be back with the dogs."

Lance made it back to his condo, swimming and wading once more. Bracing for a grueling return trip to the dental office, he found relief. An out-of-town sheriff's crew from Jefferson Parish downstate happened by in two boats and ferried him and the dogs close to the office. Lance thanked the officers and, with the dogs, made it back to Ronald. Little brother was overjoyed to reunite with Bobbi and Sushi, a momentary salve amid Katrina's torment.

In the days after the storm, residents reported hearing gunshots at night. All around the Madison brothers, homes and offices had been ransacked and stores had been looted. The air, it seemed, was filled with menace. Some survivors seized US Post Office trucks. Romell's office was dry, but, with electricity out, the air choked on itself. In the post-hurricane tropics, the brothers' refuge became oppressive. They were cut off from family. The phone lines were down. As their food and water supply dwindled over three more nights, Lance and Ronald Madison charted their next move.

On the morning of Sunday, September 4, 2005, the sun gleamed upon New Orleans. The brothers saw it as a sign. They ventured out once more, leaving the dachshunds with food and water. They would make their way to their mother Fuki's home, hop on bikes, and pedal as far as possible from the misery.

To reach 4833 Lafon Drive, they would first cross the Danziger Bridge, the seven-lane lift bridge a stone's throw away. Nearly three-quarters of a mile long, the Danziger Bridge connects with Chef Menteur Highway and runs east to west over the Industrial Canal. Danziger runs parallel to another well-traversed New Orleans bridge, the I-10 high rise, which spans nearly one mile.

In post-Katrina New Orleans, two miles seemed like two hundred.

SHERREL AND JJ: TOGETHER, THEN SEPARATED

With no ride out, JJ Brissette had stayed through the storm with his mom at the home of a schoolmate on Burgundy Street in the Ninth Ward. Filled with a teenager's curiosity, he ventured out from the house, each time a little farther, to take in the flooding with his own eyes. "Mama, you should see that water!" he reported after one trip into the city. "It's up to here on me," JJ said, pointing high on his wiry frame.

"JJ, stay out of that water," his mother implored. "I can't swim, and I'm not going to save you."

Not long after that interchange, JJ said good-bye and headed out once more. At dusk, Sherrel awaited his return, eyeing the front door. "I cannot go to sleep. I'm waiting for my son," Sherrel said. "He could come back at any moment." Days passed, but no JJ. Armed authorities began directing

Sherrel to evacuate, but she resisted, hoping the front door would spring open and her seventeen-year-old son would flash a mischievous smile, just as he had at age three after dousing her kitchen floor with all that Spic and Span.

Finally Sherrel knew she had to find the safety of higher ground. She departed in the back of a military truck. "When he brings his butt back here, hold him here!" she told authorities, thinking ahead to her reunion with JJ.

"That's the last I saw of my child," she said. "After he left that Tuesday, I never saw him no more."

BUNKERED IN SQUALOR

When the levees broke, the water flooded so high outside Susan Bartholomew's home it swallowed a fence around the apartment building, reaching higher than Susan's head. The water swirled higher, snaking its way into their apartment. The second floor no longer offered refuge.

Nephew Jose punched a hole in the top of the ceiling and climbed to the roof. From there, like the Madison brothers had, he feverishly waved for help. His pleas were not answered.

Soon, a savior arrived. A boat, navigated by NOPD officers, motored up outside their building and carried the group to drier ground along Chef Menteur Highway. The family had never been so relieved. Two of Jose's uncles worked for the New Orleans Police Department, and it felt as though family had come to the rescue.

Now on drier ground, they searched for a roof to shield them. At the first hotel they happened upon, shouting filled the air, leaving Susan uneasy. "You could hear them yelling out really loud," Susan said later. "There's no electricity, so the streets are dark, and you don't know what's going to happen next." Nephew Jose wasn't as taken aback. "I stay in the Ninth Ward and you hear a lot of gunshots and violence and stuff like that, so it kind of seemed normal to me," he said. Fearing the commotion would explode into gunfire, Susan Bartholomew looked for another hotel. The group settled at the Family Inn, just off the Danziger Bridge. It was a Katrina-soaked dump: no power, no water, filthy carpets, and toilets that wouldn't flush. It did offer a roof and adjoining rooms. They took it.

By now another person had joined the group, James Brissette Jr. JJ had crossed paths with his close friend Jose after he left his mom that Tuesday. Jose was out that afternoon with Susan and the family, when a voice shot out. "Jose! Jose!"

From a distance, Jose didn't initially make out who was calling his name, not recognizing JJ, who had recently gotten a new haircut. But then he knew. When JJ flashed every one of his teeth, Jose could tell how happy his friend was to see him. JJ told his buddy he too had been rescued in a boat, and asked if he could tag along. Inside the Family Inn a little beyond the Danziger Bridge, on the other side of the overpass from where the Madisons were staying, the Bartholomew family made room for one more.

They needed medicine. Susan's mother, a diabetic, had been scheduled for a hospital visit before the hurricane, but the procedure had to be cancelled because of Katrina. Inside the grimy hotel room, her feet began to swell, and she began to throw up. We need to get out, Susan said. We need medicine for Mom—Glucerna, a nutritional drink for diabetics—and cleaning supplies for the rooms. The Winn-Dixie, just over the bridge, was said to be open.

As the family set off for supplies that morning, they were joined by JJ. Thinking of his mom, James Brissette hoped to find the rescue boat and make his way back to check on her. He looked ahead with a teenager's optimism. "We were in a happy mood, making the best out of things, laughing and joking," Jose said.

AN OFFICER DOWN, A "KATRINA BROTHERHOOD"

On Tuesday, August 30, in the late afternoon a day after Katrina's flooding plunged New Orleans into historic despair, veteran officer Kevin Thomas and a partner, John Mitchell, saw several women looting a Chevron gas station at General De Gaulle Boulevard. They stopped the looters, took their names, and made them give back the beer.

As his partner checked inside, Thomas, a black officer wearing an NOPD baseball cap and police badge, stood outside. Just then, four men approached. Thomas stopped them and started a pat-down search. One man screamed obscenities, then pulled a .45 caliber pistol from his pocket and fired a bullet into Thomas's skull, sending the officer tumbling to the pavement in a pool of blood. Hearing the fire, Officer Mitchell managed to strike one of the fleeing men in his left shoulder and radioed for help as the criminals sprinted off.

Rushed to West Jefferson Medical Center in critical condition, Thomas survived, and a massive police search hunted down the culprits. The shooting, occurring in a city flooded with water and buried in lawlessness, put police on a red-alert edge. "We were scared," one NOPD sergeant later confided.

Some officers began sleeping with their side arms. The chain of command that ruled their lives had vanished. The police communication system collapsed with the storm, leaving officers to connect through handheld radios. "It was chaotic, overcrowded. People are talking on top of each other," a police lieutenant explained. "It was hard to get in and speak with the dispatcher because there was so much communication going on." When three officers became trapped in floodwaters, their radio batteries died, killing their connection with colleagues. "It was totally out of control for people used to being in control," said one lieutenant.

The chaos bonded the Katrina police corps in palpable ways. NOPD officers ventured out each day with two core missions: to save the stranded from the floodwaters, and to shut down the scofflaws ransacking the city.

Robert Faulcon Jr., now part of this core, knew Kevin Thomas as a friend and viewed the post-Katrina days as his brothers did. It was us against them. It was war.

Heeding a call to find higher ground, Faulcon spent his first days after Katrina at the Comfort Suites with his partner. The hotel charged them for the lodging, but the accommodations were bleakly spare. Faulcon arrived to a room without power and suffocatingly hot. The windows did not open, so Faulcon and his partner jimmied the air conditioning unit out of the wall to allow a whiff of air to circulate. He slept in the same police uniform he was wearing when he had kissed his fiancée good-bye.

After the levees broke, Faulcon peered from his third-floor hotel window and saw his police car submerged in water. His police service revolver, dunked in the water by accident, wouldn't fire. He was now, it seemed, a hostage to Katrina: no power, no food, little air, and no way to communicate as the sun set to stifling, eerie black nights.

"I saw the water get up to the—halfway up the wheel of the car, our police car, and then after I saw the police car being submerged in water, at that point, I knew we were in trouble. . . . The water continued to rise until it got to the roof of the houses," Faulcon explained later. "We didn't have any ventilation. We didn't have any food. We didn't have any plumbing. And basically at nighttime it was just hot, stifling, and just dark, black, pitch-black dark."

He didn't know it, but his son, Rashad, was born the day after Hurricane Katrina's arrival. With power dead, the officer had no way to connect with his family. Instead, thinking of his pregnant fiancée and absorbing his bludgeoned surroundings, he awaited his mission and sought his own survival.

Two days in, a police boat appeared outside his hotel. Faulcon and his partner, Paxton, waded into the water and climbed inside. "Somehow," Faulcon thought, "they found us."

The boat transported them to the Crystal Palace reception hall, at the intersection of Chef Menteur Highway and Read Boulevard. Faulcon's possessions comprised the clothes on his back: stinking, wet, and dirty. It would be days before a trip to Walmart brought fresh underwear and T-shirts. Some patrolmen later moved to a retirement home, evacuated after Katrina, where they slept at night and returned to the Crystal Palace in the morning. This banquet hall was now the police department's anchor in this corner of east New Orleans.

The Crystal Palace reception center stands back off Chef Menteur Highway, US 90, surrounded by palm trees and an expansive parking lot, with a soft peach exterior. Not far away: used auto-parts stores, a collision body shop, Popeye's and Church's Chicken, and Chef Cash Advance. Some homes rise in the vicinity, but the section is mostly industry. On one side of the road on a typical summer day without hurricanes, men sell whole watermelons from the back of a truck, a hand-lettered sign listing the price at six dollars. Across the street, a laborer grabs a respite under the shade of a tree. A few people walk here and there, but this is lower Louisiana, not New York City or Washington, DC, and, in normal times, it moves at its own pace. Louisianans will get there, but on their own terms. Right across from the Crystal Palace stands Capt. Sal's Seafood & Chicken, featuring po'boys and daiquiris. Lucky's Lounge is a mile and a half up the road.

It is a straight 3.3 mile drive, like a beeline, to the Danziger Bridge.

From this nerve center, with the hurricane forcefully reconfiguring the landscape, Faulcon joined other officers. "We immediately went into rescue mode."

Sometimes they traveled in boats, their weapons at their side, looking to rescue survivors or arrest looters. Other times they traveled passable streets in vast Budget rental trucks commandeered from a hardware store near the Winn-Dixie. Police sometimes stopped cars and trucks traveling through New Orleans. If the driver could not prove the car was his, officers assumed it was hot. They took the keys. "If we found a vehicle that we could get started, we pretty much used it," Officer Michael Hunter explained. Navigating a city ravaged by winds and water, Faulcon was stunned by what he saw. New Orleans was unlike anything he had witnessed in the US military.

Women, children, and the elderly were living on the I-10 service road. "They were just there. They had nowhere to go," he said. Faulcon and his colleagues pulled them in and took them to shelter, most often to the Superdome downtown. "We did that around the clock."

In his rescue missions, Faulcon and his partners sometimes passed dead bodies.

"It was pretty much like nothing existed. There was no life, I mean just—it was just nothing. It was just devastation," he said. New Orleans turned pitch dark at night, powerless and foreboding. As Faulcon retired to the Crystal Palace after another long day of rescue, he heard gunfire crackle the air and glimpsed signs of looting around him.

At the Palace, Faulcon was surrounded by his brethren, but the federal government was nowhere to be seen. He didn't notice any state officials, either. It was just the men and women of NOPD, trapped by the storm. He felt abandoned, betrayed. His partners were now his brothers, and the only ones he had. They sat around the Palace at night, sharing a meal of Vienna sausages and breathing heavily after another day.

The word spread that looters were shooting at Black Hawk rescue helicopters. Then the officers heard that a well-known colleague had taken his own life after the hurricane. With even the police communication system operating on life support, it was nearly impossible to separate fact from fiction. But as they set out into flooded streets and a powerless city, the officers expected the worst.

As he tried to find sleep, Faulcon's head spun.

"We just went through a major storm. I had nothing but the clothes on my back. I didn't know where my family was. My wife was nine months pregnant. My friend, Officer Thomas, was shot in the head across the river by looters," he said. "I was just trying to keep myself together mentally."

Days after the hurricane, Faulcon was able to connect with his parents by phone. I feel homeless, he told his father. "Leave the area," Robert Faulcon Sr. implored. Faulcon said many co-workers had already fled. He had taken an oath.

The officer awaited whatever the next day would bring.

CHAPTER 6

108

Officer in Distress,
a Race to the Bridge

BEFORE HURRICANE KATRINA, Detective Jennifer Dupree's job was investigating crimes against people, including shootings, robberies, and assaults, in Police District Three, an area covering the communities of Lakeview, Gentilly, and Westend and encompassing a cluster of colleges, including Dillard University and Southern University of New Orleans.

After Katrina, her job was rescuing people.

Early Sunday, September 4, she hopped in the back of a truck and headed toward District Seven, abutting the Third District and covering a wide swath of east New Orleans, on a rescue mission checking on family members of police staffers. The Danziger Bridge connects the two police districts; the west side of the bridge is part of District Three, and the east side marks the beginning of District Seven. Two trucks, driven by civilian volunteers, towed airboats that Dupree, other officers, a supervising lieutenant, and the volunteers would use that day to pluck survivors from their upper story windows and roofs.

Interstate 10 runs parallel to the Danziger Bridge, and this morning, the police and civilians took the I-10 to head into District Seven, the smaller expanse clearly visible off to their left as they drove east. As the truck rolled down the high-rise, Dupree spotted a pack of cars stopped at the foot of the I-10.

"Get down. They're shooting at us!" a man yelled as Dupree's truck pulled up, flagging them down from the roadway. "They're trying to take our boats!" Dressed in full police uniform, the man said he was from a sheriff's office upstate.

Dupree heard the popping of gunfire, jumped out of the back of the truck, and ran to the side of the I-10 facing away from the Danziger Bridge.

She looked down and saw four black males on the ground below the bridge. When someone yelled "Police!" two of the men looked up. One wore a red shirt, and the other had on a black shirt and carried a backpack. Both were armed. Dupree heard more gunfire and ducked for cover.

"Kick it in!" her supervisor ordered, and Dupree, a six-year NOPD veteran, did just that.

"One-o-eight!" she called into the police radio, kicking in the call for help. "Officer needs assistance. Officer's life in danger!"

The two men sprinted under the I-10, and Dupree lost sight of them. She repositioned herself on the other side of the I-10, now facing the Danziger, but still couldn't see them. As fellow officers scanned below, a man with a video camera, who happened to be atop the I-10 at that moment, turned to Dupree. "There they are," he said. Dupree looked down and re-spotted the men, a red shirt and a black shirt. They were running toward the Danziger Bridge. In between the two expanses, the men sprinted over ground covered with storm debris and cluttered with trailers and cars. Dupree followed them with her eyes, calling in updates over her handheld radio, as other officers took off in pursuit. "It became kind of chaotic at that point," she said.

Armed with a Glock .40 caliber pistol and her police-issued shotgun, Dupree strained to follow their path as the men ran past a pack of dogs, calling in more updates as fellow officers shared what they saw. "The guys with the red shirt and the black shirt, I specifically kept my eyes on them," she said. "I lose sight of them because they're running in between the trailers. So you would catch a glimpse of them, lose sight. I tried to give the locations where they were." She relayed that officers were running down toward the suspects, and kept repeating her description of the two men—one wearing a red T-shirt, the other a black shirt with a black book bag. Years later in court, Dupree reported that she never said the words "Officer down." Despite the gunfire, no officers had been struck.

Dupree—sturdily built, focused on her targets—held her shotgun at the ready, but did not fire. From day one in the academy, the rules were clear: fire with deadly force only when you face it yourself. With their backs to her, fading off into the distance, the gunmen were not a direct threat. "I was too far away," she said. Then she lost sight of them entirely.

At the Crystal Palace, the officers, gearing up for another day of duty, heard the call: 108. A comrade under fire. Sergeant Kenneth Bowen, among the first to hear the bulletin, rushed inside the Palace. "One-o-eight! Chef and Downman!" he screeched. Officers began sprinting toward a Budget truck parked outside.

"It's a call that you never want to hear," said Officer Faulcon. Though Dupree said she never broadcast that a colleague was down, officers racing to the scene assumed the worst, and feared what awaited them. Some believed a comrade, indeed, was down. Faulcon, for one, interpreted the dispatch as "an officer down, shots fired, 108, officer needs assistance, multiple armed subjects."

Faulcon hopped in the back of the boxy Budget truck, a white behemoth with dashes of color around its logo. Two officers drove up front, and nine crowded in the cargo area in back. With the truck's back doors ajar, the officers in back could see buildings getting smaller behind them. Faulcon was sandwiched between both veteran police sergeants and patrolmen relatively new to the force.

The officers barely spoke, the truck's gears grinding over pavement as it sped the three miles separating the Crystal Palace from the bridge. Faulcon gripped a twelve-gauge pump-action shotgun. In the days after Katrina, NOPD officers had been fired at, some hit, and Faulcon braced for a battle.

"I knew we were going into a bad situation because of the fact that it was a 108. And once we arrived, I just expected to be shot at because of the fact that the description that the officer gave when she said multiple armed subjects."

The shotgun wasn't his but borrowed from another black officer, Anthony Villavaso II, after his own weapon had been dunked in water. "Vil," as his partners called him, crouched near Faulcon with an AK-47. Vil's partner, a young black officer named Robert Barrios, toting a Remington shotgun and wearing a Philadelphia Eagles cap backward, sat in the back alongside other armed officers.

Michael Hunter, a twenty-eight-year-old white officer who had served a six-month stint in the US Marines at age nineteen, jumped in front and drove. Days earlier, Hunter bade farewell to his wife and four young children, who headed to Houston. He had his police-issued Glock .22 caliber handgun as well as his own AK-47, a thirty-inch military assault rifle, which he wedged between the two front seats in the Budget truck each time he headed into the city. As the officers sped to the bridge, Sergeant Bowen, the lean, steel-faced white officer who alerted his comrades to the 108 call, sat beside Hunter. A decade earlier, Bowen served in the Marine Corps Reserve, and mates said he embraced its motto and creed: *Semper Fidelis*, "always faithful," to God, corps, and country. Now, at age thirty-one, Bowen looked toward major life changes. His son was due to be born in four months. And, like his father, Kenny Bowen worked as an officer by day and studied law by night. Having graduated from Loyola University College of Law, he was due to secure his Louisiana State Bar license the next month.

Four years earlier Bowen had survived his own brush with the criminal justice system. Just before midnight on December 13, 2001, Bowen had shot to death a fleeing black man when the suspect turned and pointed a pistol over his shoulder, the officer stated. Bowen fired a single shot from his .40 caliber Glock, sending a bullet through Sylvester Scott's back shoulder and out his chest. Paramedics found Scott face down in an alley, in handcuffs, with a nine millimeter handgun and packets of pot nearby. The twenty-six-year-old was pronounced dead at Charity Hospital. Police said Bowen shot Scott, an ex-con, as they struggled, after a chase that began when Scott fled a bustling crowd outside a lounge as Bowen and a partner pulled up.

"NOPD killed my son," said a placard handed out at a community demonstration a week later. Friends of Scott said he put his hands up in surrender to the pursuing officers. The police "didn't say, 'Stop. Freeze. Get down. Nothing,'" one friend said.

The New Orleans Police Department cleared Bowen, by then a five-year veteran serving the Second District. "Exonerated," said the NOPD Public Integrity Bureau's case report. Prosecutors were not convinced, deeply questioning the police account and the finding of a gun near the dead man. They secured an indictment charging Bowen with second degree murder. "There's nothing on that gun that links Sylvester Scott to it," a district attorney prosecutor said. Prosecutors suspected police planted it.

In November 2002, an Orleans Parish Criminal District Court judge ruled that prosecutors failed to present evidence to support their case, putting too much weight on a single witness's testimony. The judge's ruling, finding no probable cause to prosecute Bowen, doomed the charges and cleared the officer. The police fraternity cheered the news. To the NOPD, the charges were an insult to those carrying a badge.

Now, fewer than three years after being cleared in Sylvester Scott's death, Bowen turned and asked for Hunter's AK-47. Bowen, once Hunter's supervisor, had his own police-issued Glock, but wanted the AK-47 instead. Hunter hesitated, but then relented. Robert Gisevius Jr., another white police sergeant in the truck who had been cleared of a string of abuse allegations, brought his own M4 high-powered assault rifle. He too preferred it over his police-issued handgun. Other officers gripped twelve-gauge shotguns, police-issued .40 caliber semiautomatics, and AK-47s.

They were armed for war.

TWO FAMILIES ON THE BRIDGE

With the Sunday weather greeting her like a reprieve, Susan Bartholomew headed out with a brood of six to buy Glucerna, the nutritional drink for diabetics, for her mother, who stayed behind at the Family Inn. She also needed cleaning supplies for the hotel rooms. Susan began walking to the Winn-Dixie, just over the bridge going west, along with her husband, their two oldest children, nephew Jose, and his friend JJ.

Susan wore a T-shirt, borrowed from JJ, and bright orange sweat pants. Leaving the hotel, she spotted a shopping cart in the road and began pushing it, planning to use it to hold the supplies she'd buy. Her children skipped and hopped in the fresh, freeing air. Jose challenged his buddy to a race. It was no contest. Jose beat him easily to the foot of the Danziger Bridge, with JJ stopping midrace to catch his breath. *Cigarettes,* Jose thought, *they're slowing that boy down.* Now ahead of the group, Jose had time to grab a seat on a rail dividing the bridge from a pedestrian walkway, lean over, and tie his shoes.

As he did, two men walked past him heading in the same direction, over the bridge going west. Lance and Ronald Madison. A full week since the family debate over whether to stay or flee, the brothers, now physically and psychologically exhausted by the storm, had stepped out in a search for escape: from the heat, the water, the hunger.

On foot earlier that Sunday, they had crossed the Danziger Bridge going east, passing St. Mary's Academy, a private Catholic school, and reached the subdivision where Ronald and their mother lived.

They could not get to the house through the still-flooded street. Nearly beaten, they turned around, now heading in the same direction as the Bartholomews. Along the way, Lance picked up a shovel and then saw a flat cart discarded from a Home Depot or Lowe's store. He put the shovel in the cart and began pushing it. "I brought the shovel to clean the debris that my brother had in his office. And I brought the cart back to help the people that was at the hotel," he later testified.

Making their way back over the bridge to return to Romell's office on the Third District side of the Danziger, the Madisons passed a young man sitting on the railing tying his shoes, and they saw a group of people coming up from behind. "They had kids with them," Lance said. "I didn't know if they was a family or not. I just saw it was a group of people."

The bridge now connected the families and the police. The Madison brothers and Susan and Leonard Bartholomew and their extended clan tethered by a spare bridge that connects to a commercial strip like an appendage and looks up toward the I-10. Below the Danziger the waters of the Industrial Canal roiled. Three miles away, the police were heading their way, racing to respond to the 108 call.

The two families—traversing a bridge they had passed all their lives, and a week after Katrina, simply trying to endure—did not know each other or share a single word that morning.

CHAPTER 7

THE SHOTS ON THE BRIDGE

Lives Intersect—Two Dead, Four Maimed,
Endless Barrage of Gunfire

AS SUSAN AND FAMILY joined up with Jose at the foot of the bridge, a large Budget rental truck roared toward them. Behind the wheel, more than a football field away, Officer Hunter glimpsed a group of people ahead on the bridge, walking. Pulling closer, Hunter saw no weapons, sensed no threat. "Where are they?" he asked. Where are the gun-toting thugs police are hunting? Then he heard a call over the radio: "That's them right there, right there, right there." The officer had no idea whose voice was on the other end of the radio or where the caller was positioned. Instantly he assumed the people walking on the bridge were the criminals firing weapons earlier that morning. Roaring closer, Hunter leaned out the driver's window and, without saying a word, fired warning shots from his police handgun to scatter the family in front of him. He steered with his right hand and fired with his left.

The Bartholomews, stunned by the gunfire, raced for cover behind a three-foot concrete barrier separating pedestrians from the traffic. Hunter then saw Bowen firing his AK-47 from inside the cab of the truck. Big Leonard inched his head up to take in the scene. Just then, Bowen unleashed several rounds.

Susan's fourteen-year-old son, Leonard IV, heard a swerving of the truck to his left, barreling toward the family. "And, when it was coming up, I saw a rifle pointed out the window," the son said later. He crouched behind the barrier, and then dashed down the bridge and tried to scamper back toward the motel, his arms up in the air. The bullets kept coming.

The truck screeched to a halt so abruptly one officer in back, Robert Barrios, went tumbling to the floor. Then a pack of officers, some black, some white, adorned in blue police-issued uniforms, jumped out. Without warning, they began unloading their weapons at the black family of six now scampering for cover.

"Jump over the barrier!" Susan yelled to her children, screaming as they hurdled the barrier separating the bridge from a walkway. Susan vaulted her body over, but before she landed, a bullet struck her arm. Her husband and daughter jumped down beside her. "I could hear them crying out," she said.

JJ and Jose hit the ground.

Robert Faulcon Jr., seated in the back of the truck, stepped out onto the concrete and fired his shotgun. Then he pumped, and fired again. Another pump, another blast. Then a fourth pump and blast. He fired with precision. As James Brissette Jr. lay on the ground, blasts from Faulcon's shotgun tore into the back of JJ's head and the bottom of his feet. He blasted a hole in Jose Holmes's face and lodged pellets into the back of Big Leonard's head.

Police officer Anthony Villavaso II, seated in the back along with Faulcon, stepped out, assault rifle at the ready. As his feet hit the pavement, he fired at least nine shots from his AK-47, rapid fire: *pop, pop, pop, pop, pop, pop, pop, pop, pop*. Like Faulcon, Villavaso aimed at the people—JJ, Jose, and the Bartholomews—lying unarmed on the pavement. He issued no warnings.

Villavaso's partner, Robert Barrios, was poised to join the fire but froze as a bullet whizzed past his ear. A black officer sitting near him, Ignatius Hills, had leaned out the truck to take aim as Little Leonard raced down the embankment. Hills targeted the boy's back. He missed. Another officer in the truck, a white patrolman named Kevin Bryan, turned to Hills. "What the fuck are you doing?" he demanded. "What the fuck are you shooting at?"

"I tried to pop that little N——," Bryan would testify Hills replied.

Screams mixed with gunfire. The mother, father, and daughter, Lesha, cried out, bloodied and in pain. A bullet grazed Big Leonard Bartholomew's head. Another tore into Lesha's stomach.

More gunfire ripped into Susan Bartholomew's right arm, nearly severing it from her shoulder, her limb held together by skin. Lesha, at seventeen years old, one inch shorter than Susan, lay atop her mother, trying to shield her as bullets tore through the concrete barrier.

"I got closer," Lesha said, "so she wouldn't get shot again." The bullets kept coming. "Lord, help us," her mother whispered.

Why is this happening? Lesha couldn't fathom the answer. Then a bullet ripped into her buttocks.

Sergeant Robert Gisevius, seeing two men sprinting up the bridge, fired his M4 at the backs of Lance and Ronald Madison. Hunter fired toward the Madison brothers, as well. Then Gisevius turned and aimed closer, firing a bullet into Susan Bartholomew's leg, and another into James Brissette Jr.'s leg as the teenager lay on the pavement, defenseless, authorities said.

Bullet after bullet shredded JJ's body from the heel of his foot to the top of his head; the teen now lay dead on the pavement. Seven gunshot wounds and even more pellet wounds, fired from multiple weapons, tore into JJ's right leg, right buttock, and right elbow; pierced his left arm and shredded his neck; and lodged in his brain. His wiry body was left unrecognizable. Faulcon fired some of the shots. Bowen fired another, from the borrowed AK-47.

Jose Holmes, shot in the jaw, arm, and elbow and down near JJ, felt the most severe pain of his life. He lay still, praying the gunfire would stop. "I heard my auntie and my cousin Lesha, I heard them screaming. I heard my Uncle Leonard, he was screaming too."

Suddenly Officer Hunter shouted, "Cease fire!" Using a motion he learned during his short stint in the US Marine Corps, Hunter, with a mop of brown hair over his head, moved his arms up and down to signal the command. The gunfire was so raucous Hunter thought his fellow officers couldn't hear his command, so he flapped his arms to be sure they did.

The shooting stopped. For five seconds.

Sergeant Bowen, the dark-haired, pale-skinned officer who had been so tense in the truck, kept pursuing. Holding the AK-47, he leaned over the concrete railing and began "firing indiscriminately" at the residents cowering on the sidewalk, Hunter said.

Jose Holmes looked up and saw a man lean over the railing, his finger on the trigger. Holmes clenched his stomach, told himself to breathe, and braced for the fire.

"I saw like a shadow, a person run over, and I looked up and I saw a barrel of a gun. And so I looked away and they shot me twice in the stomach," Holmes said later. His thought: "Man, they really want me dead. I paced my breathing because I knew—I thought if I panicked really bad that I would die. So I had enough mind to pace my breathing."

Blood gushing over his body, he lay on the ground, "wondering if I would survive. You know, praying to God that he would get me through this."

Bowen's AK-47, borrowed from Hunter in the truck with a full magazine of thirty bullets, was now empty. When Hunter went to retrieve it, the assault rifle was hot to the touch.

Officers raced to their victims, and standing over them, ordered them to shut up, not to look up, and to raise their hands in the air.

Susan Bartholomew thought it a death sentence.

"They were telling us to hold our hands up, raise both our hands up, and, of course, I couldn't because my arm was shot off, and I just thought they were gonna—gonna kill me, and they said that they would kill us," she said later. "We weren't allowed to look to see who they were, turn our heads the other way."

"I raised the only hand I had."

In the madness, Bartholomew glimpsed the garb of one officer. It was NOPD.

Lesha lay still. One officer barked that if she moved "he was going to blow my head off," Lesha said.

Officer Hunter stood beside Susan and Lesha Bartholomew as they lay on the bridge, clutching each other and wailing in pain. Lesha suffered a gunshot wound in her leg so wide "I could stick my fingers in it," Hunter would later testify. The officer said nothing to the women. He didn't call for help. He was taken aback by what he saw. "I thought it was kind of messed up, that the females got shot," he said. "It was just the first reaction I had. I'm not used to dealing with seeing females with gunshot wounds."

Kevin Bryan, son of a deceased NOPD officer, later caught up with the younger Bartholomew. He pointed his gun at Little Leonard, ordered him to freeze, and get on his knees. Then the officer slapped the black youth with an open hand and put the fourteen-year-old in handcuffs. Little Leonard hadn't threatened Bryan or any officer. He was scared. Why did Bryan hit him? "The heat of the moment, adrenaline pumping," said Bryan. When the moment passed, he felt horrible for slapping the teenager. Bryan moved Little Leonard, still cuffed, behind a car wash, to shield him from any more fire that may come. "They had all kinds of gunfire going on, and I didn't know which direction they were coming from," the officer said.

The Madison brothers had been halfway across the bridge when the gunfire unleashed. Stunned, Lance Madison had spun around to see heavily armed men pile out of the truck and prey upon the group he and his brother had passed moments earlier. In the frenzy, Lance initially assumed the younger people he saw moments earlier had fired first, and he thought he saw an object in one of their hands. Why else would these men be hunting us like animals? He didn't have time to stop and think.

Lance and Ronald sprinted to escape the bridge. Lance Madison ran faster than he had in his football days, believing a pack of criminals had stormed the bridge to shoot unarmed residents and steal their possessions. "Run, Ronald!" Lance yelled to his little brother. "They're shooting at us."

As the Madisons made their way down the other end of Danziger, Officer Dupree, who kicked in the initial 108 call, spotted them. Lance, wearing black spandex shorts and a black short sleeved shirt, and Ronald, in jeans shorts and a white shirt, did not match the description of the gunmen Dupree saw earlier. One of those men wore a red shirt, and the other had a black book bag on his back. But, believing they might be linked to the earlier turmoil, she called in an update: subjects fleeing the bridge. Faulcon heard the call and believed these were the same men whose earlier gunfire prompted the initial 108 call. The radio transmission became more urgent. "That's them," Faulcon heard an officer say. "They're getting away, they're getting away. Hurry, hurry!" Dupree kept calling in updates but, by now, officers had their targets in their sights. One officer radioed back to Dupree. "Shut up!" he screamed. "We got them."

Lance glanced over and saw that Ronald was already pierced by gunfire and bleeding through his white shirt, struck by fire from the men who spilled from the truck. Ronald wailed in pain. Lance raced over, lifted him under the shoulders, and tried to rush him to cover. Ronald, breathless, stopped him. "Tell Mom I love her," he said. He shook big brother's hand, and said to tell their brothers and sisters he loved them.

"We got to go!" Lance shouted. "These guys are coming after us." He and Ronald began descending the bridge, crossing paths with a man pushing a cart in the opposite direction. Lance yelled to turn around, people were firing at them. "We just kept running." He glimpsed a car coming behind but didn't look at it closely. "I was trying to run, get out of the way from being shot," he said.

As he descended the bridge, Lance led his brother toward the Friendly Inn, at 4861 Chef Menteur Highway, just off the foot of the bridge's west end and right next to their brother's dental office. "I'm going to get help!" Lance told Ronald, trying to calm him. "Just be quiet. You're hurt real bad." Lanced turned a corner toward a hotel courtyard, with Ronald staying behind. Separating from his brother would haunt Lance Madison as the most wrenching choice of his life. He ducked through the hotel lobby and searched for someone, anyone, who could help. Behind him, the gunfire continued.

Faulcon and other officers, finished with the Bartholomew family, now pursued the Madison brothers. As officers headed up the bridge, they spotted a Louisiana state trooper, Sergeant Michael Christopher Baron, behind the wheel of a black Chevy Impala. State police had been in the area earlier that morning for another reason, responding to unconfirmed calls of sniper fire on a Coast Guard helicopter at a Holiday Inn at Chef Menteur Highway and the I-10. Strikingly, the two dramas played out in the same pocket of New Orleans that Sunday morning, reports of snipers aiming at a helicopter and then, afterward, the 108 call.

Baron, all clear on the sniper call, got wind of officers under fire on the Danziger. He pulled onto the bridge, parking behind a police cruiser under the trusses at the expanse's halfway point.

Baron rolled his window down to ask what was happening. Then he heard gunfire and ducked in his seat. Faulcon jumped into his car, sitting up front, holding his shotgun. Gisevius and Hunter jumped in back. Hunter now had his AK-47, and Gisevius held his M4.

"Let's get them!" an officer told Baron. He pressed his foot to the pedal, pursuing men running ahead, on high alert, the morning's tensions all now converging in his mind.

Racing ahead, he saw a man running parallel to him, wearing a white T-shirt splotched with red blood, holding his right hand under his left arm, almost wobbling as he ran. It was Ronald Madison. By this time, Lance had sped off looking for help.

"That's him, right there," trooper Baron heard one of the officers say.

To Hunter, it looked as though the man was bleeding from his left arm. He was expecting a gunfight from inside the trooper's car, but Hunter didn't see a weapon or sense an immediate threat. In the back, Gisevius told him to hold his fire.

The man kept running. "I got him," Faulcon said, eyeing the figure in the T-shirt.

Baron began to slow the car to a stop. Soon the trooper heard a shotgun blast. He looked up and saw Ronald Madison tumble to the ground and Faulcon standing outside the Impala, his shotgun raised to his shoulder.

Hunter had been looking at the ground, with his door ajar waiting for the car to come to a complete stop so he could step out, when he heard the same blast. "I looked up, and the guy in white was on the ground." Faulcon had shot him. Later Faulcon would say he feared being ambushed, with the second figure, Lance Madison, no longer in sight. He contended Ronald spun his head around several times to glance at the car. Faulcon never issued a warning.

IN MOMENTS SERGEANT BOWEN, by now on the west side of the bridge, stepped out of the Budget truck and walked over to Ronald Madison, as Officer Hunter witnessed the scene unfold. The forty-year-old Madison, hit several times in the back, was wheezing, breathing his last breaths.

"Is this one of them?" Bowen screamed, his eyes filled with fire, his closely cropped, jet black hair contrasting his pale complexion. Ronald Madison, donned mostly in white, from his T-shirt to his white socks and tennis shoes, lay slumped in the hotel driveway next to an abandoned Chevrolet van. Nearby, discarded cars were submerged in water reaching their floorboards.

Hunter watched as Bowen, wearing his police issued boots, stomped on Ronald Madison's back, again and again.

Officer Hunter was startled. "He was stomping on him with his foot. On his back. It was several times. He was very angry. He had a very malicious look in his eye," he later testified.

He yelled at Bowen to stop.

Ronald was dead, but Lance did not know it. Desperate to find help for his brother and racing for his own life, Lance spotted several feet of water flooding one section of the hotel courtyard. He dove into it, trying to hide. Then he escaped around the back of the hotel.

Just then Robert Rickman, a maintenance worker, security guard, and all-purpose troubleshooter for the Friendly Inn, happened to be snapping pictures of the hotel's water damage for insurance purposes. Rickman heard gunfire crackling in the air and looked up to see Lance treading through water with officers in pursuit. Moments later Rickman stepped outside and saw Ronald Madison's bloodied body on the ground. Rickman had two cameras with him, one in hand and the other in his pants pocket. He began snapping photos, focusing his lens on Ronald's body and on the mass of law enforcement swarming the bridge.

An officer rushed to the scene, ordered Rickman to get away from the area, and snatched the camera from him. Then he stomped it to pieces on the ground. The other camera remained in the worker's pocket.

Finally, the shooting stopped.

Lance spotted officers he thought were with the National Guard, but they were actually SWAT team members with the state police. He dashed to them, pleading for help. Just then New Orleans police officers raced over. "Arrest him!" they said. "He was shooting at us." Officers threw him to the ground and handcuffed him. Lance looked up and saw a cluster of officers now circling him. They were NOPD. Bowen, the dark blue sleeves of his uniform rolled up, stood to one side. Hunter, in a lighter blue police shirt and his weapon in his hand, stood to the other side. For a moment Lance Madison closed his eyes, helpless prey engulfed by police.

"You're making a terrible mistake," Lance pleaded, braced on his knees, handcuffed behind his back. "You have the wrong guy."

There, in the middle of the street, Lance Madison begged for a lie detector test or gunpowder residue check of his hands. "I'm innocent, I was not shooting," he pleaded. "My brother's been shot and he needs some type of medical attention."

Officers ignored him. "Shut the fuck up," one said. Madison peered toward his armed accusers with a face flush with fear, bewilderment, and shock. Later, an irony would haunt him. If he knew it was police spilling from the Budget truck, he never would have run. "I wouldn't be here to-day because they would have shot and killed me."

Morrell Johnson, a private security officer staying at a nearby hotel, had been returning from the Winn-Dixie that morning when he heard so much gunfire he felt as though he was in a war zone. "Like you was in Vietnam the way it was going on. Nothing but just shooting, just noise," he said. Johnson is the man Lance saw going the other way up the bridge.

After police stopped firing their weapons, they threw Johnson to the ground and put cuffs on his wrists so tight they bled. Johnson, black and unarmed, said an officer grazed his forehead with a boot as he lay on the ground. He saw Ronald Madison slumped on the ground.

Later, Johnson rode in a bus to a police lockup with the young Bartholomew and Lance Madison.

Lance turned to him.

"Did you see my brother? A little short guy you saw me on the bridge running with?"

"That's your brother?" Morrell Johnson asked.

"Yes," Lance said. "He's handicapped."

"I'm sorry to hear that."

"Did you see him?" Lance needed to know.

"Yeah," Morrell told Lance Madison. "He was lying on the side of the old van over at the motel under cover."

"Did he move?"

"No," Morrell said. "He never moved."

Lance began to sob. Johnson tried to comfort him. Don't cry, he told the stranger. Don't cry.

Lance Madison, readying to face attempted murder charges, told himself: Remember this man's name, Morrell Johnson, and the boy's name, Leonard Bartholomew IV. "So I just kept on saying it over and over to myself until—I say I'm going to need these people to be a witness for the crime that was committed against us."

Packed inside the police truck, with his hands behind his back, Madison turned to an officer. "Why were you all shooting at us?"

"I should have shot you," one of the officers told him, "and I wouldn't be going through this." If Lance were dead, he'd have nothing to explain. Lance's handcuffs were so tight they cut into his wrists. He asked police to loosen the cuffs. They ignored him again.

At police headquarters, a female officer set Morrell Johnson and the younger Bartholomew free with food and bottled water. She told them to catch a bus out of town. Johnson looked after the Bartholomew son, who he had never met before that day. "We was just walking, walking down Loyola. And I asked him, I asked where he was going, what he was going to do, where he was going. Because he didn't have nobody, nowhere to go," Johnson said.

On the other side of the bridge, paramedics tended to the Bartholomew family. Susan's arm would have to be amputated. Her daughter and husband were also rushed to the hospital, where their wounds required immediate attention.

A supervising paramedic took one look at Jose Holmes—shot in the abdomen, legs, arms, hand, elbow, neck, and stomach—and told his partner to move on to someone else. Jose was too far gone.

"Don't give up on me," Jose whispered.

Stanton Doyle Arnold, an EMT (emergency medical technician) from upstate Louisiana who volunteered to serve in New Orleans after Katrina, saw all the blood and could not believe the teen was still alive. "He's been shot so many times," the paramedic saw. He didn't expect the patient to make it. Jose continued to breathe.

Arnold, armed with a .380 Colt himself because of the chaos in the streets, had prayed in the ambulance as it raced to the scene of the shooting. Now he leaned over Jose Holmes, focusing his care on his patient's upper thoracic cavity, and then helped put him on a stretcher and into the ambulance.

Soon the NOPD would have some business with the teenager. Jose Holmes, clinging to life with a stomach wound that would require surgery, was poised to face charges of attempted murder. The officers who fired on him would claim Jose, like Lance Madison, was a criminal.

Officer Kevin Bryan made his way back up the bridge and saw a man on the ground, covered in blood. EMTs pressed one side of the victim's chest. Blood squirted out the other side. Bryan, on the force for two years, felt nauseated. He never fired his gun, nor did at least three other officers in the truck.

Officer Dupree raced to the scene.

"I was the one that kicked it in," she said. "Do you all need anything?"

"No," she was told. "Keep going."

The police brass assigned to investigate the shooting—which left two dead and four gravely wounded—decided it was unnecessary to question the officer whose call set the events in motion that morning. Just as it failed to question state trooper Baron or other officers, like Bryan, who did not fire their weapons. "If you didn't shoot," an NOPD sergeant told the trooper, "I don't need you."

A police log would later catalogue the bloodshed.

- Susan Bartholomew, black female, date of birth 3/5/67, three gunshot wounds to the left leg, one gunshot wound to the right arm, fractured left femur, amputated right arm.
- Lesha Bartholomew, black female, date of birth 6/25/88, one gunshot wound to the middle of stomach, one gunshot wound to the left lower buttocks, one gunshot wound to the middle of the buttocks, one gunshot wound to the left middle back.
- Leonard Bartholomew Sr., black male, date of birth 12/22/60, one gunshot wound to the left heel, one gunshot wound to the upper back, one gunshot wound to the head, exiting above the right ear.
- Jose Holmes, black male, date of birth 6/13/86, gunshot wounds to his left hand and elbow, right elbow, neck area, and stomach.
- JJ Brissette, black male, deceased, gunshot wounds to the right elbow, right flank, and back of the neck.
- Ronald Madison, black male, deceased, multiple gunshot wounds to the back "consistent with a shotgun blast."

"On the scene, the bodies of the two deceased perpetrators remained with no Coroner's Office support available to retrieve them," police reported. Officers from the Seventh District briefly watched over the bodies until a lieutenant later took them to the coroner's office in Jefferson Parish. From there, JJ Brissette and Ronald Madison were moved to Saint Gabriel, Louisiana, where they lay in a temporary morgue for victims of Hurricane Katrina.

For some time police were not clear about the names or ages of the two men they had just killed. Initial reports listed JJ as "Name Unknown, black male, approximately 20 years of age," and Ronald Madison as "Name Unknown, black male, approximately 25 to 30 years of age," underestimating his age by a full decade. Police would identify Ronald

Madison through dental records within days, but months later, the department could report only modest progress in learning the identity of the teenager who had died of his gunshot wounds.

"Let it be known, during this investigation, the names of James Barsett, James Barest, James Bartert, and James Bastert have been mentioned as a possible name of the unknown black male who was fatally wounded on the Danziger Bridge. Attempts to identify this individual have been met with negative results," said a report filed months later. "This inquiry is ongoing."

AS AMBULANCES SPED TO the hospital, filled with the still-breathing victims bloodied from the gunfire, Sergeant Bowen walked over to Hunter. "I'm sorry. I was out of line," Bowen said. "We're not animals like them," Hunter shot back. "We're better than that."

Do we have a problem? Bowen asked. No, Hunter said. No problem at all. *It is what it is*, he thought. He didn't say another word.

Later, Bowen would deny stomping on Ronald Madison, would deny leaning over the railing and spraying gunfire at innocents. Those images, he said, took place solely in Hunter's mind.

Racing to the bridge after the 108 call, Hunter had felt his insides fill with fury, stunned that, once more, police appeared under attack. That mix of fear and rage engulfed the Budget truck, coursing through officers black (Faulcon, Villavaso, Barrios, and Hills) and white (Hunter, Bowen, and Gisevius). In the months to follow, the focus would be on these seven, not the four other officers who didn't fire.

What enraged Hunter most was that the call came in the aftermath of Katrina, as police scrambled to keep peace amid the flooding and chaos. "I wanted to send them a message," he would later testify. "Don't mess with us." Officer Ignatius Hills, who aimed his service weapon at a five-foot, eighty-five-pound fleeing teenage boy, said he fired out of fear.

"It was an intense situation," Hills said about those moments.

"You intended to kill him?" he was asked.

"Yes."

"You wanted him dead?"

"Killing him is not—wasn't my intention. I didn't want to kill him."

"You wanted to shoot him in the back?"

"Yes," Hills admitted.

Soon after, a veteran white NOPD supervisor ordered a criminal records check on some of the citizens on the bridge that morning. The sergeant assumed the run would produce criminal rap sheets. It came back clean.

IMMEDIATELY AFTER THE GUNFIRE STOPPED, another caravan of officers arrived at the Danziger Bridge. The group had been headed to the Crystal Palace to report for duty, steering a commercial shuttle bus commandeered from a limousine service, when they passed the Budget truck speeding by in the other direction. Officer Taj Magee, a lifelong city resident driving the bus, told his partners to turn on the police radio. Gunfire and shouting filled the air. Magee turned around and headed, cautiously, to Danziger.

Magee stepped from the bus and witnessed the remnants of a massacre.

He saw Holmes, blood pouring from his mouth, trying to breathe. He saw JJ, motionless, blood-soaked. "He had several gunshot wounds to the torso and one that was—that I remember vividly was the fact that his elbow had been blown out where it was exposed, where you noticed in the joint, you could see the bone and you could see the flesh. And that kind of stood out to me."

Nearby, he spotted a woman on the ground. "She was attempting to crawl, I would think, and she was riddled with bullets."

On the other end of the bridge, he made his way near Ronald Madison, slumped over, the back of his white shirt turned dark red. "He was pretty much on his butt leaning forward, slumped over." Madison was dead.

Instantly, the images the officer took in didn't add up. When he stepped into the street, Magee was careful to check for bullet holes in the truck, but found none. Walking atop the bridge, he saw dozens of shell casings, but recognized all as coming from police weapons. He saw no guns near Holmes, none near JJ, none near the Bartholomews, and none near Ronald Madison. It didn't make sense. He began scouring every inch of the bridge, desperate to find evidence that the victims had fired first or had carried weapons themselves. He couldn't fathom the other possibility racing through his mind.

"I didn't understand why they were shot, you know, and I didn't understand what was going on, what happened in the incident altogether," he said. "I was hoping I would find a weapon or something of that nature, or a second area where there were casings so that it would make sense to me why there was a shooting. . . . Hoping to find bullet casings, a weapon, anything that would, you know, explain and justify the incident that occurred."

He kept scouring the bridge, from one end to the other, and then began walking down the grassy area under the Danziger. Nothing. He passed by another officer and shared his findings. "Good thing you're not working for a lawyer," the cop told him.

Magee got back into the bus and drove away from the Danziger Bridge, trying to put the puzzle out of his mind. It wasn't his investigation. It wasn't his role to question the shooters. He returned to other duties. "I didn't ask anybody anything," he said. "I didn't want to know."

An old adage entered his mind: "Ask me no questions, and I'll tell you no lies."

TWO TO THREE HOURS after the gunfire had quelled, Friendly Inn troubleshooter Robert Rickman walked back outside. Ronald Madison's body remained on the pavement. No officers were around, the lifeless figure left unguarded. Rickman pulled camera two from his pocket and began taking pictures. He snapped photos of the forty-year-old man lying before him and of shell casings around the body. No one from NOPD asked him a question about that morning, but Rickman kept the photographs. They might be important one day, he thought.

CHAPTER 8

TRIAGE

AT WEST JEFFERSON MEDICAL CENTER, the alert blared over a loud speaker. "Dr. Thompson, come to the emergency room stat." The victims of the police gunfire were being rushed to the hospital for emergency care.

Craig Robert Thompson, the lead surgeon, had been living in the hospital since Katrina destroyed his home. Responding to the call, he quickly scanned the four surviving gunshot victims. Performing emergency triage, he decided three—Jose, Lesha, and Susan—faced life-threatening injuries. Leonard, grazed in the scalp and legs, was in the most stable condition. Dr. Thompson arranged for his care and focused on the other three victims.

Susan Bartholomew, even in her dire condition, fading in and out of consciousness and her right arm severed and hanging, was more stable than her daughter or nephew. The doctor arranged for a plastic surgeon to amputate her arm, while other doctors treated her remaining gunshot wounds.

Lesha was alert, but the doctor saw that bullets had penetrated her abdomen, legs, and bottom. The gunshot to her abdomen was the most worrisome, since the bullet had settled near major organs. Dr. Thompson feared she was bleeding to death within her abdominal cavity. Opening her up, he discovered a bullet that pierced her liver and blood in her abdomen. Like her mother, Lesha would need surgery.

Jose Holmes's injuries were the most severe. "He was no longer responsive. He had very low blood pressure," the doctor said. "He had multiple gunshot wounds. In the order of triage, he was clearly the most in danger at that time." Jose was in shock, and Dr. Thompson could barely detect a pulse. Medical staff inserted a tube into his trachea to help him breathe. The teenager suffered a gunshot wound to his jaw, just above his neck, and multiple gunshot wounds to his abdomen. His liver was hemorrhaging, and his colon had been perforated as well.

"I thought we could save him," the doctor believed. "But I also knew that Lesha was also seriously injured, and I knew we could save her. So my instructions at that time were that I was going to take Jose up to the operating room. And then in about fifteen minutes, I asked them to bring Lesha up and take her and put her to sleep in another operating room, believing at that point that I was either going to have enough time to stabilize Jose and then step out of that operating room and go over to Lesha's operating room, or at that point Jose may have expired and Lesha would be ready to go."

Dr. Thompson performed surgery on one part of Jose's body after the next, back-to-back-to-back procedures to close his gaping holes and settle his traumatic injuries. When the physician was nearly done, he checked one last part of Jose's body, his right elbow. He found a bullet there too.

CHAPTER 9

NOPD TRIAGE

The After Action Reports

THE EMERGENCY ROOM DOCTORS at West Jefferson were not the only ones performing triage after Hurricane Katrina.

Six weeks after the deadly storm, in October 2005, the New Orleans Police Department examined how well prepared it had been for Katrina. The answer was obvious. If a blueprint for failure for hurricane preparation existed, it was spelled out in the After Action Reports filed by NOPD supervisors who had, in some instances in the immediate wake of the storm, issued pleas for help in all capital letters.

"There did not appear to be a preplan for this event," Captain Jeffrey J. Winn, a commander in a tactical unit, wrote in his "Hurricane Katrina After Action Report." "Communications failed at the most critical time. Back up systems did not work at all."

The radio system crashed. With no central communications system working, officers had to keep contact through handheld police radios, as Dupree did when she "kicked in" her assistance call.

"This was critical to the operation and seriously hampered rescue operations," Winn explained. "Lack of communication placed officers in extreme danger without an avenue for assistance."

Logistics and support were nonexistent. There had been no preplanning for food, water, weapons, and medical care. No central distribution point was set up to move supplies to the field, and no one thought ahead to such basics as the officers' needs for personal hygiene and restrooms.

These officers saw firsthand how those failings put lives in danger. The first night after the storm, the department lost contact with three officers trapped in rising waters. Their radio batteries had died, and colleagues spent a fruitless night searching for them. After wading through five miles of water that sometimes reached their chests, the officers found their way back by morning.

The force had no aerial views to tell the officers where the waters rose highest, leaving them to guess where they were most needed.

"The New Orleans Office of Emergency Preparedness failed," said Captain Timothy P. Bayard, commander of the Vice Crimes–Narcotics Section. "We were not prepared logistically. Most importantly, we relocated evacuees to two locations where there was no food, water or portable restrooms. We did not utilize buses that would have allowed us to transport mass quantities of evacuees expeditiously. We did not have food, water or fuel for the emergency workers. We did not have a back-up communication system."

"We drove trucks, piloted boats and walked past bodies in the first fourteen days of the storm," Captain Bayard wrote in his After Action Report. "We did not have the proper clothing, equipment or training to attempt body recovery. We notified the communications section where human remains were and secured the bodies to unmovable objects. No one knows when these bodies were recovered or if they were even in the location initially reported."

The lack of planning left officers in the lurch, bereft of fresh clothing and hustling for food, just like the residents held captive by Katrina. A Third District commander, Captain Donald J. Paisant, said the officers were forced to fend for themselves. "The only food and water we had were the ones the individual officers provided," Paisant wrote.

"Many of our officers lost their families, their property, and basically everything they had to their name," reported Sergeant John F. Deshotel. "But they had to put on their game faces and handle the mission despite their own growing grief. There was absolutely no counseling or compassion being offered by the supervisors to the victimized officers."

At one point, Deshotel had three people pass out at his ankles from heat exhaustion while waiting for buses to evacuate them. "That incident was truly overwhelming for me, considering I had absolutely no medical resources available to me."

More than anything, he said, the chaos, the exhaustion, and the stress pointed up the need for counseling. Without it, police officers are torches poised to ignite.

"Some officers who should have been decommissioned and sent for counseling were given rifles instead and allowed to continue working while choosing their own assignments."

PART II
MAKING IT ALL GO AWAY

CHAPTER 10

THE COVER-UP

WHEN THE 108 CALL screeched over the radio that first Sunday after Katrina, sending an urgent alarm about officers under fire, Lieutenant Michael Lohman stood outside the Crystal Palace handing out assignments for officers to venture out on boats to rescue survivors. The grandson of a police officer, Lohman was raised on the West Bank in Jefferson Parish in the suburbs of New Orleans. He joined the NOPD in 1988, at age twenty, after logging several semesters at the University of New Orleans and then Louisiana State University in Baton Rouge. Lohman exudes the look of a man raised in a law and order family: sturdily built, with dark eyebrows and close-cropped gray-black hair framing his white skin and accentuating his masculine jaw. A cop's cop with a commanding presence. With Hurricane Katrina looming, Lohman had sent his wife and five- and eight-year-old daughters to stay with family in Prairieville, Louisiana, an hour northwest of New Orleans. "I had to work," he said.

That morning Lohman saw the pack of officers race off to the Danziger Bridge, and he felt the force was plentiful enough to handle the call. He finished handing out the last of the rescue missions. Then he headed for the Danziger Bridge himself.

As the ranking officer on duty, Lohman would supervise any internal inquiry likely to surface should officers, indeed, engage in a gun battle likely to come with the 108 distress call. By the time Lohman arrived, the gunfire had quieted, and blood and bodies covered the overpass.

When he pulled up to east side of the Danziger Bridge, Lohman glimpsed five people on the ground, paramedics working on the bodies. Police hovered around the area. Lohman instantly began looking for guns, just as officer Taj Magee had. The difference was that Lohman was now officially lead supervisor in charge of reporting what had just happened.

He didn't see any. "I was concerned," the lieutenant said later. "If these were the perpetrators, where were the guns? How come we weren't locating any guns?"

By this time another white supervisor, Sergeant Arthur "Archie" Kaufman, who worked under Lohman's direction in the department's Seventh District leading the homicide section, arrived on site. After twenty-seven years as a police officer, Kaufman was no longer the fit army enlistee he had once been, but retained a head of thick, wavy hair. That morning Lohman assigned Kaufman to lead the review into the shootings on the bridge.

Atop the bridge, Lohman huddled with Kaufman and Sergeant Kenneth Bowen, who was also under his supervision in the Seventh. Both told him the same story, Bowen from a first-person perspective and Kaufman telling what he learned shortly after arriving. "When they arrived on the scene of the bridge, they saw a group of pedestrians on the bridge who were armed with weapons. The pedestrians fired at them and they returned fire, and as a result, the individuals who were lying in the pedestrian walkway were struck with their gunfire," Lohman later recounted, encapsulating the police line that quickly took shape that morning.

What about the guns? Lohman asked. We're still looking for them, came the reply. The lieutenant scanned the area. He didn't see police officers searching for guns, or, for that matter, any evidence to back up their account.

Lohman walked across the bridge and down to the expanse's west side. There, he saw Ronald Madison sprawled on the pavement between two vehicles near the Friendly Inn. Bowen filled him in here too. The dead man had been part of the pack of people shooting at police on the other side of the Danziger, Bowen said, and then tried to flee pursuing officers over the expanse of the bridge.

"As he ran across the bridge, Officer Faulcon, along with other officers, pursued him over the bridge," said Lohman, repeating Bowen's account. "And as he turned into the driveway of the motel, he reached into his waistband. Officer Faulcon thought he was going for a weapon and fired one shot, striking him."

That morning Faulcon shared the same account with Lohman. "When the guy turned into the entrance of the hotel, he reached into his waistband," Lohman recounted. Faulcon said he believed he was going for a gun, and fired.

Once more, Lohman searched for a gun near the victim. Once more, he came up empty-handed. His concern, sparked on the other side of the bridge, was now fully stoked. Lohman spent two hours that morning on the bridge, and as the minutes passed, his gut told him he had stepped into a police shoot gone horribly wrong. In his mind, he began tallying all the missing pieces of the police story's puzzle.

"The fact that they responded to a scene and it was alleged that these people were the perpetrators who had fired at them, yet there were no weapons located by the perpetrators or on the perpetrators," he said. "No one could tell me which one of the perpetrators was actually armed with the weapon, whether it was all of them, one or two of them, or just one of them."

Lohman and Bowen now huddled on the west side of the bridge near the motel and Ronald Madison's limp body. Suddenly Bowen came up with a story to explain the missing guns. "Well, what about this, what about if I kicked the guns over the side of the bridge?" Bowen offered, Lohman would later testify under oath.

Why, Lohman pressed, would you kick the guns over the side of the bridge?

"Well, it was a hot scene," Bowen proffered. "It was still hostile and chaotic. There were people running around. I didn't know to what degree the pedestrians were injured. They could possibly re-arm themselves with the guns or someone else on the scene could pick up a gun and arm themselves and start shooting at us. So to secure the weapons . . . I pushed them over the side of the bridge with the intention of going down there and getting them once the scene is under control."

So why, then, couldn't police find the weapons he kicked? Bowen had an answer for that too. "Someone apparently came by and picked up the guns and left with them," said the officer, a month away from earning his Louisiana State Bar license.

Bowen simply didn't have any place on his body to place the hot guns, he told the supervisor. Lohman looked over his colleague, and saw that Bowen was attired in his NOPD uniform—with six pockets in the cargo pants, plenty of room to store any found guns. It was another fiction in plain sight.

That morning the police supervisor, a college-educated lieutenant who had advanced through the ranks, made a decision.

"I knew this was a bullshit story, but I went along with it," Lohman said. The blue line of the police brotherhood was stronger than any remorse he might later feel for lying, or any guilt he might have about the victims. "The guys who were involved in this were co-workers, and some of them were friends of mine," he said. "I didn't want anyone to get in trouble; I didn't want anyone to have to have any problems, including them and myself, and that's why I participated and went along with the cover-up."

That morning on the bridge, Lohman went back to confer with Bowen and Sergeant Robert Gisevius Jr., another white officer under his command, who had just sprayed gunfire at the unarmed victims. Bowen and Gisevius directed patrols in high crime hot spots for the Seventh District's task force. Unlike Sergeant Kaufman, who worked attired in jacket and tie, they turned out for duty in the full "BDU style"—battle-dress uniforms, with blue pants, cargo pockets on the side, and police patches on both sleeves of a blue shirt.

"You two guys need to get together and decide what happened," Lohman told them. "You need to calm down, collect your thoughts and decide what happened, and come back and let me know what happened."

The veteran lieutenant already knew how the story would play out. He didn't expect the truth.

Lohman was careful not to tell his underlings precisely what to say, but, instead, to give them room to find a believable account. "Had they came back and said, 'Look, we made a mistake, we screwed up and we shot the wrong people,' that's the way the story would have went," he explained. "In my heart or in my gut, I knew that wasn't what they were going to come back and tell me, though. I knew they were going to come back with a story explaining their actions."

Archie Kaufman, just assigned to investigate the shootings, was reaching quick conclusions about how the case would come down.

"Twenty-one NAT, babe," Kaufman told Lohman, using police lingo that, translated, means the case will be closed. NAT: necessary action taken. Twenty-one: miscellaneous complaint. In Kaufman's mind, and in the police narrative rapidly taking shape that morning, what just happened atop the Danziger Bridge was nothing more than twenty-one NAT, babe.

The two supervisors mulled over the idea of gathering evidence. Kaufman had a thought. "Look," he said. "We're just not going to collect anything because we'll write it off on Katrina since the crime lab wasn't available." Again, Lohman went along.

Blaming Katrina became shorthand, allowing the NOPD to explain away the lack of investigation of a fusillade of fire that morning, which left two residents dead and four wounded. Standing atop the bridge, Kaufman figured at least some of the residents handcuffed or sprawled out before him would have police records, and that would make it easy to cast them as criminals, not victims.

Typically, when police engage in gunfire and victims are left bloodied on the pavement, a small army of supervisors, experts, and technicians instantly scour the crime scene, snapping photographs, collecting and tagging shells and firearms, interviewing witnesses, brushing for fingerprints, and taking note of every minute detail. But this was no normal shooting, and it was no normal time.

A detective assigned to work with Kaufman, his friend Jeffrey Lehrmann, said Kaufman made a conscious decision not to worry about collecting evidence just yet.

"Because of the hurricane and the lack of resources of the police department, he wasn't worried about collecting shell casings, or photos, or anything," Lehrmann said. "And even at that time, he didn't even intend on putting anything on paper."

Kaufman pulled Lohman aside once more. He had an idea about how to deal with the lack of weapons found on the victims. I have a gun, Kaufman confided. I can put it on the scene.

"Is it clean?" Lohman asked him.

Yes, Kaufman assured his lieutenant, the gun he had in mind was clean, untraceable.

"If you're going to do it, do it," Lohman whispered. "You don't need to talk about it with anyone else or involve anyone else in it." Lohman knew what would come next. "He was going to plant a gun on the scene to make it look as though the people that had been shot were armed."

. . .

THAT SUNDAY MORNING, the police officers returned to the Crystal Palace. There, all the officers who fired weapons on the bridge gathered around a table, brought together by Kaufman. Lohman told the crew Kaufman was going to be handling the investigation. "Homicide isn't coming out," Lohman said. "It's going to be handled internally. Everything's going to be okay."

Officers who had not fired their weapons were barred from the session. One of them was Kevin Bryan, who had become nauseated witnessing the blood gushing out from victims. Not long after the meeting, Bryan saw all the officers huddled around Bowen, clutching reports in their hands. When Officer Ignatius Hills passed him, Bryan asked for a copy. The two had graduated from the academy together. Hills refused to share any report.

Bryan was stunned. The report was a public record. It was standard for police to read each other's reports. "I felt that something was trying to be hidden," he later testified.

Instead, the small cadre of shooters and supervisors kept their work a closely held secret. In that first meeting, Lohman asked the officers who did fire to speak up, to recount how many times they shot at people. Hunter spoke first. He had fired multiple rounds, the first flurry of "warning shots" to scatter the family of six at the foot of the bridge, and then more shots toward the two men racing over the expanse.

"Hold on. Let's stop for a minute," Lohman burst in, stunned by what he heard. He pulled Kaufman, Bowen, and Gisevius outside the room.

To Michael Hunter it was clear why Lohman suddenly halted the group powwow. "We can't have this looking like a massacre," he heard the lieutenant say.

The cover-up took full bloom, and the shooters themselves could see the police narrative unfolding as clearly as the Sunday morning sky. "I mean, it was pretty obvious that they were initiating a cover-up," Hunter said. "They didn't separate us and ask us questions individually. Nothing was collected from the scene."

Over the coming days, weeks, and months, the NOPD began crafting multiple written versions of what happened atop the bridge. Versions, plural, because the officers and brass had to labor through rewrites and more rewrites to strike up a cover story they believed would hold water.

The police story that began to emerge in black and white was more like an airbrushed Hollywood screenplay than an official recounting of that devastating morning, filled with jolts of creativity, invented witnesses and evidence, phony names, and fabricated facts. And like a screenplay going up the line in the studio for notes, the police reports went up the line to supervisors, who sent back comments, wrote through confusing passages, and strove to craft a Hollywood ending. At times, like the director and stars hovering over the film editor's final cut, the whole NOPD crew—from the officers themselves to their supervisors—stood together over a computer terminal, looking to strike just the right key. In their story, the police were unquestioned heroes, standing tall amid nature's fury to save their city from looters and shooters.

As supervisors began creating those reports, starting in October 2005, the officers supposedly under review would stand at their side, helping to shape the story. The department had no hunger for an independent review. What it wanted, more than anything, was to keep the massacre out of public view and to cast the officers on the bridge as public servants doing their job during the torturous days after Katrina. It took a fair amount of sweat, and occasional bickering, to strike the right tone.

That October Kaufman filed a thirty-two-page report for Lohman's approval. "It was a horrible report," Lohman saw. "It justified the police shooting, but it was full of holes and inconsistencies, and it—although he cleared the police officers, it really didn't justify their actions. It didn't make any sense. It wasn't logical."

As he read the report, the lieutenant internally began ticking off the holes he saw filling page after page. "They couldn't identify who had what weapon or who was actually armed with a weapon. It really didn't provide any details about anything. Basically, it was a general summary of: The police arrived on the scene—responded to the scene of a 108. Upon arrival, they encountered gunfire and they returned gunfire. That's basically what it said. It provided no details."

For police purposes, the report did contain useful sections, including some tales that would stick for years as police gospel. The report said a gun had been recovered under the bridge, a day later, by Kaufman. That story would stick.

And, the report included a lengthy recounting of events attributed to Bowen.

> The truck proceeded to the area of the Danziger Bridge at which time the truck stopped and Sergeant Bowen shouted for the subjects to raise their hands in the air. The subjects immediately went for cover while arming themselves and fired upon the officers. The subjects then all jumped behind a cement barrier for cover to ambush the officers exiting the rear of the truck.
>
> To protect his own life and the lives of other officers exiting the truck, Sergeant Bowen fired several shots into the concrete barrier to deter the subjects from standing and aiming at the officers. Sergeant Bowen began to shout to the subjects to throw their weapons off the side of the bridge.
>
> Sergeant Bowen observed a young male subject jump from the bridge onto the grassy area several feet below to flee. Sergeant Bowen heard . . . gunfire from the immediate area. Officers Faulcon, Villavaso, and Barrios engaged the armed subject behind the cement barrier and then ceased firing.
>
> Sergeant Bowen also observed two males running west over the bridge while gunshots could be heard coming from those two subjects. Sergeant Bowen exited the truck and cautiously peeked over the cement barrier. He observed two dark colored handguns lying on the cement next to the stationary subjects. Sergeant Bowen jumped over the cement barrier and kicked the weapons over the side of the bridge.
>
> Sergeant Bowen ran down the bridge and into the tall grassy area on the side of the bridge to look for the young male subject. While walking through the grassy area next to the bridge, Sergeant Bowen observed several handguns lying in the grass near the bridge.
>
> Sergeant Bowen could see that the officers were still chasing the other two male subjects on foot over the bridge, when he observed one of the subjects being chased, later identified as Lance Madison, discard his weapon over the bridge into the Industrial Canal.
>
> Once in front, Sergeant Bowen observed that one of the two subjects who had fled over the bridge was stationary just inside of the apartment complex. The officers lost sight of the second subject who had run north in the floodwaters. Shortly thereafter, Louisiana State

Police SWAT team located the second subject attempting to escape outside the west side of the police perimeter. This subject was arrested by state police without incident.

That second subject, of course, was Lance Madison, whose brother lay dying as Lance pleaded for help.

As police constructed their story, they occasionally shifted the narrative's setting and scenery, moving from the Danziger Bridge to hospital bed interviews with the Bartholomew family. These east New Orleans residents, clinging to life on an eighth floor hospital ward, pointed the finger at nephew Jose Holmes as unleashing the gunfire, the police reported. Kaufman and the detective assigned to work with him, Jeffrey Lehrmann, had visited the Bartholomews as they recovered from surgery days after the shootings.

Lehrmann, raised in the New Orleans suburb of Metairie, had joined the New Orleans Police Department in March 2005, fewer than six months before Katrina, and Kaufman was his link to the force. The two had bumped into each other performing off-duty work at a Marriott Hotel when Lehrmann worked for a neighboring sheriff's office. Early in 2005 Lehrmann told Kaufman he was thinking of transferring to the department. "Well, if you don't have anywhere to go or you don't really know anybody, you can come out here and work with me," Kaufman told him. "Okay. That sounds good to me," he replied. So, Lehrmann, a white, thirtyish officer with a puff of light brown hair, went to work in the Seventh District.

When Kaufman left Susan Bartholomew's hospital room after one visit, he made an announcement, in a booming voice loud enough for nurses and fellow investigator Lehrmann to hear. "She just said Jose shot at the police."

So now, in the hospital charged with bringing the Bartholomews and Jose Holmes back to life, the word was out: Jose had shot at police first. Soon a veteran nurse scolded the teenager for shooting at police.

"Mrs. Bartholomew stated that she recalls her nephew was shooting at the police officers as they approached on the Danziger Bridge," an NOPD report said. "Mrs. Bartholomew stated she doesn't remember what happened after that and later woke up in the hospital."

The police reports included more embellishments from other members of the Bartholomew family. The father said that, as the family began walking to the Winn-Dixie, nephew Jose "started shooting at military vehicles that pulled up behind them. He stated he did not remember anything after that," police reported. "Mr. Leonard Bartholomew Sr. mentioned he was unsure why his nephew was shooting at the military."

When Kaufman and Lehrmann entered the room for one visit, they found the parents and their daughter, Lesha, sitting together. Lehrmann felt a chill coming from the teenager, who didn't say a word. "She was still, basically, afraid of me," the detective saw. "Because we shot them—they shot them."

Detective Lehrmann knew the truth. The Bartholomews had never said Jose was shooting. He had no weapon and fired at no one. Kaufman was inventing testimony and taking a starring role in spreading the tales, at times with dramatic flourish.

The NOPD's storyline ensnared Ronald Madison as well. In one police account, Susan Bartholomew told police that Ronald and Lance Madison were friends of Jose Holmes and were with the family on the east side of the bridge when the shooting began. In truth, the Madisons, who did not know Jose, were heading toward the other side of the bridge.

"As they walked on the bridge, her nephew, Holmes, and his two friends began shooting at police officers. She said she was then shot from what she thought was a military helicopter. She indicated she remembered nothing beyond that."

The officers employed their most vivid creative writing to place Ronald Madison on that side of the bridge with the Bartholomews, saying he and some of the family members headed out together to loot a store for food. The idea was to place the two families together and pretend that the shooting all began on one side of the bridge. That story was easier to believe than having two dead victims on opposite sides of the bridge, two separate crime scenes in which no guns were found near either James Brissette Jr. or Ronald Madison. "The reason he was chased to the west side of the bridge in the first place is because he was part of the initial group that were shooting at police officers," Lohman explained. "I think it would have been unbelievable—more unbelievable to think that there were two separate groups on either side of the bridge."

Other invented scenes filled the accounts.

"Two of the subjects, one later identified as Jose Holmes and the other who remains unidentified, continued to fire in the direction of the officers from behind the barrier, while the two remaining subjects continued to run towards the top of the bridge also firing at the officers.

"At this time, Officers Faulcon, Barrios, Hills, and Villavaso tactically moved to the concrete barrier, as Sergeant Bowen laid down suppression fire, and engaged Holmes and an unidentified black male who also brandished a handgun. The officers fired several rounds as the two perpetrators returned fire, striking all five subjects."

The larger story was taking shape. Still, the initial thirty-two page draft needed tweaking, required an editor's eye. Lohman scrawled notes on the report and handed it back to Kaufman for reworking. "Clarifying things, adding details," he said. "Making it more believable."

Soon after, Kaufman handed him a forty-six-page report. It was, again, "horrible," the lieutenant saw. "It didn't provide any details or justify any of the officers' actions. Although it cleared them of the shooting—in the shooting, it didn't justify their actions or what they did."

A racial divide became clear in the forty-six-page report. Only the black police officers, Faulcon, Barrios, Hills, and Villavaso, were said to have struck the civilians with gunfire, while a white officer, Bowen, laid down suppression fire.

The white officers huddled together and created the report—led by investigators Kaufman and Lohman, with input from shooters Bowen and Gisevius. All worked in District Seven.

"As of this writing, it appears that officers Faulcon, Villavaso, and Barrios are more than likely the officers whose rounds struck the perpetrators," the report said. It made note that Anthony Villavaso was armed with an AK-47, but neglected to say that white officers were too.

Lohman didn't like the newest version either. He took matters into his own hands, that November crafting his own seventeen-page police report. He typed over what was already there on the computer document, adding or subtracting information after conferring, once more, with trusted aides Bowen, Gisevius, and Kaufman. As he rewrote the reports, the officers under his command sat with him, the group bouncing ideas off one another. They made sure to talk out of earshot of officers they feared would not go along. Within the NOPD, naysayers likely to question the unfolding Danziger Bridge narrative were cut out.

The seventeen-page report now nearly finished, Lohman told Kaufman to meet with each officer named in the report, to make sure they were good with how their actions were portrayed. Kaufman reported back, "They were all okay with what their role was in the report." Lohman signed this report and handed it to Kaufman to submit up the line.

Without telling anyone, Lohman had made copies of each report that took shape, from the thirty-two- to forty-six- to seventeen-page version he assumed would be the final initial report. Even as he stood by the blue line of police brotherhood, something nagged at him, so much so that he stored copies of the reports without telling anyone. "I had concerns about this case all along and about what had taken place," he said, explaining why he kept copies.

Unbeknownst to Lohman, Kaufman took out his own editing pen and filed a slimmed-down seven-page report, replacing the seventeen-page version, to further tighten the police script while keeping the core story intact. Lohman never signed that report. Later, he learned that his signature was there, nonetheless—thanks, he said, to sleight of hand. The face sheet from the seventeen-page report was removed, and then placed as the cover sheet on the seven-page report.

It took the investigators four tries to get the initial report right. And that was not even the final word. That initial report was a precursor to a larger, fifty-four page supplemental report that would be filed in May 2006 and become the final document.

Publicly, the department's Public Affairs Division issued a two-page press release on October 4, 2005, one month after the shootings, under the letterhead of Superintendent Edwin P. Compass III. The press release would later disappear from police archives. But, for now, it was the official police version, prepared for public release. That statement, updating information on the "attempted murder" of eight officers, said the police were met with gunfire from "at least four suspects at the base of the bridge. The officers positioned themselves and began an exchange of gunfire."

An unidentified gunman sustained a gunshot wound and died on the scene, the press release said. That was JJ Brissette; the press release implied he'd been shot only once.

The other unidentified gunman was Ronald Madison. "The suspect reached into his waist and turned toward the officer who fired one shot fatally wounding him." Ronald Madison had seven gunshot wounds. Lance Madison "was seen discarding his handgun into the Industrial Canal," the release said, and was apprehended.

"When Jose Holmes is released from the hospital, he will be arrested on eight counts of Attempted Murder of Police Officers, along with Lance Madison," it said. The others on the bridge that morning were not charged. "However, the District Attorney is being consulted."

"Investigators are still [in] the process of establishing an exact motive for the incident," the release concluded.

"GIVE ME A NAME!" Kaufman hollered out one day, seeking to create a star witness as he worked to hone the final report about the shootings on the bridge. Lehrmann, Kaufman's underling, heard his colleague's question. Lehrmann had arrived on the bridge after the shooting began and then, once it stopped, started to put handcuffs on Ronald Madison. Suddenly realizing the slight figure was dead, he took the cuffs off. The episode embarrassed Lehrmann. Kaufman told him not to worry, that he wouldn't mention it in his report. Now Lehrmann was part of the crew assigned to investigate the shootings.

"Lakeisha," Lehrmann blurted out.

So there it was. "Lakeisha Smith" was promptly listed as a witness to the shootings on the bridge. In Kaufman's narrative, she saw Ronald Madison reach into his waistband and turn toward police before they fired. For good measure, Lakeisha Smith reported Lance and Ronald Madison had been looting and terrorizing people since the storm.

"Mrs. Smith advised Sergeant Kaufman that she was in the process of relocating to Dallas, Texas, to live with her sister at an unknown address," Kaufman reported. "Sergeant Kaufman mentioned Mrs. Smith could add nothing further."

Lakeisha Smith was a fiction, like much of the official fifty-four-page report Kaufman and other supervisors ultimately created to explain away the events of that Sunday morning. The second eyewitness police cited was "James Youngman." Kaufman and crew gave Youngman a local address, at a Michoud apartment complex, but transposed the apartment number so the given address was unreachable. "Just part of the fun," Lehrmann later said in court. In the report, Youngman said he "observed several black males shooting at police officers near Downman Road and then fleeing over the bridge. Youngman advised that he also observed the police officers return fire and chase the males over the Danziger Bridge."

Police listed no phone or Social Security numbers for their two star witnesses. If anyone ever tried to track down James Youngman or Lakeisha Smith, well, good luck. They were ghosts. "Sergeant Kaufman related this was a brief verbal statement, as Officers were unable to obtain any audio or video taped statements due to post storm conditions," the report explained.

The official police version said Lance Madison and Jose Holmes fired first that day, and that officers were fully justified in responding. Around the Crystal Palace, that story stuck. Already, fellow officers were patting Bowen, Hunter, Hills, and the other gunmen on the back, thanking them for protecting their hurricane-ravaged city from looting gunmen.

Lance Madison was accused of trying to kill seven New Orleans Police Department officers who pursued the two families, along with the man dressed in police garb, who initially flagged officer Dupree for help from the I-10. He was charged with eight counts of attempted murder of the same mob of NOPD officers who shot Ronald in the back, James Brissette Jr. from heel to head, and four others from the Bartholomew family. Jose Holmes was still in the hospital recovering from surgery. Once he was released, the department planned to charge him with attempted murder too.

The fact that the accused and the victims Ronald and JJ were not criminals with lengthy rap sheets and multiple trips in and out of the city's justice system presented a serious flaw. "You have these—these great charges against this man that's never been arrested," said Lehrmann, referring to Lance Madison. "That's going to present problems."

Kaufman had a solution.

"Hey, let's take a ride," Kaufman told officers around the Crystal Palace one afternoon, planning to make good on his earlier promise to Lohman. So, Kaufman, Lehrmann, Bowen, and Gisevius took a ride to the sergeant's own house. He parked the car, opened the garage, and rummaged around large Tupperware storage bins. He walked back holding a brown paper bag.

"What's this?" Lehrmann asked.

"A ham sandwich," Kaufman replied. The bag passed from hand to hand until it landed in evidence. The Colt Trooper Mark III revolver was now, police said, the firearm Lance Madison used to try to kill police. It was untraceable.

In the police department log, Lance Madison's weapon was recorded as one blue steel Colt .357 magnum Model Trooper MKIII revolver, five-inch barrel, six shot handgun, serial number 84044J. "The weapon was confiscated by Sergeant Arthur Kaufman on Monday, September 5, 2005 at about 10:00 AM, from the scene on side of the Danziger Bridge. It was subsequently submitted in to Central Evidence and Property," police reported. "At this time, no purchase information on the weapon or history has been obtained."

The gun landed in the evidence room six weeks after the shootings, but Kaufman had an explanation. He found the weapon in a search of the bridge a day after the shootings, but left it in the back of his car for six weeks. He simply forgot to put it in evidence right away.

More problems. The supposed officer who first flagged Dupree with the distress call on the I-10 high-rise and who pulled onto the Danziger Bridge riding atop the front of a police car to help identify the suspects, although dressed in full state sheriff's uniform, was no officer at all. He was Marion David Ryder, a convicted felon who convinced police he was one of them. No matter. In the official fifty-four-page report, David Ryder was listed as a deputy sheriff who swore Lance Madison was the same man who had fired those first shots that morning. Ryder likewise said Ronald Madison was also shooting a gun. Like the seven officers who aimed their weapons, Ryder was listed in the police report as a victim. The phony officer, in fact, was listed as Victim #1.

Detective Lehrmann was there when Kaufman learned Ryder was no sheriff's deputy. Kaufman was, again, not happy; but he refused to change this story line. "If [Ryder] made those claims and he can't back them up, then that's on him," Kaufman told his colleague.

IN AN ABANDONED, gutted New Orleans police office shortly after the calendar turned to 2006, Kaufman delivered a message to the squad: We've got you covered. "Get your stories straight." This was on January 25,

2006, as the officers on the bridge prepared to give formal audiotaped statements about the shooting to New Orleans officers. First, they huddled together. Kaufman, Lehrmann, and another investigating sergeant, Gerard Dugue, a black officer lately assigned to help with the Danziger inquiry, met with Bowen, Gisevius, and Villavaso. Bowen took the lead in describing the story, and other officers chimed in. Hunter, Hills, and Barrios were there too. Among the seven officers who said they fired their weapons, only Robert Faulcon, who had left New Orleans late in 2005, was not present for the powwow.

"I call it a secret meeting because Dugue told us in the meeting, he said, 'Look, this never happened. I'll never admit this meeting occurred,'" Detective Lehrmann would later testify. "And what the meeting was, it was, basically, 'Okay, this is the story, everybody read the report, everybody know what you're going to say, so we can put it on tape and take the statements.'"

Once the taping began, the officers did their part to help advance the story. Sergeant Gisevius, who fired his M4 at the Madison and Bartholomew families instead of his police-issued handgun, was asked whether he shot his weapon that day. His answer was artful avoidance. "No," he replied. "I did not fire my service weapon, no." He later turned in his police revolver to evidence but not the M4 assault rifle.

One after the other, the officers shared their stories that Wednesday afternoon, their accounts recorded for posterity.

Starting at 2:45 p.m., Barrios gave his statement to two detectives. Shortly after, Bowen began giving his, answering questions from Dugue and Kaufman. At 2:57, Villavaso gave his statement to two other detectives, who then turned the tape recorder on for Hunter. As Villavaso was sitting down, Officer Hills began fielding questions from Detective Lehrmann. And then, at 3:30, Dugue and Kaufman queried Sergeant Gisevius. The statement lasted fifteen minutes.

Like clockwork the police story came together, neatly tidied up as officers sat down to answer questions from fellow New Orleans Police Department officers.

AS THE POLICE CLIQUE cemented in the months to follow, most of the officers went back to work, and as they did, they were celebrated for protecting the city and doing honor to the force during a time of unprecedented chaos. They were treated "pretty much like heroes," Hunter admitted. "Nobody thought we did anything wrong. They thought we did our job. You know, we stayed for Katrina."

Robert Faulcon Jr., whose son was a Katrina baby and who fired the fatal shotgun blast into Ronald Madison's back, was no longer part of the blue line. Faulcon soon left New Orleans and gave up the badge, moving to Houston, Texas, to be with his bride, young child, and two stepdaughters and doing all he could to put the gunfire and death out of his mind.

"It was a traumatic event. It's something that you try and get over. It's something that you don't want to be reminded of," he said. Trained in the military and grounded in police work, Faulcon was getting as far away from the life as possible. In Texas Faulcon enrolled in truck driving school, graduating that December. The man wired for police service was giving it up.

CHAPTER 11

SHOCK, FUNERALS, POLICE VISITS—AND A FAMILY'S QUEST FOR ANSWERS

AS POLICE PUT THEIR story into the record, victims planned funerals and grappled with the unknown. Finding the body of their son and brother Ronald took the Madisons more than a month. For more than nine months, Sherrel Johnson did know where her son JJ was.

When Ronald and Lance stayed behind in the condo, the rest of the Madison family rode out the storm in Lafayette Parish, a 140-mile journey through Bayou low country west of New Orleans. There, sheltered in a hotel in Scott, Louisiana, they heard nothing. The Madisons had always been close with police. At his dental practice aside the bridge, Romell had treated NOPD officers as patients for years. One of the officers on the bridge, Ignatius Hills, had been a patient as a child. A brother-in-law was an officer, and cousins wore the badge. Romell called some of the police he knew and asked them to check on his brothers. A female police representative rang back. Ronald was dead and Lance had been arrested.

Romell knew something had gone wrong. His brothers were no outlaws.

He phoned his sister, Jacquelyn Brown. Inside her hotel room, Jacquelyn dropped the phone upon hearing the news from Romell. Their mother, Fuki, collapsed into the arms of Jacquelyn's husband. "We cried," Jacquelyn later said. "You know, we had to give each other encouragement to let us know that, you know, this wasn't the end for us. That we were still determined to seek justice and we would go to the next step."

Days before Romell's phone call, Jacquelyn had told her family of two dreams that stirred her from sleep even before Hurricane Katrina's arrival, dreams later recounted by her daughter, Brittney Brown:

Dream 1
My mother woke up crying to my father. She told him that in her dream she walked out onto the front porch of a house. The wind was blowing and the sky was getting dark, then it begins to rain. It was like a storm was approaching. As she stood on the porch, a little girl walked up to my mother. She said she could not see the young girl's face because it was covered with a veil. The young girl held a flower up to my mother and said, "Everything is gonna be okay," then all of the petals blew away.

Dream 2
Once again my mother woke up crying to my dad. This time she was at a funeral and all of our relatives were there. My mother walked up to the casket and her brother Ronald was laying there; she had no idea how or why he passed away.

Now, drowning in loss, the Madison family was equally racked by uncertainty. One brother was dead, another locked up, and they had no idea why. They didn't know where Ronald's body was, and simply learning where Lance was being held would require persistence and contacts. Through a series of phone calls to police, friends, and judges they knew, they got wind that Lance had been transferred upstate in the vicinity of Baton Rouge. They knew little more. Knowing the details they were hearing could not possibly be the full story, they searched for answers.

Their drive was led by Romell, the oldest son, the civic leader. The Monday after the shooting, Romell reached out to Nathan Fisher, a one-time prosecutor and longtime defense attorney with an office in downtown Baton Rouge. The family wanted a lawyer outside New Orleans. "We didn't know who we could trust," Jacquelyn said. "So we had wanted to get an attorney that was outside the area."

Fisher attended Ole Miss when James Meredith became the first black student to attend the university in Oxford, Mississippi, and the young Jewish man witnessed Meredith's enrollment triggering riots. "It was a hell of an education, watching that," Fisher said.

Now, the lawyer took the call from Romell Madison, sharing news that one brother had been killed and another locked up. "There's absolutely no way this happened the way they said it happened," Romell told Fisher, trying to absorb the little the family knew at that point. The first challenge was to find Lance, and, in the insane days following Katrina, with power still out and communication in the dark ages, it took Fisher and Shannon Fay, a law student working with him, some time to do that. "I don't believe I've ever felt as inept as an attorney as that first day, when I couldn't find that guy," Fisher said.

Working his criminal justice sources, Fisher confirmed Lance was being held in the Elayn Hunt Correctional Center, about fifteen miles away.

After Lance's arrest, officers initially held him at the Crystal Palace for more than an hour, keeping him in handcuffs outside the building. Lance spotted a New Orleans police officer he recognized from his football days. He started telling him what happened. "I know this guy," Lance heard him say. "He wouldn't do something like that." The officer went off, Lance assumed, to share his findings. But later, when Lance saw him again, "he said he couldn't talk to me."

Next, Lance was taken to "Camp Greyhound," the temporary jail compound at the Greyhound bus station. He was held in a cage with a portable toilet. German shepherds circled the cage.

Finally he landed at Hunt Correctional Center. There, Lance was being held in a special camp set aside for Hurricane Katrina criminals. At Hunt, Lance Madison stood with his back against the wall, peering out toward anyone coming toward him. He feared someone would try to kill him before he could tell the truth about what happened on the bridge.

It was another day before the lawyers met with Lance. "I didn't do this," he told them. "They shot my brother. These people just showed up in a truck and started shooting at us."

Fisher, Fay, and their defense investigator would look under every rock and follow to the end every thread they could find to test whether the law enforcement version of events was true: that Lance Madison was an attempted murderer. "This family is the salt of the earth. They got hammered," Fisher told me. "If that had been you and I going across that bridge, that would not have happened."

By the time he and Fay finished peering under the NOPD's veneer, Fisher would come to a stark conclusion. This was about the worst abuse of police power that he had ever seen. Fay quickly picked up on clues of a police shoot gone wrong.

Fay is a confident young blonde, a digger who was committed to helping the Madison family uncover the truth. The shootings on the bridge would serve as a real-life case study beyond anything Fay's professors could dream up in the classroom at Southern University Law Center in Baton Rouge, the same college Lance had graduated from decades earlier. In law school Fay studied contracts, property, criminal, and other legal matters, working for the Nathan S. Fisher Law Firm by day and taking classes at night. The story she was beginning to see unfold—the police fictions, the killings of innocent people, and the cover-up—opened her eyes. "It definitely left a lasting impression," she said. "This was all we lived and breathed for months."

First, they represented Lance during a hearing to set his bond while the formal charges against him played out. When Fisher had first gone for the hearing, he bumped into the judge assigned to rule. "I can't go against the police department," the judge confided. Fisher stalled, saying he needed more time to prepare. What he really needed was a judge who hadn't already decided the matter before hearing a shred of evidence.

On Wednesday, September 28, 2005, another judge was assigned the hearing. Fisher didn't know what to expect.

Magistrate judge Gerard J. Hansen presided over the hearing that would set the bond and determine whether Lance had any chance to be released in a legal system buried in Hurricane Katrina backlogs. Hansen, with soft tufts of white hair and a soothing Cajun cadence, grew up working in the family's Sno-Bliz counter on Tchoupitoulas Street in New Orleans, shaving ice from the oldest sno-ball stand in the United States. As a judge, Gerard Hansen went on to earn the distinction of setting the most bonds of any jurist in Louisiana history.

In the hearing this day, twenty-four days after the shootings on the bridge, Sergeant Kaufman testified first, called to the stand to outline the gravity of the charges against Lance Madison and to help the district attorney seek a steep bond for his release. From the witness stand, Kaufman recounted the 108 call. The Budget truck headed out first, racing to the bridge. Kaufman jumped into a police car and called for an ambulance to follow him, arriving after the shootout.

"A gunfight ensued," Kaufman told the judge. "The officers identified themselves; they were fired upon by four of the seven subjects. Handguns were used by the subjects."

There were eight residents, not seven. Kaufman left the Bartholomew son out of the narrative, the teen who escaped down an embankment and avoided bullets whizzing by his back.

"Five people were shot at the foot of the Danziger Bridge, four critically wounded, one killed," the sergeant continued, first describing what happened to the Bartholomew group.

Then he recounted the Madison brothers' path up and over the bridge. "Two of the perpetrators continued up the bridge firing at the officers. They were chased into the Friendly Inn, which is on the Third District side of the Danziger Bridge. It's right at the foot of the bridge. One subject turned, reached in his waistband, turned on the officers— returned—actually fired; killed him on the spot in the driveway."

Kaufman described how Lance Madison continued through the driveway, wading through water and toward the back of the hotel. Kaufman said he pulled onto the scene in time to see Ronald Madison shot and killed in the driveway.

"At that point, of course, chaos ruled," he said. "And we were making sure that no officers were shot."

State police stormed the bridge in an armored vehicle, and some fifteen Louisiana State Police troopers spilled out, donned in SWAT-team regalia. They had been in the area earlier responding to the unconfirmed sniper call and, once they heard of the fracas from the 108 call, went to the bridge. In the bond hearing, Kaufman connected the sniper fire to the shooting on the bridge, another web to tangle the victims into the police account. "Once we got everything under control, we realized that the gunfire coming from the hotel and the incident that we encountered were one and the same. That was the same group of people," Kaufman told Hansen.

Officers swarmed the area and apprehended Lance Madison behind a business. By this time, one hundred officers were on scene, Kaufman said, answering questions from assistant district attorney Donna Andrieu. He said that David Ryder, the man who flagged down officer Jennifer Dupree, setting the initial call in motion, was brought to where officers surrounded Lance Madison. Ryder identified Lance Madison as among the people shooting at him that morning, Kaufman testified.

Did police find a gun on Lance Madison, the family's attorney, Nathan Fisher, asked. "Not with him, no, sir," Kaufman replied. But they did find one later, he said.

"We have one," Kaufman said, figuratively putting a weapon in Lance Madison's hand. "It's a revolver," he continued. "It was retrieved by one of the other officers that was involved in the incident."

Fisher asked about the polygraph Lance Madison had begged for that morning. "There's a possibility he may have asked," Kaufman answered, dismissing the question's significance. "It was irrelevant at that point."

Then Fisher asked Kaufman about a curious one-page report, a brief police summary of events known as a Gist Sheet filed that first day to support the attempted murder charges against Lance Madison. Scanning the sheet days before the hearing, the family lawyers noticed two sets of handwriting on the single page. The newer handwriting filled the bottom three lines. "The perpetrator fled and threw his handgun into the Industrial Canal and was apprehended a short time later," it said. The report was authored by Ignatius Hills, one of the officers on the bridge that morning, and approved by Sergeant Kaufman.

"We saw there is clearly a different handwriting," Shannon Fay said. "That's when we knew something wasn't right." This was not only odd, the lawyers knew, but potentially revealing, perhaps a first sign of a larger cover-up. They retained a handwriting expert to confirm that the Gist Sheet was scrawled in two different hands. In court twenty-four days after the one-page report was written, they found no need to call the expert to the stand. Kaufman confirmed he wrote the second set of notes.

"And the last three lines, would you read those to me?" Nathan Fisher asked.

Kaufman looked at the report and read them aloud for the judge to hear. Those lines, for the first time in the report, introduced the idea that Lance Madison was armed.

Why, Fisher wanted to know, were the report's first twelve lines written in one hand, by Officer Hills, and the last three in Kaufman's?

Sergeant Bowen told him about the gun after Hills first filed the Gist Sheet, Kaufman said. So he added the detail.

That Wednesday in the bond hearing, defense lawyer Fisher decided to take an unusual step. "Your honor, you know I've been practicing for thirty years. And I never thought that I would put on a defendant at a Preliminary Hearing but I'm going to call Lance Madison," he told Hansen.

By taking the stand, Lance opened himself up to cross-examination by the state prosecutor, a potential quicksand trap for any defendant facing attempted murder charges. Typically it's better to keep your mouth shut and force the state to prove its case. Lance Madison, silenced on the bridge, wanted to speak. He raised his right hand to swear to tell the truth.

Little more than three weeks after the Sunday morning shootings, the events and facts remained a blur in Lance Madison's mind. At that point, he assumed the teens he saw that morning had fired first. He couldn't imagine police simply opening fire without cause and aiming at unarmed targets. He also thought he saw something in the teens' hands.

"We tried to run for our life," Madison testified. The men he later learned were police, "they shot the little kids up. And then they saw me and my little brother going up the bridge and one of the officers shot my brother in the shoulder. And I had to pick him up to try to run down the bridge to find some help.

"And my little brother was shot. And I had to put him down and told him I'd be right back. 'I'm going to get you some help!' And that's when I ran trying to find some help for him through the hotel. And that's when the police officer came and I don't know if they shot him again or not."

As he ran through the hotel, Madison was chased by bullets. He looked up and saw officers from the state police.

"I felt comfortable so I was running to them to explain to them that my little brother's been shot and he needs some medical attention," Lance testified. "And they threw me on the ground and arrested me."

I had no gun, Lance told Judge Hansen. He did own a gun once, but it had been stolen in 1988. He filed a police report then and had not owned a weapon since.

"Did you, in fact, shoot at some policemen?" Fisher asked.

"No. I didn't have a gun at all. My little brother didn't have a gun. We was running for our life," he answered.

In court, Lance said he had no idea where his brother's body was. He did not know that a day earlier, his siblings Romell and Jacquelyn had gone to a morgue to view Ronald's body. They were denied that request and told they needed a court order to view the body of their dead brother. Fisher had to file a motion to allow the family to view and identify Ronald Madison.

On the witness stand, Lance told the judge how he desperately tried to convince police he and his brother were the victims, not the shooters. "I kept telling them—I said that y'all have the wrong person and I'm not that person."

The NOPD had no interest in Lance Madison's plea. "They kept cursing me and told me to shut up. They don't want to hear nothing from me. They just cursed, kept cursing me."

The police didn't want to hear from Lance Madison, but magistrate judge Gerard Hansen did. He was struck by the story he heard that day. "Listening to your client's testimony and looking at your client, it's hard for me to believe that he would be the type of person that would be up shooting at people," Hansen said.

Still, based on Kaufman's statement that Lance threw a gun into the canal, "I'm going to have to find that there was probable cause for his arrest," the judge said. "But the bond, I think, is excessive under the circumstances. The bond today is $800,000, am I correct?"

Hansen cut the bond in half. The family would put up property to meet the bond, freeing Lance as he waited for the case to move through the legal system.

"Sir, you will be free but I have to take some safeguards and security because of the circumstances," Hansen said, speaking directly to Madison. "And the charges are serious; they're extremely serious."

"Thank you," Lance said.

"If I actually thought you were up there shooting, I would raise the bond to two million dollars, all right. If I actually felt that, I would raise the bond. Okay. I don't think you're one of the shooters. I don't think that, okay.

"I could be wrong but I've been doing this for thirty-two years and I think I have a gut reaction on this."

Lance was released on bond the next day, September 29, 2005.

In all, Lance Madison spent twenty-five days behind bars. "The twenty-five days I spent at Hunt's prison felt like years. I was sick every day, filled with anxiety. I thought I'd spend the rest of my life in prison. I couldn't breathe, and was certain I'd lose my mind," he said. "I still feel like I'm in prison . . . still struggling daily to put this nightmare behind me." He remains haunted that he left his brother's side. "To my dying day, I will regret that I didn't stay with Ronald," he said. "These officers shot Ronald down like an animal, and I had to make the awful decision to leave my injured brother's side to try to find help."

That same day, Romell and attorney Fisher went to the morgue to view Ronald Madison's body. His body had been moved to another location, they were told. An Orleans Parish coroner would not tell them where. Romell asked to see the autopsy. The coroner said it wasn't yet typed. Romell asked to see the written notes. The office said no. In two days, the coroner said, he would call Fisher to arrange for the family to view the body.

It wasn't until the first week in October that the morgue called to confirm the identity of Ronald's body. The family had to file a court motion to view the autopsy and see Ronald. When the autopsy was finally released, it said the Orleans Parish Coroner's Office concluded Ronald Madison had seven gunshot wounds in the backside of his body, five in his back and two in his upper arm and shoulder area. Two wounds were penetrating, and five perforating. Attached to the autopsy, a diagram placed the fatal gunshot strikes. Six clustered to the right of his spine, and one to the left. The Madisons arranged for a second autopsy, taking every step to confirm what happened to Ronald. On his Louisiana death certificate, the cause of Ronald Curtis Madison's death is listed as "Hurricane Katrina related. Multiple gunshot wounds."

His funeral cost the Madison family $9,216.50.

WHEN FAMILY AND FRIENDS gathered for the Mass of Christian Burial on November 2, 2005, at Our Lady of Guadalupe Chapel in New Orleans, they mourned Ronald's death and celebrated his life inside the city's oldest church building, whose mortuary chapel had first risen in 1826 to bury victims of yellow fever. "God, in His own way, for His own purpose or reason, and in His own time reached down in our midst early Sunday, September 4, 2005, and called Ronald Curtis Madison home to a sweet and glorious rest," said the booklet from the morning ceremony.

"We are, in a small way, comforted in knowing that he joins his family in heaven—his father, James Madison; brothers, Ronald 1 and Theodore Madison; sisters, Loretta Madison and Barbara Madison Woodfork; and nephew Lance Madison."

A final inscription reads, "He has gone to a land that is free from pain and sorrow." Looking back upon Ronald's life, mourners took a moment to soak in family pictures on display. In one grade school photograph, Ronald is smiling, with his hands clasped over each other just like any other child would for his school portrait. In a later picture, he is adorned in cap and gown for his graduation. In others, he is surrounded by his family, his protectors.

At the service, brother Lance was among Ronald's pallbearers.

Lance's release from the Hunt facility motivated the family to push even harder to unmask the truth they knew was hidden that morning on the bridge, even as police were telling the public they had ample cause to fire at the citizens.

In the coming days, an investigator for Nathan Fisher traveled from his Baton Rouge office to New Orleans with Shannon Fay to visit the crime scene. Questions, not answers, were all around. "We took pictures. Bullet casings were still on the ground," Fay said. "Clearly there had been no crime scene worked up."

As the Madisons pushed for answers, some NOPD brass became fearful of what could come. Lorna Humphrey, one of the Madison sisters, was just then going through a divorce with a New Orleans officer; her husband was once a partner with the then NOPD superintendent Edwin Compass. Romell and Compass had been fraternity brothers years earlier, and Compass, a former football player himself, worked out at the same gym as Lance Madison. He had attended the funeral of their father, James Madison. "We're sorry," Compass told Lorna in a phone call, the family said. "We hope you don't sue us."

Said Shannon Fay, "You knew something wasn't right when the police chief called up and said, I hope you're not going to sue us."

The Madison family was determined to get a full accounting of what happened on the bridge. With Ronald's passing, five of the ten children born to James and Fuki had died. Jacquelyn's daughter Brittney cited a piece of scripture that was driving them. "For there is nothing *covered*, that shall not be *revealed*; neither *hid*, that shall not be *known*" (Luke 12:2, King James version, italics added).

AS ROMELL MADISON AND his family pressed for answers, Susan Bartholomew, her daughter, and Jose Holmes Jr. were hospitalized for months recovering from their injuries and the surgeries they had to undergo.

When Susan was first whisked into the hospital room, a nurse walked in and Bartholomew clung to her fiercely. "She just seemed like an angel, a godsend. I asked her and begged her to just to not leave me, and she said that she wouldn't," Susan said later. Then she lost consciousness.

In the days after the shooting, Officers Kaufman and Lehrmann twice entered Susan Bartholomew's room. Leaning over her bed, they asked, "Who did this?"

She looked up and saw it was NOPD.

"I'm not sure," she said. "I think it was the National Guard."

Bartholomew knew the shooters were New Orleans Police, not the Guard. She was scared, and their direct questions chilled her. *These are the same people who shot off my arm, fired at my husband's head, and tried to kill my two children. I'm going to trust them?* "I felt threatened," she said. "I felt intimidated, just the way they . . . their approach."

After the first two visits, she asked a nurse to stop the officers from coming back. The nurse promised to help.

A few days later, the police returned. The nurse turned her back and walked away. The officers closed the door and stood over Bartholomew. "Who did this?"

"The National Guard," Bartholomew said. They asked her husband the same question. "The National Guard," Leonard III said.

For nearly two weeks, Susan had no idea where her son, Little Leonard, was, and she woke up each morning jolted by worry. After Morrell Johnson looked out for the boy that Sunday morning, Little Leonard met a woman who was driving people out of New Orleans in buses. The woman, Carla, heard his story and took him into her home in Baton Rouge for a week and a half. She and her boyfriend cared for him and put a notice on the Internet about a missing child. In Texas, his uncle Jerome saw the notice and came to get him. Jerome drove Leonard Bartholomew IV directly to the hospital.

His mom was in a wheelchair, her right arm gone. His sister Lesha was in a hospital bed, unable to walk. Cousin Jose, his close pal, lay in his own hospital bed, unable to talk, with a metal plate in his jaw. Surrounded by loss, the teenager was suddenly engulfed by guilt. Why wasn't he shot too?

Looking toward his cousin Jose, he started crying.

"I'm sorry," Leonard told him. "I should have been shot, too. It isn't right that I got off like that but everybody else has to go through all of this pain. And I'm just walking around, I'm fine. I don't have to worry about injuries. It just isn't right."

Jose looked at his cousin, lifted an arm, and gave a thumbs-up. You didn't do anything wrong, he was saying. None of us deserved this.

When Jose had first been rushed to West Jefferson, a gush of wind snapped him to as the hospital doors whisked open, and he looked up to glimpse lights and doctors encircling him. Then the images faded, and doctors scurried to save his life in surgery. Now Jose lay in his hospital bed with a metal rod in his left arm, a jaw fixator to hold his face in place, deep scars across his stomach, a tube to help him breathe, and a colostomy bag. "A poop sack," he called it. Nurses ordered Jose to move even when he didn't want to, to begin the painful process of rebuilding his muscles. One nurse refused to let Jose be lazy, and he was thankful she pushed him. Yet the same nurse chastised him for firing at helicopters, repeating the line Sergeant Kaufman so loudly uttered after one visit to Susan's hospital room.

Another hospital staffer told Jose he needed to get healthy because, once he was released, he would be arrested on attempted murder charges.

In the weeks after the shooting, Jose was barely able to speak. Other than a BB gun at age fourteen, he had never owned a gun. In the hospital bed he tried to muster strength to tell the nurse what the police were saying about him was not true. "And I just kept shaking my head because I couldn't talk to her," Jose said, "but she kept insinuating I was shooting the helicopters." More than anything, he didn't want the people working to bring him back to life believing he was a killer.

.   .   .

AS 2005 SPUN INTO 2006, Sherrel Johnson heard nothing from JJ. He had vanished, and the family feared the seventeen-year-old had been buried by Hurricane Katrina's floodwaters. She had no inkling he had been gunned down on the bridge.

James Brissette Jr. was not the only family member killed during the hurricane and its aftermath. His brother-in-law, Lawrence Celestine, who was married to JJ's sister Andrea Celestine, was a well-respected, eight-year NOPD veteran who had died in the first days after Katrina. Initially police ruled his death a suicide, an event that captured the attention of the *New York Times* and was cast as a symbol of the city's painful, depressing spiral. A forensic expert, conducting a psychiatric forensic autopsy, concluded that "Officer Celestine's death by suicide was the result of an 'Acute Stress Disorder,' brought on by the extreme catastrophic circumstances of the aftermath of Hurricane Katrina and the duties he had to perform in the course and scope of his employment as a NOPD officer," a Louisiana Fourth Circuit Court of Appeals ruling noted five years later.

Some other experts did not share this assessment, finding no sign that Celestine suffered from mental illness and seeing no evidence to support the diagnosis.

The circumstances of Celestine's death are filled with coincidences. The seven-page NOPD report on his death was written by the same Sergeant Kaufman helping lead the department's probe of the shootings on the bridge. Officer Celestine was related by marriage to Henry Glover, a New Orleans resident shot by police and later set on fire in the days after Katrina. The accused shooter served in the same police district, the Seventh, as Celestine. Glover and Celestine died the same day.

Citing these and other unusual circumstances, Celestine's widow pressed the city to investigate her husband's death as a murder, not a suicide. A decade later, the case remains unresolved.

MONTHS AFTER THE SHOOTINGS on the Danziger Bridge, Sherrel Johnson knew only that her nerdy, book-loving teenager was no longer around.

By Mother's Day weekend 2006, Sherrel submitted her DNA sample to a network formed by the Louisiana Department of Public Health following Katrina to connect families with missing loved ones. The state set up the Find Family National Call Center in a one-time sporting goods store in Baton Rouge and, every time the center linked a family member with a missing loved one, a worker would ring a bell. Sometimes the family member rang it, the clang a visceral confirmation of one more family tie knotted.

Using dental records, fingerprints, medical records, and other resources, the state's Victim Identification Center also worked to positively identify the remains of unclaimed Hurricane Katrina victims. By December 30, four months after Katrina, forensic experts at the center had positively identified 735 remains.

"When all other means have been exhausted, a technique called kinship DNA analysis will be used to assist in the identification of victims. This process involves analyzing DNA from family members and then comparing these samples to DNA taken from the unidentified deceased," said the Louisiana Department of Public Health, which took mouth swabs to collect the DNA.

Sherrel had resisted going to the center, fearing the worst but still holding out a mother's hope. Displaced to Tennessee for weeks after Hurricane Katrina, she took the time to fill out paperwork enrolling JJ in public school there, saving a place for him when her boy came home.

When Sherrel finally did submit her DNA sample, she did so with her mother at her side, a cushion of familial strength. A match came back. On June 6, 2006, Sherrel was told JJ had died. She initially assumed her son had drowned. She didn't know police had killed him, a fact she would learn only later.

An autopsy report, written by the Coroner's Office of the Parish of Orleans and signed in March 2006, said the deceased had arrived clad in black tennis shoes, blue shorts under a pair of gray-black shorts, and wearing a white T-shirt. JJ had a wooden pendant hanging from his neck. "IRIE," it said, Jamaican patois that means "all right," to be at peace with yourself. "There are seven gunshot wounds to the left upper arm, right posterior neck, mid posterior neck, left anterior upper arm, right buttock, right upper anterior leg and right elbow," the report said.

A subsequent exam of JJ's X-rays would reveal even more pieces of shrapnel lodged in him. "They broke my heart," Sherrel said. "In November, he was going to be eighteen. He was going to get his first car. I'll never get to see the grin on his face when he's waving his keys." Katrina ravaged the homes of Sherrel and her daughter, Andrea, and most of their possessions. With JJ in the morgue, the family had one photograph of him left to hold on to. It was taken at Andrea's wedding. In the picture, James Brissette Jr. is nine years old.

CHAPTER 12

VICTIMS SHINE A LEGAL LIGHT

AS THE CALENDAR TURNED to summer, and Hurricane Katrina's one year anniversary greeted a city still mired in a painful recovery, the police story stood firm. Lance Madison and Jose Holmes Jr. remained suspects in eight counts of attempted murder, and the public at large viewed the shootings on the bridge as one in a flurry of Katrina tragedies that forever changed their city.

In May 2006 Sergeants Arthur Kaufman and Gerard Dugue had filed the department's fifty-four-page report supporting their charges of attempted murder against the two men, and logging the evidence—the Colt .357 Magnum "confiscated" by Kaufman a day after the shootings. The report included interviews with all the officers, who supported the police line.

The final police report never listed a motive for the shootings. Instead, it cast the spotlight upon the hurricane. "The motive for the attempted murder of several police officers is unknown. It should be noted that after Hurricane Katrina passed, the City of New Orleans was in a state of chaos and confusion. Officers throughout the City of New Orleans were taking fire from pockets of insurgent citizens which remained after evacuations were complete." These officers were listed as victims:

- "Deputy" David Ryder, white male, age forty at the time of the shootings
- Sergeant Kenneth Bowen, white male, thirty-one
- Sergeant Robert Gisevius, white male, thirty-three
- Officer Robert Faulcon, black male, forty-one
- Officer Michael Hunter, white male, twenty-eight

- Officer Ignatius Hills, black male, twenty-eight
- Officer Anthony Villavaso, black male, twenty-eight
- Officer Robert Barrios, black male, twenty-four

The report said other officers on the scene, including Officer Dupree and police riding with her that morning, were likewise victims. "Let it be known there were relief workers who were being fired upon by the assailants, but fled the area before they could be interviewed," Kaufman and Dugue reported. "None of the law enforcement officers or relief workers sustained any injury from being fired upon."

The officers' narratives filled the report, one after the other describing their actions as by the book. This report, built from the earlier versions, sharpened the story line to clearly cast the police as responding to an attack.

"Police!" the report quoted Bowen as shouting that morning. "'Show me your hands. . . .' He stated the subjects immediately went for cover, while arming themselves, and fired upon the officers. Sergeant Bowen mentioned he began to shout to the subjects to throw their weapons off the side of the bridge."

Bowen saw two men running—the Madison brothers—"who were shooting back at the officers on the bridge," the narrative continued.

"Sergeant Bowen stated he exited the truck and cautiously peeked over the cement barrier. He observed two dark colored handguns lying on the cement next to stationary subjects. Sergeant Bowen jumped over the cement barrier and kicked the weapons over the side of the bridge."

Other officers told similar tales, each relating how they identified themselves before firing, and each describing how their targets were armed.

"With the apprehension of Lance Madison, as being one of the subjects shooting at police officers and rescue workers, and the arrest of Jose Holmes being imminent, this case is considered solved."

On the report's cover sheet, an *x* is typed in next to the words "Cleared By Arrest." To police, the case was closed.

From Baton Rouge, lawyer Nathan Fisher and Shannon Fay kept digging for details to prove the police conclusion was an utter fraud and to show that their client Lance Madison was innocent. Reading the fifty-four page police report, they saw "Deputy David Ryder," of the St. Landry

Parish Sheriff's office, listed as the first victim of attempted murder by Lance and Jose Holmes Jr. Their investigator plugged Ryder's name into databases and could find no evidence he was a police officer. Instead, he found the same Marion David Ryder had a police record—arrested in 2002 for battery of a police officer and in 2003 for possession of cocaine and simple battery in St. Landry Parish two and a half hours upstate from New Orleans. He found other criminal cases in Texas. "We were trying to run him down," Fay said.

She and Fisher pulled apart other threads from the police story. "'Oh, we kicked the gun off the bridge,'" she saw, reading Bowen's account. "Oh," she wondered, "that's what you were trained to do?" She added, "We knew it was bad but we had no idea how bad it was until we started seeing the internal investigative reports. When all of a sudden a gun appeared, we're like, where did this come from?"

They kept pressing, reaching out for any pictures or video footage that may have captured what happened that morning. This digging hit pay dirt. The lawyers uncovered never-aired footage from an NBC affiliate that helped paint, in broad strokes, what happened on the bridge. The footage was too fuzzy to reveal individual faces, but it showed in a larger sense police officers in pursuit, not retreat. "You can see what's happening," said Shannon Fay. "You can't see who it is, but you can use it as a guide."

Fisher and Fay looked for the police's supposed star witnesses, Lakeisha Smith and James Youngman. "Obviously, we didn't find them," Fay said; another big question mark in the police account.

They kept pushing and meeting with the district attorney, professing Lance's innocence and seeking his exoneration. "Each day was something new," she said. "It was also such a blur."

As the lawyers pressed for evidence, Lance Madison took care of a small piece of personal business. On September 18, 2006, he sent a fifty-dollar check to Winn-Dixie for the food he took as he and Ronald struggled for survival in Romell's dental office. "I would like to thank you for your honesty concerning the food you and your brother took during Hurricane Katrina in your time of need," Joey Medina, a Winn-Dixie regional vice president in New Orleans, wrote him back. The company returned the money, noting that its losses were covered by insurance. "We hope you will use it to continue shopping with us," Medina wrote. "Again thanks for your honesty."

Lance was falling into a difficult depression. He never returned to work at FedEx at the airport, even though the company had kept his job open for him, and began to undergo therapy to try to work through the horrors he and his brother experienced that morning on the Danziger Bridge. His family and lawyers told Lance to keep telling the truth, stressing the greater purpose in his words. "You were able to speak for Ronald."

AS FAY AND FISHER worked to clear Lance's name in criminal court, a second legal front was brewing in civil court.

Behind the scenes, the Madison family, the Bartholomew family, Jose Holmes, and Sherrel Johnson worked to challenge the police-created perception, laying the groundwork for a series of lawsuits against the city, Mayor Ray Nagin, Superintendent Edwin Compass, other top NOPD brass, and the police officers who unleashed their weapons. These lawsuits, which were beginning to be filed around the one year anniversary of Katrina, were the first public signal that the police story might not be true.

Fisher and Fay shared their findings with Mary Howell, a New Orleans–based civil lawyer with a grainy Cajun cadence to her voice and deep history of challenging police misconduct and deadly shootings. Howell had built a name taking on police corruption in her city, and her work was often recognized. She had once chaired the Civil Rights Section of the Louisiana Trial Lawyers Association and had many honors on her resume, including the ACLU of Louisiana Benjamin E. Smith Civil Liberties Award.

Howell worked from a small blue-colored office on South Dorgenois Street near the courthouse, a cozy setting with hardwood floors, colorful rugs, and aged, handsome cabinets. From this quaint office Mary Howell had taken on some of the biggest police abuse cases in New Orleans history, representing the families victimized by the department's overreaching.

Now, exploring the shootings and the cover-up, she put her experience and expertise into action. On September 1, 2006, she filed a thirty-seven-page civil rights lawsuit on behalf of Lance Madison and his mother, Fuki.

"This case involves a terrible tragedy which unfolded in the aftermath of Hurricane Katrina," the lawsuit begins. "It involves two brothers, life-long residents of the city, who were first victims of the storm and then victims of the City of New Orleans, its failed leadership and its collapsed police department.

"This tragic incident resulted in the death of Ronald Madison, an innocent, mentally retarded, unarmed man who was seeking safety and shelter at his brother's dental office on Chef Menteur Highway and who was repeatedly shot in the back by officers of the New Orleans Police Department and left to die.

"As if the incident itself was not sufficiently terrible, the NOPD officers and supervisors involved in this incident embarked upon a desperate plan to attempt to cover-up their misconduct, by lying and fabricating evidence and attempting to frame an innocent man whose brother they had just killed," she wrote, "an attempted cover-up which continues to this date."

The lawsuit detailed how the police-driven truck "suddenly, without warning," pulled to the foot of the bridge, and how police piled out and started unleashing gunfire. "Prior to opening fire on the Madison brothers, the shooters made no announcements, gave no warnings, and issued no verbal instructions."

The lawsuit said the seven shooting officers hatched a cover-up, and it called out David Ryder's lies. He was no officer, but a convicted criminal.

The suit blamed Mayor Nagin, police superintendent Compass, and NOPD brass for systematically allowing the command structure to collapse. "They were aware that many officers were mentally, emotionally and physically exhausted and on the verge of collapse," the lawsuit said. "Yet they failed to conduct any screening or evaluation of officers to determine their fitness for duty and instead permitted officers, including those who were not fit, to obtain and use non-departmental approved weapons."

Nagin, a black man, had handpicked Compass for the job in 2002, elevating a black officer from the ranks of the NOPD into its top role. In so doing, Nagin departed from his predecessor, former mayor Marc Morial, who had hired his police chief from outside the department and quickly introduced the new superintendent to FBI agents investigating corruption festering inside the NOPD. Morial's chief, a police executive from Washington, DC, named Richard Pennington, did not want to be friends with his officers. "Pennington had ice water in his veins when it came to discipline," said Morial, who focused on cleaning up the department, and purposely chose an outsider not tied to the force. Nagin's path, hiring a friend and local football star he had known since grade school, sent a different signal. Compass was a police brother, a man who would embrace fellow officers with a bear hug and exclaim, "Give me some love!" He was known for backing his brethren, white, black, or Hispanic.

Nagin had won the mayor's seat in 2002 by edging the same Richard Pennington in a race that drew fifteen candidates, among them a funeral home operator, a onetime actor, a plumber, a gardener, and a pastor. Nagin, a cable company executive running on a pro-business platform, won the support of the local *Times-Picayune*'s editorial pages. He became the first New Orleans mayor in fifty years elected to run the city without prior political experience. Among his first acts was to tap a police insider to run a force with a history of civilian abuse cases stretching back decades. Morial said Nagin instantly shuttered the reform programs put in place by his mayoral opponent, former chief Pennington.

Nagin's chief did not last long after Katrina. Superintendent Edwin P. Compass III, battered by criticism that he and Mayor Nagin overstated the degree of chaos and crime in the Superdome, had resigned September 27, 2005. "I served this department for twenty-six years and have taken it through some of the toughest times of its history," Compass told reporters at a news conference. "Every man in a leadership position must know when it's time to hand over the reins. I'll be going on in another direction that God has for me."

The Nagin era ushered in a culture where officers felt empowered to patrol their turf as they saw fit, without looking over their shoulder at the FBI, police department watchdogs say. "Compass wanted to be loved," Mary Howell told me. The reforms of the Morial administration "all got undone." The lawsuit now in court was unmasking the dark side of that police culture.

Nagin and Compass contributed to the atmosphere of lawlessness, the lawsuit said, "by urging, encouraging and pushing NOPD officers to 'take back' the city by any means necessary, including the use of excessive and unlawful force, if needed."

Amid the chaos of Katrina, the mayor, chief, and other top officials communicated that the protections of the US Constitution no longer applied to the police, Howell asserted. "Officers were authorized to 'shoot to kill' individuals in circumstances and under conditions and standards which were constitutionally deficient."

The lawsuit, filed in US District Court for the Eastern District of Louisiana, sought damages for Ronald Madison's "pre-death terror and death" and for the loss of his love to his mother and brother. Lance Madison has "suffered extreme mental anguish over witnessing the death of his brother, Ronald." Among other damages, the suit sought an order that the city pay for Ronald's funeral.

The Madison legal salvo was joined by others. The day *Madison v. City of New Orleans, et al.*, was filed, Jose Holmes Jr. had brought suit in the same federal court, filed by New Orleans lawyer Gary W. Bizal. The lawsuit echoed many of the key points in the Madison case, similarly citing the state of collapse at the New Orleans Police Department.

"As Jose Holmes Jr. [lay] on the ground defenseless, he was shot multiple times by this group of armed men," the suit said. "At no time was Jose Holmes Jr. or anyone in his group armed with any type of weapon or any object that could have been perceived as a weapon." The multiple surgeries required to keep Jose alive left him permanently injured, the lawsuit said, and will reduce his life expectancy.

The Bartholomew family filed suit in August 2006, listing the officers as John Doe and seeking more than $29 million in damages from the city. After the other suits were filed by Jose Holmes and the Madison family, lawyer Edwin M. Shorty Jr. amended the Bartholomew case to include the names of the seven New Orleans police officers.

While each case sought millions in damages, the larger losses—of family members killed, loved ones permanently disfigured, and of police casting the victims as criminals—carried a more lasting toll. Lesha Bartholomew, who lay atop her mother on the bridge to shield her from more gunfire, later put this larger pain into words.

"Why is this happening to us?" Lesha wrote. "This is one of the many questions I asked as I lay on the ground, shot multiple times. This incident has had a major impact on me and my family. I never thought that I would get shot, let alone the shooters being the people whose job it is to protect me. Our lives have completely changed since that day. We now have scars and injuries we have to deal with and look at every day. The scars that I incurred as a result of the gunshot wounds have been very damaging to my self-esteem. I am constantly reminded of that day every time I undress, wear certain clothing, or people stare as I walk.

"My mom has suffered more than anyone," Lesha continued. "I know because she hasn't been out of pain since the day of the shooting. She faces quite a challenge daily. Her right arm was blown off so she is now disabled and in no way has the ability to do things as she once did before. The phantom pain she suffers becomes unbearable at times. It hurts me to see my mom in so much pain. There are days that I can still hear my dad's scream for help as we laid on the side of the bridge waiting for the ambulance. Sometimes it honestly feels like a bad dream and I just want to wake up."

The lawsuits filed by the Madisons, Jose Holmes, and the Bartholomews pointedly challenged the police department's contention that the families were criminals. For the first time, the public was hearing a different story about the shootings on the bridge the first Sunday after Katrina.

In a story published September 14, 2006, headlined "Lawsuits Dispute Fatal Shooting," the New Orleans *Times-Picayune* cited this turn of events.

> A police shooting six days after Hurricane Katrina that authorities initially portrayed as a response to sniper fire on the Danziger Bridge has spawned three federal lawsuits claiming that police killed two unarmed men and wounded four others in a hail of unprovoked gunfire.
>
> In the lawsuits, filed this month against the city, the families of the wounded and the dead, including a 19-year-old man and a 40-year-old mentally disabled man who refused to leave his dogs during the storm, offer accounts of the incident that contradict the police account. The incident remains under investigation by the Orleans Parish district attorney's office.

FOR POLICE, FOR THE VICTIMS, for the city, the question was now in the hands of the parish district attorney's office. Would the DA dig deep, as the families had? Or, would prosecutors side with the police account?

In New Orleans, the DA's office had drawn attention on the spectrum between fame and shame, depending upon the times. Jim Garrison, the Orleans Parish district attorney from 1962 to 1973, believed conspiracy-minded culprits had plotted the assassination of President John F. Kennedy and was portrayed by Kevin Costner in Oliver Stone's movie *JFK*.

In 1974 Harry Connick Sr., father of the New Orleans jazz musician, took over. The elder Connick, a crooner himself, was indicted on racketeering charges in 1989 for returning gambling records, seized in a police raid, to the accused gambler. Charged with aiding and abetting the gambling operation, the DA said he gave the forms back so the accused criminal could complete his tax returns. His case went to trial a year later, and as jurors stepped out to deliberate a verdict, Connick filed for reelection. The jury cleared him, and he was indeed reelected.

Eddie Jordan, a former federal prosecutor who won notoriety for convicting former governor Edwin Edwards of corruption charges, was elected district attorney in 2002, becoming the first black to hold that position in New Orleans. Now the Danziger Bridge matter fell under the legal domain of the prosecutor who had finally nabbed the elusive Edwin Edwards.

Edwards always had a way with words, and of getting the last one. He once chided a political opponent as being so slow it took him "an hour and a half to watch *60 Minutes*." Edwards professed little in common with another well-known Louisiana politician, David Duke, with one exception. "We're both wizards under the sheets." After serving eight years in prison for extorting $3 million from casino companies seeking state licenses, the former governor walked out of prison and, in Bayou fashion, recast himself anew. At age eighty-three, Edwards wed a blonde bride, aged thirty-two. Then in 2014, at age eighty-six, he ran for Congress. He lost in a runoff to a politician not even half his age. "It's not the end of the world for me," Edwards said after his first political defeat, still savoring the journey. "I love this state." Once more Edwin Edwards got the last word, but Eddie Jordan was forever known as the prosecutor who slowed him down, at least for a spell.

Raised in the Ninth Ward of New Orleans, Jordan entered office with a vow to take the city's streets back from criminals and to ratchet up convictions in an office plagued by stressed caseloads and small conviction rates. Earlier, as a federal prosecutor, he had been the one to bring the case against the brutish officer known as Robocop.

But Jordan's postelection glow faded quickly. Once in the job, he ordered an office shakeup that entailed firing white staff members almost exclusively. That housecleaning earned Jordan his share of public ire. It also cost the taxpayers in court when a jury, just four months before Hurricane Katrina's arrival, issued a $3.7 million wrongful termination verdict against the DA's office.

Now Jordan faced his biggest test, the shootings on the Danziger Bridge. The prosecutor who won fame in federal court in the Edwin Edwards trial and the case convicting Robocop now set his attention on what the families, and the police, were saying about the events of September 4, 2005.

That summer of 2006, one year after nature's force altered the landscape and history of New Orleans, one other truth was certain: the NOPD family was keeping a close eye on every step the district attorney would take.

CHAPTER 13

THE DISTRICT ATTORNEY BRINGS CHARGES–AND THE POLICE BROTHERHOOD FIGHTS BACK

AS DISTRICT ATTORNEY JORDAN explored the evidence, Lance Madison's lawyers made sure to meet with the DA's office, sharing their findings. Romell Madison and his sister Lorna Madison Humphrey sometimes took part, as did the family's civil attorney, Mary Howell.

In those meetings, the state prosecutor handling the case, Dustin M. Davis, and his investigators were coming to the same conclusions, based on their own research. This was a bad shoot, a chief investigator told the lawyers frankly during one meeting. Davis assured them he was conducting his own investigation and not depending on the police account—an account that appeared fishy, he believed.

On December 28, 2006, the story of what happened on the Danziger Bridge underwent a torrential turn. In the Parish of Orleans, a grand jury convened by the office of Eddie Jordan returned charges of first degree murder, attempted first degree murder, and attempted second degree murder against the seven officers who spilled out of the commandeered Budget rental truck that morning. No longer cast as criminals, the Bartholomew family, Jose Holmes, JJ Brissette, and Lance and Ronald Madison were now described as victims of police violence.

In rat-a-tat fashion, the charges rolled out that Thursday:

- Kenneth Bowen, Robert Faulcon Jr., Anthony Villavaso II, and Robert Barrios, charged with attempted first degree murder of Susan Bartholomew, her husband Leonard, daughter Lesha, and nephew Jose Holmes Jr.

- Ignatius Hills, charged with attempted second degree murder of Leonard Bartholomew IV.
- Faulcon, Bowen, Villavaso, and Robert Gisevius Jr. charged with the first degree murder of James Brissette.
- Bowen, Michael Hunter, and Gisevius charged with attempted first degree murder of Lance Madison and attempted first degree murder of Ronald Madison.
- And Robert Faulcon, who sent his pregnant fiancée away and stayed behind to serve his city as Hurricane Katrina roared near, was charged alone with the first degree murder of Ronald Madison.

Now, these police officers' photographs were filed as mug shots, like criminals.

"We cannot allow our police officers to shoot and kill our citizens without justification, like rabid dogs," Orleans Parish district attorney Jordan said in announcing the charges. "The rules governing the use of lethal force are not suspended during a state of emergency. Everyone, including police officers, must abide by the law of the land."

Lance Madison, released on bond after twenty-five days behind bars, was now officially vindicated. On the same day they charged the police officers, the grand jurors impaneled by assistant district attorney Dustin Davis issued a "No True Bill" to charges that Lance Madison attempted first degree murder against the seven officers and David Ryder. No True Bill: no truth to the charges, the refrain Lance Madison tried to ring out while on his knees, handcuffed behind his back, as the officers finished off killing his brother Ronald and ignored his plea for a lie detector test.

Those three words were vindication for a family that had pressed for the full story from the moment they received the call that Ronald was dead and Lance apprehended. With Lance's release the family could celebrate the closing of the charges against him. Yet the Madison family now had to officially confront the horror that Ronald, the man they watched over like a child, had been gunned down by the New Orleans police officers, and the reality that the police lie could have held as gospel.

The Madison team had kept nagging police for information, and kept sharing its findings with state prosecutors. "'We need these documents. When are you going to close this report and submit it to the DA's office?'"

family lawyer Shannon Fay recounted. "We kept pushing and pushing—that's when they did the crime scene." They were pests, because they had to be to tear down the police façade. Fay believes this relentlessness, driven by the Madison family, was instrumental in the charges being brought.

"The state grand jury refuted the New Orleans Police Department account of what happened on Sept. 4, 2005, which had been portrayed by officers as an appropriate response to reports of both sniper fire and people shooting at police officers near the bridge, on Chef Menteur Highway in eastern New Orleans," the local newspaper reported after the charges became public.

How far the local DA would go in punishing police misdeeds remained under question. District attorney Jordan announced the state would not seek the death penalty for the four officers facing first degree murder charges—Faulcon, Bowen, Villavaso, and Gisevius. Life in prison was a possibility if the charges became convictions, prosecutor Dustin Davis said.

Faulcon, who had resigned from the force, was relieved to learn the state would not try to put him to death. "It would have defied all precedent had they sought the death penalty for a police officer who was in his line of duty," one of Faulcon's lawyers said.

"We feel they deserve the death penalty," Lorna Madison Humphrey, Ronald's sister, said after hearing the news. "But we'll settle at seeing them spend the rest of their lives in jail. They executed my brother. They shot him for no reason."

For the families, even seeming slam-dunk victories were not fully cause for celebration.

Soon, the six officers still on the payroll would return to their jobs. They were not allowed to wear uniforms, make arrests, or carry weapons, and court-ordered ankle bracelets tracked their every move. But they could return to the force, draw their pay from the city, and continue as members of the union that supported them.

That even one of the accused officers remained on the force unsettled the Madison family. Romell Madison wanted the city mayor, Ray Nagin, to ban them from the department altogether. "These men have been indicted with first-degree murder and attempted first-degree murder charges by a grand jury of the Orleans Parish Criminal District Court system," Madison said, standing outside the criminal courthouse alongside his sister Lorna Madison Humphrey on the last day of January 2007. "For them to be allowed to resume their jobs is a slap in the face of justice."

Lorna Humphrey contrasted the treatment of the accused police killers to that of her brother Lance, who, dogged by depression since witnessing his brother's death, had been unable to return to work at Federal Express at the New Orleans airport. "First he watched his brother gunned down, then he was arrested. He's been out of work seventeen months now, but the police are back," Lorna said. "Is that fair?"

From police headquarters Warren Riley, the former deputy superintendent who rose to lead the force after Eddie Compass's departure, issued words of caution and asked the public not to rush to judgment. "I would like to remind everyone, this is but one step in the judicial process that will determine the future of these officers," Superintendent Riley told reporters. "This is not when it ends."

The police brotherhood would make sure of that.

TWO DAYS AFTER THE charges against police were logged by the DA, Mike Glasser, the president of the Police Association of New Orleans, sent out word in an urgent bulletin. "There is no issue facing ANY Public Safety Officer, law enforcement or medical professional, more serious than an indictment for Murder for doing your job," he wrote that Saturday, December 30. "NOW is the time to show our brother officers that we are there, we will not forget, we will not stop and WE ARE ONE NOPD."

To Glasser and his brothers and sisters at the police association and the Fraternal Order of Police, the charges were not just an affront to officers who served their city during catastrophe. They were a drummed-up fiction driven by a district attorney, Jordan, with a deliberate agenda to hurt police. "In the meantime, I want to assure everyone, that the Police Association of New Orleans is fully dedicated to the complete support of these officers and their families," Glasser wrote. "PANO and FOP are completely unified in their support efforts, both legally and financially."

Signal 26, an online message board for city police, was soon filled with criticism of the district attorney and an unqualified support for the officers. "Jordan has committed a legal atrocity by indicting our brothers on murder. . . . Is it for this that our Seven must be sacrificed? Not on my watch. Or yours," one wrote under the heading "They've Picked the Wrong Fight." The writer added, "This travesty must not only be rectified, but it must be avenged."

"Is it me, or are they trying to send police the message that they aren't supposed to do their jobs?" another writer asked. Yet another officer told Signal 26 he was stunned his brethren stood as accused criminals after staying behind to serve after "the worst natural disaster in U.S. history" and finding themselves "in the middle of a gun battle."

"These guys stepped up where most would have tucked tail and ran," the writer concluded. "Today I lost outlook on life here in New Orleans. This could have been me."

That feeling echoed like a 108 call for the street officers watching their colleagues face murder and attempted murder charges. "It could have been me" was a refrain that would play out deep and wide for the force. Their fellow officers stayed behind during Katrina, and their thanks was to engage "a bunch of wild looting thugs" on the streets and now, after the gunfire on the bridge, to confront the prospect of life behind bars.

The department would stand up for these men, and not just with words.

For one thing, the police association's Glasser told fellow officers, he would send out details about fund-raisers to aid the accused. At the same time, the Fraternal Order of Police was creating a system where officers could contribute to the Danziger 7 defense fund through payroll deductions.

But for now, the association leader said, police should flex their muscle on Tuesday, January 2, 2007, as the officers walked to the city lockup for the initial booking of their charges.

"I am requesting that EVERYONE, civilian, military, sheriff's office, federal agents, state and local police, and especially NOPD, come to the area of South Broad and Tulane Avenue, before 10:00 a.m., the earlier, the better," Glasser wrote. "We will begin lining the streets from Central Lockup at South White and Perdido Street, up South White, to Tulane Avenue, then on Tulane towards South Carrollton Avenue. The officers will follow this route in and I am requesting that EVERYONE wishing to show their support for these officers and for ALL of the Public Safety and First Responders, come and line the streets as these officers come to surrender themselves."

The association president added, "This request is not just for law enforcement, but for ALL CITIZENS who disapprove of their public safety officers being treated in this fashion. Just get in line as you arrive, wherever there is space. I hope by 10:00 a.m., there is no space all the way to Jefferson Parish."

His clarion call was heard, loudly and clearly.

That morning, in the first days of the New Year, the accused officers, most dressed in coats and ties, gathered with a swarm of supporters at the PANO headquarters and, after a short ride to a parking lot, began walking in unison to the city lockup. As they headed to be booked on the charges, Faulcon, Bowen, Barrios, Gisevius, Hunter, Hills, and Villavaso were mobbed. One supporter hugged defendant Robert Barrios, putting one hand atop his head like a father comforting a son. Gisevius shook hands with one police brother as two others put their hands on his back, support beams against the charges. The sergeant walked ahead, stone faced, a focused intensity framing his face, wearing a suit and tie. Many clapped as the accused officers walked by. Bowen, also in suit and tie, reached out to clasp hands with police brethren white and black. Hunter, more casually attired in a zippered jacket, looked a little overwhelmed as hands reached out to him from all directions. Faulcon likewise had his brothers reaching out for him in front and tapping him on the back, a well of camaraderie so deep the retired officer broke out in a smile.

The show of support from the force and its larger message were unmistakable. The charges against the Danziger 7 were charges against all of us, every officer donning the BDU uniforms. "They stayed, served & sacrificed," said one placard hoisted that morning. "Don't let it be water under the bridge."

Nearby, the throng hoisted signs that spoke of their backing for the accused.

"Heroes," they said.

CHAPTER 14

FROM NARCOTICS COP
TO POLICE ATTORNEY
An Insider's View

FOR SEVENTEEN YEARS, Eric Hessler worked the streets of New Orleans as an NOPD officer handling narcotics investigations, homicides, and SWAT missions. In the neighborhoods he patrolled, the residents sometimes called him "Shorty," a reference to his diminutive stature. Hessler, a white man, patrolled the urban core with ready eyes and taut instincts, and he knew how it felt to pull his weapon.

Hessler retired as a sergeant in 2001. During his years patrolling New Orleans, he eyed the fragile levees with a knowing wariness. One day, he knew, those levees would fail. And then hell would truly arrive in his city. "It was bound to happen," Hessler said. "When I was in the job, we had numerous close calls. And occasionally, we really believed it was going to be the one that breached the levee."

Now it had happened, and the world was bearing witness. Hessler had fled New Orleans before Katrina's arrival, heading to Mississippi, and returned ten days later. Teaming up with a former police partner, he volunteered to join the narcotics unit, headed by Tim Bayard, and went to work. "We would go through looking for bodies, going through houses," he said. He and the ex-partner did this work for four or five days straight. As the days rolled slowly into nights, the power still shot in New Orleans, the stress and misery mounted. "It seemed like Armageddon," he said. "I couldn't stay any longer. It was devastating from an emotional standpoint."

In those days navigating the city, with Katrina's fingerprint on every corner of New Orleans, Hessler was stunned by the lack of support for the men and women of the NOPD, the troops he once called partner. "I saw the dysfunction," he said. "I saw there was absolutely no chain of command. There was a complete command structure failure. The officers, you can only imagine the stress they went under at that time." Ten days after Katrina, "no one knew what was going on. No one knew who was in charge."

Many officers were survivors themselves before heading out to report for duty, and Hessler blamed the police department and city brass for their condition. Instead of placing officers at a central command post with the hurricane churning toward New Orleans, they sent many officers home on Katrina's eve "to avoid paying overtime costs," he said. "You would think when the mother of all hurricanes was coming to New Orleans, all the officers would be on duty. They are at their house, told to come back at six."

When he left the force in 2001, Hessler did not slip quietly into retirement. He became a lawyer, with a specialty of defending police officers. Hessler tells his clients he knows what it's like to sit in the defendant's chair. "It's easy to stay out of trouble if you stay behind your desk," he said.

In 1989 he and a partner were charged in state court for failing to protect an inmate in their custody who suffered a battery, allegedly at the hands of another officer. The trial judge tossed the charges. Then the federal government took up the matter. Again, Hessler persevered and was acquitted at trial. Years later, he said, the victim tried to hire him as his attorney.

Late one night in 2000, after searching for a suspect earlier that evening, Hessler fired a shot that killed a black man running with a gun. Hessler said he was driving home, passing through a rough neighborhood, when he looked up and saw a man firing a gun. Hessler said he pulled over and, as he exited his Jeep, the gunshots continued in his direction. He fired five shots, striking the man once. A witness called the shooting a tragic mistake, saying the victim, Steven Hawkins Jr., and his girlfriend had been carjacked at a tire shop, and Hawkins was racing back to his car. The sole witness said he told Hessler he had shot the wrong man, and the officer replied that he couldn't have shot the wrong man because the subject was firing a gun. The witness said Hawkins—though he did fire his gun—did not aim at the officer. Hessler said he yelled, "Police! Drop the gun," but the witness reported not hearing that warning. The police force cleared Hessler. A civil judge granted Hawkins's family a $700,000 judgment, but an appeals court overturned that ruling.

Hessler had fired his weapon before, but this was his first fatal shot, a stark reminder that police sometimes face split-second decisions. "It happens so quickly you don't have time to think of the danger. You just react." He wonders if politics played a part in the earlier state battery case, which was filed by the office of then district attorney Harry Connick Sr. The NOPD's vice squad had investigated the DA. "Police work is a challenging job by any measure," he said. "In New Orleans, you have the politics: political politics, racial politics. All of which I find more dangerous. That's what I worried about the most, the political side."

Hessler served through a series of mayors, and the biggest reform plus, he said, is having a mayor who allows the superintendent to call the shots. He saw that under Marc Morial and was promoted during his tenure. "Morial, he brought in an outsider. He let the chief be the chief," Hessler said. With subsequent mayors, "you had a police chief, but he was the puppet. That's where the problem comes in."

And now, after Katrina, the force felt rudderless.

Hessler served as legal counsel for PANO, the Police Association of New Orleans. And, with the officers charged in state court after the Danziger Bridge shootings, Eric Hessler signed on as lawyer for Sergeant Robert Gisevius Jr.

Before Katrina, police files show Gisevius had run into more than his share of abuse complaints—seven in a five-year period from 1999 to 2004. "Allegedly spit on subject," said one report from 2004. "Officer allegedly used unnecessary force," said another complaint a year earlier. Each time, the department cleared him of wrongdoing.

Hessler sees a different side. A solidly built cop with crisply cut dark hair, Gisevius had graduated from a Catholic high school in the area in 1990, then enlisted in the Louisiana Army National Guard Reserve. He went on to raise two sons, tended to his ailing parents, and joined the force.

Trapped inside a hotel room by Katrina, Gisevius swam to safety, using fence posts as paddles to rescue colleagues.

Racing to the bridge that morning, expecting a shootout, the officers did as they were trained to do, Hessler said. The call came at a time Mayor Nagin, his police chief Compass, and the national media were relaying horror stories of lawlessness in New Orleans, telling tales of rapes and brutality at the Superdome. Many of those tales proved to be just that. The officers did not know that: the mayor and superintendent were saying it was true. Then came the 108 call.

"When you're dispatched you realize this is the call, and this is real," Hessler said. "Perception is this guy's reality. The reality of what was occurring during Katrina. I think it became really real when you are in the back of a boxed-in truck" barreling ahead, and officers up front have already begun firing their weapons. When he stepped out of the back of the truck, Gisevius believed he and his fellow officers were under fire, Hessler said. "It combined for the perfect storm for a situation like this to occur."

Handling the case now from the other side, as a lawyer representing an accused officer, Hessler came to a conclusion about what happened that morning on the bridge.

"I believed firmly this shooting was justified," he said. A fighter who had beat back cases when he was on the force, Hessler would join the defense counsel representing the other officers, and the larger police department family, to make that case.

CHAPTER 15

JUDICIAL TIES, PROSECUTORIAL ERROR, AND THE NOPD WALKS FREE

IN THE ORLEANS PARISH Criminal District Court, the case of *State of Louisiana v. Kenneth Bowen et al.*, was assigned to Criminal District Court judge Raymond Bigelow. Three days after the police officers were hailed as heroes in the streets, Judge Bigelow was filing a report in the courthouse disclosing the many ties between his office, the officers, and their counsel. Suddenly the criminal justice system in Orleans Parish was feeling very much like a family affair, according to the January 5, 2007, report the judge prepared.

"In an effort to apprize the prosecutors in the captioned matter of relationships which exist between members of my staff and individuals identified with defense, the Court files this notice into the record," Judge Bigelow declared.

Sergeant Bowen, the judge noted, was represented by the law firm DeSalvo, DeSalvo, and Blackburn. "These attorneys are the father, brother and husband, respectively, of one of my minute clerks, Emily De-Salvo Blackburn," Judge Bigelow reported. A minute clerk helps keep the court's official records.

The spokesman for the Fraternal Order of Police, Sergeant Donovan Livaccari, "is the husband of my other minute clerk, Claire Livaccari." The FOP was a major source of support and fund-raising for the officers facing charges.

The lawyer for Officer Ignatius Hills, Bruce Whittaker, "was the longtime law partner of my law clerk, Michael Riehlmann, until August, 2005."

The judge said these tentacle-like ties would not impede his handling of the "Danziger Bridge 7 Indictments," among the most closely watched police corruption cases in New Orleans history. "Notwithstanding these relationships, the Court, confidently assures all parties in this matter that it can conduct all necessary proceedings in an entirely fair and impartial manner," the judge wrote, signing his name, Raymond Bigelow, at the bottom of the one-page report.

Bigelow was not overjoyed when the case landed on his desk through the random allotment of cases on the criminal docket. "I wasn't real thrilled. I knew it was going to be a headache of a case," he said. Bigelow felt it unfair to simply recuse himself and shuffle the case over to another judge. So, he disclosed the ties between his office and the defense team and would have stepped aside if either side asked him to.

The defense was not likely to make the request. DA Eddie Jordan's office, the side far more likely to object to ties between the judge's office and the defense team, didn't file a motion either, at least not right away. "I felt I was elected to handle the easy cases as well as the tough cases, so I didn't want to dump this on any other judge. It wasn't like I tried to hide anything from anyone in the public," Bigelow explained. "If any one person had made the motion I would have recused myself from the case."

The case stayed with him.

That same Friday afternoon Bigelow issued a first important ruling. After each of the seven officers pleaded not guilty, the judge granted bond to all the accused, including the four facing first degree murder charges, setting them free from spending time behind bars while their case traveled through the system. Bond in a murder case is highly unusual, but Bigelow granted it to all of them.

The district attorney's office did not challenge the bond ruling, just as the office of DA Jordan had not filed a motion requesting Judge Bigelow step aside and allow another judge to hear the case—another judge without three clerks with ties to the law firm for one accused officer, the lawyer for another, and the FOP union that had lambasted the charges now before the bench.

"Everyone is entitled to a bond, you don't automatically get a bond, but the defense had filed a motion for bond in the case," the judge said.

"And I met with the DA and the defense attorneys. Mr. Jordan, do you wish to agree to have a bond set? And he agreed to have a bond set in the case."

His bond ruling was welcome news to the police association. "The officers were released and reunited with their families. There are some restrictions and court imposed requisites relative to the bond, which will not interfere with the officers' ability to return to work in administrative capacities, pending final resolution of the matter," wrote Glasser, the association president. "The officers wish to thank everyone for their support and I would like to remind everyone that the fight is just beginning and continued support will be crucial."

EVEN AS THE CASE sprung to life with the state court charges, the Madison family did not sit idly by and watch the Orleans Parish legal system unfold. The family was troubled that the judge granted bond, troubled by his office's ties to the defense team, and troubled that the DA was doing nothing about it, at least not yet.

By February 2007, a month after Judge Bigelow's disclosures, Romell Madison and his supporters were pressing for a federal civil rights investigation into the shootings on the bridge. They didn't trust the local DA's office to right the wrong.

One of Madison's phone calls was placed to Marc H. Morial, the former New Orleans mayor who had risen to become president and chief executive officer of the National Urban League in New York. Morial was twice elected mayor of New Orleans, following the path cleared by his father, Ernest "Dutch" Morial, the first black man to hold the office. The younger Morial entered city hall in 1994 vowing to clean out corruption "with a shovel not a broom," and eyeing the police department in particular. He had hired Pennington to help clean the mess and, on Pennington's first day as superintendent, introduced him to FBI investigators embedded in the department's Public Integrity Bureau.

Morial was outraged by what happened on the bridge, by the shootings of innocents trying to survive the hurricane. What most troubled him was the cover-up.

"It's almost as though a bad police department has an instinct and a culture of covering up misconduct," he said. "When a department is covering up corruption they are operating like a criminal enterprise. Because that's how the Mafia operates."

Morial knew the justice system in New Orleans had a spotty record of convicting rogue officers. Convictions in the Algiers 7 case, when officers responded to the death of a white colleague by killing four black residents, came only when the case moved out of New Orleans and was held in Dallas. Algiers 7 unfolded while Morial's father ran the city.

"In order to convict a police officer, you don't have to convict him beyond a reasonable doubt. You have to convict him beyond all doubt," the younger Morial said. "The history of New Orleans in police corruption is you have to have the Justice Department in order to have a just outcome. History teaches us that."

A police brutality case that came to light shortly after he took office showed how outlaw officers had been allowed to wear the badge and rule with impunity. In December 1994, in a corruption case touted as the largest in the city's history, nine police officers were charged in federal court with pocketing nearly $100,000 in bribes to protect a vast cocaine operation. The problem, for police: the cocaine center was actually run by undercover FBI agents. The investigation began a year earlier when two officers, one named Len Davis, began extorting bribes and offering protection to a drug dealer. That dealer then turned federal informant, and the sting was hatched. As the undercover operation unspooled, even federal agents were taken aback by the brazen police tactics. Davis, his partner, and seven other friendly officers they recruited stood guard over the supposed cocaine center, sometimes while on duty and in uniform. The federal sting prosecution was led by the same Eddie Jordan now serving as the city's DA.

The undercover probe was abruptly halted after federal investigators discovered that Davis, in October 1994, had ordered the execution of a thirty-two-year-old woman who had filed a battery complaint against him. The woman, seeing Davis and other officers manhandling a neighborhood boy, had tried to come to the teen's rescue when, she said, Davis roughed her up. Kim Groves filed a complaint against him. Seething, Davis turned to one of his criminal informants. "Get that whore!" he told the triggerman, who killed the young black woman in front of her home in the city's Ninth Ward, firing a bullet into her head.

When the victim was killed, Davis uttered words Sergeant Kaufman had replicated on the bridge. "NAT," Davis said. Necessary action taken.

Before the shooting, Davis had been the subject of at least twenty brutality complaints over five years; nearly all were dismissed by police. "He's got an internal affairs jacket as thick as a telephone book," an officer told a reporter covering the case, "but supervisors have swept his dirt under the rug."

After the hit on Kim Groves, victims of police brutality were wise not to complain about abusing officers. The execution of Groves made sure of that. The police-ordered hit may never have come to light had the FBI not been monitoring Len Davis and his troupe of badge-wearing cocaine protectors.

Davis, who had already come to be called Robocop, was sentenced to death for the murder, but that sentence became entangled in appeals and legal wrangling for decades. Sentencing for the gunman had not even been finalized thirteen years later in 2007 as Morial set his sights on the newest police scandal in New Orleans after receiving a call for help from the Madison family.

Morial had staked his two terms on uprooting corruption—winning widespread voter support and minimal political opposition. His hand-picked police superintendent, Pennington, tried to rise to the mayor's office. Pennington lost to Ray Nagin, and Morial contends that moment set back efforts for lasting reform within the department. "There were incidents before Katrina involving black men and excessive force by police that I would not have tolerated. So the seeds for Danziger were planted before Katrina," Morial said.

"Danziger is a symptom. The cancer is police corruption," agrees Rafael Goyeneche III, a former prosecutor who is president of the Metropolitan Crime Commission, a nonprofit watchdog group focused on spotlighting corruption and that operates directly across from the Mercedes-Benz Superdome. "You look at fifteen years before Danziger and the pattern is clear. The culture predicted Danziger."

City watchdogs say there's no question police discipline improved under Morial. Goyeneche believes the department celebrated success too soon, saying widespread change requires lasting commitment.

During Morial's tenure, the Department of Justice threatened to step in with a lawsuit that would demand change. Morial convinced the DOJ not to take that formal step. He said his reforms were more sweeping than any the federal government could adopt. The department won accreditation, stressed community policing, and took, for New Orleans, a hard line on police wrongdoing. But by not allowing the Justice Department to formally stake a role in the city, Morial left office without any guarantee of permanent change. "Had I had any inkling that Nagin would have engaged in a systematic dismissal of police reforms, I would have taken any step necessary to try to lock in the reforms on a more permanent basis," he said. "In hindsight I would have taken any step, any step to lock in those reforms had I had any sense that the retrenchment and the reversal would have been so massive and swift."

Morial knew Nagin's new superintendent, Eddie Compass, as a talented and respected district commander. Compass's tenure atop the force lasted only past Hurricane Katrina, and he left with the department under fire. Today Compass said he doesn't want to dwell on the past. When I asked him to talk about what happened, he replied tersely, "I really don't discuss Danziger, I had nothing to do with it." Compass said his attention during Katrina was focused on the human suffering at the Superdome. "Once Ray Nagin fired me from the police department, I don't discuss the police department. I've gone on with my life, thank you." Then he hung up. Nagin is now in federal prison serving a ten-year sentence for corruption for selling out his office for personal perks.

Out of the mayor's office for five years when Romell Madison reached out to him, Morial maintained a keen interest in police abuse cases in New Orleans. He knew the culture crossed racial lines among members of the force. When the Madison family contacted him, the New Orleans Police Department's racial makeup nearly mirrored that of the city. In 2007, in a city where 60 percent of residents were black, 57 percent of the force was black. Forty percent of NOPD's officers were white. But the bond between officers was based on the color of their uniform, not their skin.

"They call it the blue code. When the blue code becomes an operating principle in the department, it affects all the officers," Morial said.

And now the state judge overseeing the Danziger case was acknowledging his office's ties to the defense and granting bond for men accused of killing unarmed victims. Morial pushed for federal intervention. "I'm very, very proud and just respectful of the way [the Madisons] have refused to let this go. They have done it very intelligently, they have done it very forcefully. The fact they have suffered a tragedy beyond their control . . . It's clear you can't bring [Ronald] back, but they can get justice for him," Morial said.

On February 20, 2007, he wrote to the Congressional Black Caucus of the US House of Representatives, "to solicit your support for a federal civil rights investigation by the Justice Department of the circumstances surrounding the police killing of two unarmed African American men and the wounding of four others in an incident on Danziger Bridge in New Orleans on September 4, 2005, in those horrible days following the wrath of Hurricane Katrina. I am especially calling for congressional oversight into the subsequent handling of this case by the New Orleans Police Department and the court."

Morial told how a "forty-year-old mentally handicapped African American man named Ronald Madison was shot in the back seven times by police. . . . Mr. Madison died of his wounds, as also did James Brissette, another man who was shot by the police that day on the same bridge. According to witness testimonies, the men and women shot by the police were hurricane survivors merely trying to run away from unidentified men who were shooting at them." Morial described how, as Ronald lay dead on the pavement, Lance Madison was handcuffed and jailed.

He referred Congress to a lengthy accounting of events by the National Dental Association, a group once led by Romell Madison. Like the police family that stood up for the accused officers, the Dental Association was putting its might behind Romell Madison. "Their outrage stems from the additional injustice perpetuated by the court by allowing the police officers charged with first-degree murder to be released on bond, and the police department's decision to allow the officers charged to return to work."

Morial wanted action. "As you already know, there is so much pain and tragedy still being experienced by the thousands who were impacted by Hurricane Katrina. So much still needs to be done to restore the many institutions that affect every day life, including the criminal justice system."

On March 27, 2007, the National Dental Association sent its own plea for help to US attorney general Alberto R. Gonzales, speaking on behalf of twenty thousand dentists and calling for a federal civil rights investigation into the killing of Ronald Madison. The group detailed the massacre on the bridge and documented concern over Judge Bigelow's staff ties to the defense and his ruling allowing accused murderers to be released on bond.

"The tragedy of rogue police officers shooting unarmed citizens, mishandling their investigation of the incident, having a court that allows men charged with first degree murder to go free on bail and even back to work as police officers, and having a judge that has several serious conflicts of interest in this case yet refuses to recuse himself—all of this causes the victims, their families and the community to completely lose faith in the justice system in New Orleans," the association wrote.

"Clearly, it is time for federal intervention and oversight in this case. Clearly, the local authorities are not committed to seeking full and complete justice," wrote Robin R. Daniel, president of the National Dental Association, the position Romell had left just four years earlier.

Others joined the fight for a federal review, Daniel told the attorney general, from the New Orleans Chapter of the NAACP to the Southern Christian Leadership Conference. "I ask you to heed these calls for justice. I ask you to take action today to ensure that there is no miscarriage of justice in these horrible murders and shootings."

In Louisiana, yet other groups were seeking to get Judge Bigelow removed from the case even as the DA didn't. On February 22, 2007, a group calling itself Safe Streets/Strong Communities wrote to members of the Louisiana Supreme Court, asking the state's highest court to recuse Bigelow from the Danziger 7 prosecution.

"At a time when the national, if not global, spotlight is on New Orleans, it is imperative that the system function in a fair and transparent manner, without a hint of impropriety," the group wrote. "We take no position as to the guilt or innocence of the officers charged. Our interest is in seeing justice done, in seeing that, the victims, their families and the defendants are treated fairly by the criminal justice system. It is our belief that as long as this case remains under Judge Bigelow's control, *any* disposition of the case will remain forever tainted for the majority of New Orleanians."

In June, five months after Judge Bigelow's disclosures and three months after this group's plea to have him removed from hearing the case, the district attorney sought a new judge to oversee the biggest case of his career. Dustin Davis, the assistant district attorney prosecuting the officers, said he had begun developing concerns, particularly over the law clerk who previously partnered with one of the defense attorneys. Bigelow had removed that clerk from involvement in the case, yet Davis said that move came only after the clerk took part in one meeting on the case and conducted research for the judge. Bigelow had already offered to step aside, but by this time he was deep in the case.

That September 2007, Orleans Parish judge Julian Parker denied the motion to remove Bigelow, ruling that prosecutors failed to provide evidence showing he shouldn't preside over the case. The judge blocked Davis from asking another of Bigelow's clerks—the one married to the FOP spokesman—whether she had contributed to a legal defense fund for the officers. Attending fund-raisers or making donations are constitutionally protected rights, Judge Parker said, cutting off the questioning.

"You have not put any meat on the bones of your application to recuse Judge Bigelow," Parker told the prosecutor.

Soon after, DA Jordan called it quits, resigning his office amid problem cases and the sting of the discrimination verdict.

ELEVEN MONTHS LATER, on August 13, 2008, Judge Bigelow dismissed the entire case, ruling that prosecutor Davis tainted the grand jury process by showing a sliver of testimony to a supervisor of the officers under review.

"The violation is clear, and indeed, uncontroverted," Bigelow said. "The state improperly disclosed grand jury testimony to another police officer."

Further, Judge Bigelow said, prosecutor Davis improperly gave immunity to three officers for their testimony before the grand jury—only to have those same officers indicted. One of them was Kenneth Bowen, the officer pursuing his own legal career. And, the judge ruled, the prosecution gave flawed instructions to the grand jurors about the second degree murder charges.

Judge Bigelow read his ruling from the bench, gutting the state's case and seemingly setting the police officers completely free. As he read from his ruling, the *Times-Picayune* told its readers, the accused officers sat silently in the front row of the courtroom, betraying little emotion. Behind them, wives and supporters wiped away tears.

Moments later, one of the police defense lawyers patted another on the back, beaming widely, as they left the courthouse surrounded by television microphones and cameras.

Ronald Madison's family sat in the courtroom, soaking in the latest legal setback. "Our family today still feels that the ruling just proves again that the justice system here in New Orleans is still flawed," Romell

James "JJ" Brissette's school picture. At seventeen, JJ was shot and killed by officers of the New Orleans Police Department.

JJ, age nine, at the wedding of his older sister, Andrea Celestine.

Ronald Madison and one of his dachshunds. While the rest of his family evacuated before Katrina struck New Orleans, Ronald and his brother Lance stayed behind to care for Ronald's beloved pets, Bobbi and Sushi.

Courtesy of the Madison family.

Courtesy of the Madison family.

Ronald Madison at home. Ronald was killed by NOPD officers while crossing the Danziger Bridge between his brother's dental office and his mother's house.

Alex Brandon for the *Times Picayune*/Landov

On Sunday, September 4, 2005, Lance Madison was detained by police, including NOPD officers Michael Hunter (center), with backpack, and Robert Faulcon Jr. (right), with "New Orleans Police" printed on the back of his shirt. In the middle-left foreground, in a black T-shirt, is Sgt. Robert Gisevius Jr.

AP/Alex Brandon

Lance Madison in 2006, after state charges were filed against NOPD officers in the shootings.

Jose Holmes, then nineteen, survived being shot four times by police on the Danziger Bridge. Holmes was later accused of the attempted murder of seven NOPD officers.

Sherrel Johnson, mother of JJ Brissette, hugs Lance Madison after former NOPD officer Michael Hunter pled guilty in connection with a police cover-up.

AP/Gerald Herbert

AP/Gerald Herbert

Susan Bartholomew, who lost her arm after being shot by NOPD officers, listens as prosecutors speak outside federal court after sentences were handed down in the case, April 4, 2012.

AP/Gerald Herbert

Fuki Madison (right), mother of Ronald Madison, and attorney Mary Howell also listen as prosecutors speak, April 4, 2012.

Sgt. Robert Gisevius Jr. (foreground), along with six other NOPD officers, turns himself in at the city jail in New Orleans, January 2, 2007.

AP/Dave Martin

AP/Alex Brandon

AP/Alex Brandon

Officer Michael Hunter Jr., swarmed by supporters, January 2, 2007.

Officer Anthony Villavaso, January 2, 2007.

Officer Robert Barrios, January 2, 2007.

Sgt. Kenneth Bowen,
January 2, 2007.

Officer Ignatius Hills, January 2, 2007.

Former NOPD officer Robert Faulcon
leaves the city jail in New Orleans,
January 5, 2007.

Retired NOPD sergeant Arthur Kaufman (right) enters federal court for the start of jury selection for his trial in New Orleans.

AP/Gerald Herbert

Ted Jackson for the *Times Picayune*/Landov

Barbara "Bobbi" Bernstein, lead prosecutor for the US Justice Department, and FBI Special Agent William Bezak, lead investigator in the Danziger case, enter federal court, July 11, 2011.

Demonstrators in Seattle, April 14, 2015, carry a banner that reads "Stop Murder By Police" as they protest the recent murders of black people by police officers. The banner includes photos of JJ Brissette (top row, fourth from left) and Ronald Madison (bottom row, third from left).

Madison told reporters, after walking down the courthouse steps wearing his blue dentist's garb, his family trailing behind him. Romell said he would ask the US Department of Justice to take over the case. To the Madison family, the ruling was confirmation of their quest to convince the federal government to become involved. The family never trusted the New Orleans criminal justice system to mete out a fair punishment against its own. Instead, the officers who gunned down Ronald Madison and JJ Brissette were set free.

The local newspaper's coverage of Bigelow's ruling cited the police defense, suggesting to readers not intimately familiar with what happened on the bridge that the facts were in dispute. While noting that the families had brought lawsuits alleging a murder and cover-up, and citing questions about the police department's fifty-four-page report, the *Times-Picayune* reported:

> Police officials have acknowledged the officers shot people on two separate sides of the bridge, but said they did so only after first being shot at. A police report said they arrived at the scene that morning in response to calls over the police radio about people shooting at other officers and rescue workers.

Judge Bigelow's ruling meant the law and order story held together, and police celebrated their colleagues as free men, not accused criminals. While the case had remained active, the accused had been required to wear tracking devices to follow their every move. Now those tracking devices were removed, and the officers went back to work, unshackled from the justice system.

Four months after tossing the case, Judge Bigelow would quietly work his last day on the bench. The onetime prosecutor, who began his career working for Orleans Parish district attorney Harry Connick, hung up his judicial robes. He went to work as a federal public defender and defense attorney handling capital murder cases.

As the judge stepped aside, some feared the case would fade too. Many in New Orleans believed the book had closed on that bloody Sunday, that there were two sides to the story, as the local newspaper reported, and the answers might never be fully revealed.

Three years after the Danziger Bridge shootings, truth remained elusive. From the moment the gunfire ceased, only a tiny cluster of people knew the full truth of what had happened that morning: The NOPD officers and phony cop who raced to the bridge, four supervisors in on the cover-up, and the eight city residents captured in their fire. With Bigelow's ruling dismissing the case, the larger community remained in the dark.

Behind the scenes, in another wing of the justice system, momentum was building for a deeper look into the events of September 4, 2005.

On September 30, 2008, nearly two months after Judge Bigelow dismissed the state case, Jim Letten, the US attorney based in New Orleans, announced federal authorities were studying whether any foundation existed for a federal prosecution.

Even a member of the state district attorney's office, Keva Landrum-Johnson, had sent a letter urging the federal Department of Justice to become involved. "More likely than not, the court will quash the indictments and the State will be left with no viable option other than to recharge some or all of the defendants on lesser offenses," Landrum-Johnson wrote presciently on August 8, 2008, five days before Judge Bigelow did just that. "Admittedly, my office bears much of the responsibility for the position we are in now."

Landrum-Johnson, who would later become a state court judge, was right on two fronts. She correctly predicted the collapse of the DA's case, and she correctly called for the federal government to get involved, which it did. "We're very happy," Romell Madison told reporters. The families, he said, "have a better playing field now, with a chance of justice being reached more quickly now that we will be without the politics of the local system."

For the time being, Letten remained tight-lipped about where any case might lead. "In order to insure the integrity of the process, no additional comments regarding this matter will be made until the review is complete," the New Orleans US attorney said.

Soon, an aggressive civil rights prosecutor who put away racists and gang members, and a mechanical engineer turned rookie FBI agent, would begin digging into the events of that Sunday morning. They would be startled by what they found.

PART III
THE TRIALS

CHAPTER 16

CONSPIRACY CRACKS UNDER FEDERAL GLARE

RAISED ON THE NEW JERSEY SHORE, William Bezak envisioned two dream jobs growing up: designing airplanes or working for the FBI. Though his family was stocked with law enforcement officers, from cousins to his brother, father, and grandfather, Bezak opted for the former. He studied mechanical engineering at Villanova University and earned a master's degree in the field.

Fresh from graduate school, he landed a job in the rotorcraft division at the Boeing corporation. He was a stress engineer, designing the drive systems for military helicopters. Bezak's dream, it appeared, had been realized.

But desk work bored Bezak, and the urge to hit the streets pulled at him. Maybe it was in his familial blood, but Bezak felt an unrelenting urge to chase corruption. In 2006 he substituted Plan B for Plan A. He graduated from the FBI Academy in Quantico, Virginia, and landed his first post in New Orleans. He'd be pursuing the bad guys, all right, in the agency's White Collar Crime task force. The targets: financial crime, mortgage fraud, and civil rights violations. Police excessive-force cases were part of the mix.

Bezak pursued cases like a puzzle, using his skills as a helicopter engineer to unravel loose, fraying ends.

By January 2009 the Danziger Bridge shootings were three years and four months old and, for many, simply a memory, a story of police responding to gunfire at a horrible time in the city. None of the officers who fired weapons that day had been convicted. The truth gnawed at the victims, but their calls for resolution had not yet been fully heard, and they felt nothing close to closure.

With the state case dropped, the federal government's Civil Rights Division in Washington, DC, had decided to take a look. The review was led by Barbara "Bobbi" Bernstein, a career prosecutor with cropped dark hair, transparent eyeglass frames, and a reputation for riveting opening statements delivered without index cards. Bernstein had a way of connecting with jurors, winning points with sharply focused questions while presenting an air of approachability. "This is Bobbi," she answers the phone in the Department of Justice's Civil Rights Division.

In 2008, just as the civil rights office was officially opening the books on the Danziger Bridge shootings, Bernstein helped put away two men who pleaded guilty to violating the civil rights of a black couple and their white friend by plastering racial threats and epithets on the home where the three lived in Collinsville, Illinois, a city of twenty-six thousand some twelve miles from St. Louis. The men spray-painted "KKK" and "White Power" on the victims' home, trying to rattle them so deeply they would flee the neighborhood. For their hate crimes, Bernstein helped make sure that one man got six and a half years in prison and the other more than two years.

Two years before that, Bernstein was part of a DOJ team that helped convict four Latino gang members in Los Angeles for a six-year campaign to assault and kill black residents in the city's Highland Park neighborhood. The prosecution targeted the Avenues street gang, whose members killed two men, prosecutors said, simply because they chose to live in the neighborhood. One black man, Christopher Bowser, was gunned down while waiting for a bus, and another, Kenneth Kurry Wilson, was killed as he searched for a parking space. "Acts of hateful violence targeted at individuals because of their race will be aggressively investigated and vigorously prosecuted," a civil rights prosecutor said. Four gang members got life in prison. For her work on that case, Bernstein received the Attorney General's Award for Exceptional Service, the department's highest honor, in 2007.

And now, a year after that recognition, Bobbi Bernstein was becoming engrossed in the Danziger Bridge shootings. As she began exploring the events of that morning, Bernstein was driven by a dual quest to uncover the truth and to find justice for the victims. By the time she was done, she would view the Danziger Bridge shootings as the most egregious case of police misconduct she had prosecuted in fifteen years. She'd see the police cover-up as a stunning betrayal of public trust. Behind those acts were families left to bury two sons, and survivors living with visible scars from the police shootout.

For the families on the bridge, the civil rights inquiry felt like an answered prayer. Nathan Fisher and Shannon Fay, Lance Madison's defense team, instantly realized the significance of the federal review. In New Orleans, the local district attorney is an elected official and, as the police bulletin board and street rallies had shown, the NOPD would put its might behind fighting any charges brought locally in New Orleans. The DOJ Civil Rights Division, more than one thousand miles away in Washington, was a world removed from this local friction. The Police Association of New Orleans and Fraternal Order of Police unions held no power over the federal office; street rallies on the case meant nothing in Washington.

When Fay and Fisher met with the federal investigators, they handed over a binder an inch and a half to two inches thick containing their case research. They noticed the prosecuting team had already assembled an entire bookshelf of files on the investigation.

ONE DAY IN JANUARY 2009, still early in the federal government's exploration, Bernstein invited Bezak to join other FBI agents and prosecutors in a meeting in New Orleans with Archie Kaufman, the NOPD sergeant who helped lead the shooting inquiry. Kaufman was eager to talk. He wanted to make it abundantly clear his colleagues had every right to fire with deadly force. He shared his agency's findings that day, January 22, 2009, describing how he discovered Lance Madison's gun at the scene, even leading the agents and prosecutors on a tour of the bridge.

Bezak was not officially assigned to the case just yet. But as Kaufman talked, the gears in his mind turned. The sergeant's explanations were curious, Bezak thought, and getting more curious as he spoke. Bezak sat still, not questioning Kaufman, who spoke with his fellow law enforcement colleagues with a friendly, jovial air, as if he were among friends.

Bezak, with a boyish face, athlete's physique, and cleanly cropped brown hair, made mental notes of what the visitor was saying. Kaufman said he both witnessed the shootings and was investigating them. That's curious, Bezak thought. A witness typically doesn't then investigate the same case. Kaufman said he was not immediately on the scene that morning, but arrived after the shooting had begun.

Kaufman showed the Feds where and how he found the gun, and said he made the discovery a day after the shootings. Bezak thought this odd. In such a high profile case, wouldn't officers have done everything possible to find the supposed criminal's gun on the day of the gunfire?

The witnesses nagged at him too. Kaufman regaled the Feds with stories of his star witnesses, describing Lakeisha Smith as so attractive "the lady could have been a stripper," one meeting participant said. Smith and James Youngman, said to have seen citizens fire first, were seemingly golden witnesses for police. They saw it happen with their own eyes. Yet the police report included scant information about them—not even their phone numbers—and little in their own words. Kaufman said they might be impossible to find.

"His description of her was so complete you could practically see her in front of you," Kelly Bryson, an FBI special agent at the meeting, later recalled. "But then the next second he was like, 'I have never seen her before, I have never seen her since.' It was almost like she was instantly right in front of you and then she was gone."

Agent Bryson was taken aback when Kaufman described a hospital interview he conducted with the Bartholomews, confiding how at ease the family appeared in talking with him. "He said it was the most comfortable in all his thirty years of doing interviews as a police officer," Bryson recounted. "He said it was the best interview—the best one he had had in thirty years."

The FBI agent was stunned by what she heard. "Susan Bartholomew and Leonard Bartholomew Sr. had multiple gunshot wounds. They were actually in their daughter's room, who had been shot but not yet released from the hospital. Neither had their nephew Jose Holmes been released from the hospital. It was extremely surprising to see that he would describe it as a, you know, comfortable, wonderful interview," Bryson said. "It just doesn't seem consistent with how people would react under their circumstances towards a New Orleans police officer."

Another glaring hole involved the Budget truck that ferried officers to the scene. "Did you look at the truck?" the federal team asked their visitor. "And he said he didn't. The truck was actually brought back to the Crystal Palace too, and he didn't look at it. He didn't inspect it, and it went back into service. That's a huge truck," Bryson said. "Because the officers would have been in that area, it would have been something to, at a minimum, look at even if you are going to let it go back into service."

As Kaufman talked, Bryson's view of the case, like Bezak's, began to shift. Archie Kaufman's tale "just didn't sound right," said Bryson, then the supervisor of the Civil Rights unit in the FBI's New Orleans office.

The fifty-four page police report included no reference to Leonard Bartholomew IV, the fourteen-year-old who fled the shootings and lived only because officer Ignatius Hills missed his back. Bezak noted this discrepancy as well, but did not yet press the contradictions with the affable visitor from the New Orleans Police Department.

Not long after the casual sit-down, Kaufman bumped into Lieutenant Lohman, the supervisor ultimately in charge of the internal review, at work. He told Lohman he had huddled with the FBI. "It's all cool, babe," Kaufman confided.

A day later Bezak sat in on a second interview with another NOPD supervising investigator, Sergeant Gerard Dugue, who had shared the investigative reins with Kaufman. Again sitting as a spectator, he listened quietly as prosecutor Bernstein carved the first cut into the department's fiction.

The fifty-four-page report used to justify police actions listed "Deputy Sheriff" David Ryder as the first witness in the case. Ryder was the man, dressed in police garb, who flagged down Detective Jennifer Dupree as she descended the I-10, telling her armed gunmen were firing. Later that day Ryder fingered Lance Madison as one of the shooters.

Prosecutors confirmed the fraud. Ryder was no police sheriff but a convicted felon who convinced police he was one of them in the chaotic post-Katrina frenzy. Bernstein confronted Dugue with this revelation. Dugue began to stammer, and sweat streamed down his face. Bezak saw huge sweat stains on the sergeant's shirt.

One thread of the story was beginning to unravel under outside scrutiny.

Within a few weeks, Bezak was officially assigned to a case that hadn't stopped turning in his mind. He gathered every piece of paper NOPD filed to justify the shootings, building a body of research that would grow to four bookshelves of files. Using his mechanical engineering background, he worked to pinpoint weaknesses. He found them. The fifty-four-page report noted that five .223 caliber rifle casings had been found on the ground, but not a single officer admitted to carrying such a weapon. Yet another report Bezak ran across showed that Sergeant Robert Gisevius Jr. carried an M4 rifle. It can fire .223 caliber bullets. Gisevius never turned it over to investigators.

Bezak tried to find star witnesses Lakeisha Smith and James Youngman. He struck out. Not a single person from New Orleans matched their descriptions.

Next, he obtained a video shot by an NBC News affiliate that happened to be near the bridge that morning, the footage retrieved earlier by the defense team for Lance Madison. The video did not capture every scene of the shooting, just glimpses of it, and from a distance, but it helped Bezak connect pieces of the puzzle. From the start, officers said they were engaged in a pitched battle. The grainy, distant footage showed police in pursuit, firing their weapons—literally standing tall.

The FBI agent spotted conflicts in two statements Sergeant Bowen gave just after the shootings. In one, Bowen said he kicked the shooters' guns from a pedestrian walkway into the grass and then stood over the weapons. In the other, he said he kicked the guns and then pursued the shooters. Which was true?

Bezak and the FBI team followed every thread of potential evidence and contacted witnesses never questioned by police. The Friendly Inn near the bridge had closed after Hurricane Katrina, but agents tracked down the hotel's former maintenance worker and his wife, who had also worked at the hotel as a manager, to their new home in Tampa, Florida. One day an agent knocked on the couple's door and asked what they knew about the shootings on the bridge in New Orleans the first Sunday after Katrina. Robert Rickman described how an officer stomped on his camera that morning and how police never asked him a single question. Rickman told agents he had a second camera in his pocket and snapped pictures. The FBI collected the snapshots as evidence.

FOR THE FEDERAL GOVERNMENT, it was time to act.

They began on the outside, approaching Detective Jeffrey Lehrmann, who worked closely with Kaufman in crafting the initial reports. The

Feds could have subpoenaed Lehrmann to appear before a grand jury, but they invited him to come in voluntarily with his lawyer. At the meeting, agents and prosecutors pressed buttons, saying the official police story was pockmarked with holes.

Lehrmann rose from his seat and began pacing the room. He did not agree to cooperate, as least not yet, but Lehrmann did share a nugget. He told authorities that Kaufman and Dugue had written yet another, thirty-two page police report about the shootings, but never released it. That nugget fueled Bezak and Bernstein.

On August 5, 2009, eight months after the first cordial chat with Kaufman, the FBI obtained a search warrant to seize Kaufman and Dugue's offices and computers. Bezak found the thirty-two-page report in one of Kaufman's thumb drives and portions on a diskette in Dugue's desk. It was investigative gold, infused with details left out of the official fifty-four-page report, including the fullest description to date of which officers fired which weapons.

The media got wind of the searches and suddenly the story was back in the press. And now it came with a provocative question: Was the US Attorney's Office exploring a cover-up in the Danziger Bridge shootings?

"FBI Seizes Police Files in Bridge Shootings," the *Times-Picayune* reported two days later, telling its readers:

> Federal agents this week raided the office of the New Orleans Police Department homicide division, seizing the files and computer hard drives of two officers assigned to investigate police conduct in one deadly post-Katrina shooting episode, law enforcement sources told The Times-Picayune.
>
> Representatives of the FBI and NOPD confirmed the seizure late Thursday.
>
> FBI agents served a search warrant Wednesday afternoon for files in the offices of two supervisors, Sgt. Gerard Dugue and Sgt. Arthur Kaufman, the sources said.
>
> The two sergeants were the lead investigators who examined the shooting of civilians by police on the Danziger Bridge days after Hurricane Katrina. Gunfire from police, who were responding to reports of shots fired at officers, left two men dead and four people wounded.

Bezak savored the publicity. It could potentially turn up the heat on the insiders—the police on the bridge, the supervisors who concealed the truth.

Pressure was a powerful tool. If you corner your targets, convincing them the evidence gathered is unimpeachable, they just might crack.

The US Justice Department pressed another, very public pressure point. Four years after the shootings, on September 26, 2009, authorities shut down the Danziger Bridge and launched an hours-long search for evidence. The search didn't turn up any new evidence, but it sent a message. The government would dig for the truth, and now everyone in New Orleans knew what was happening. The US Attorney's Office and FBI were hunting a massive civil rights cover-up.

Lehrmann broke and became the first insider to cooperate. "At that time, no one had cooperated with the government. And the government was trying to get someone to cross the line. And they were having a very difficult time," said Davidson Ehle III, the Louisiana attorney representing Lehrmann.

To Ehle the choice was clear. If you're going to cooperate, be the first, and set yourself up for the best plea deal possible. "If you're going to do it, do it sooner than later," he said. "Jeffrey was the first one, but there were some close seconds."

Roiled by the events on the bridge and his role in the cover-up, Lehrmann felt "great relief" when he finally turned, Ehle said. "He knew there were some miscarriages of justice. He seriously felt bad. Terrible, in fact."

Once he turned, Lehrmann told agents how the gun, listed in evidence as fired by Lance Madison, had actually been retrieved from Kaufman's garage. He told them about the phony witnesses, and he started wearing a wire.

For three hours Lehrmann broke bread with Gisevius at Lucy's Retired Surfers Bar & Restaurant on Tchoupitoulas Street two blocks from the Convention Center downtown. The tape recorder, hidden on Lehrmann, rolled the entire conversation as they huddled in a local haunt that stays open Saturday nights "till the cock crows."

"Archie submitted a bullshit report," Gisevius told Lehrmann. "Now, if he was fucking dumb enough to put the report you and him wrote on that fucking computer a year or so afterwards."

"I don't think he would do that, would he?" Lehrmann replied.

"I hope he wouldn't," Gisevius said.

"I would think he would have fucking deleted it, to be honest with you," Lehrmann surmised.

"What weak link could sink the ship?" Gisevius wanted to know, and one by one he went over the names of other officers under the federal microscope. He had no clue Lehrmann had already turned.

With the tape rolling, Gisevius delivered an expletive-filled description of the prosecutor pursuing the case, Bernstein. "You've never been hit like that by the fucking grand jury," he told Lehrmann. "You never had a D.C. zealot coming after you who thinks you're a dirty cop."

Bernstein, he noted, was based in Washington, occupied by "tree huggers" and "old Jewish families" who, in Gisevius's view, had no earthly clue what life was like patrolling the streets of New Orleans.

"They want a fight, dude? I'm ready to fight," he charged.

Gisevius, wary of the federal investigation, asked Lehrmann if he thought the Feds were tapping his phone. They weren't. But the tape recorder was rolling that night. For the federal team, it was another notch in their investigative belt. An officer under investigation admitting the police report was "bullshit"—confirming, in the process, that a cover-up had been hatched.

The next to flip was Lieutenant Michael Lohman, Kaufman's boss. The federal investigators first met with Lohman on May 27, 2009, probing his role in the cover-up. Lohman turned them away. Several months later, the federal government came back with a subpoena, and a message. "You're in trouble," Bernstein told him. "We got you." Lohman was about to be indicted. At first the lieutenant thought Bernstein was bluffing. Then he realized the Justice Department, indeed, had him. He was guilty. He agreed to cooperate. It was, he knew, "the right thing to do." Lohman had read the initial police justifications and spotted so many contradictions in the reports, they flunked the laugh test. One day he pulled Kaufman and Bowen aside. "You all go get your story straight, go decide what happened, and then come back and tell me," Lohman said. In deciding what happened, the police brass wrote multiple drafts before filing the finished fifty-four page document. Those earlier drafts, not released publicly, contradicted the later version. They were proof of a cover-up. Now Lohman, who had quietly kept copies of all the reports generated in the days and weeks after the shootings, was turning over yet another such police report and telling Bernstein and Co. the back story of the cover-up.

The agreements with Lehrmann and Lohman marked a significant— but not complete—break for investigators. Agents had yet to convince any of the officers who fired their weapons to cooperate. Getting supervisors to unravel the cover-up was huge. Yet getting the shooters themselves would elevate the inquiry to another level. It would take agents and prosecutors inside the Budget truck and help them retrace the footsteps as police spilled out of the vehicle and began shooting at families.

On March 4, 2010, agents applied pressure directly to the source, fanning out to the homes of three of the seven officers who stepped on the bridge with their weapons drawn and helped hatch a criminal cover-up: Robert Barrios, Anthony Villavaso, and Michael Hunter. They knocked on Barrios's door and chatted with Villavaso on his front porch.

At nine that evening, agents tapped on Hunter's door. He peeked out the window and then came out through the garage. "Am I under arrest?" Hunter asked, shaken. "No," Bezak said.

"Am I a target of the investigation?"

"Absolutely," the agent replied.

Hunter had been wrestling with demons from that morning in September 2005. After officers were first charged in state court, he was assigned desk duty doing paperwork while the criminal matter coursed through the court system. Villavaso worked alongside him.

Each day officers would come by the office, shaking their hands and ripping into the DA for persecuting police doing their job. One day Hunter had enough. As Villavaso and fellow officers celebrated the police actions of that morning, Hunter rose from his desk and stormed to the bathroom. Villavaso followed him.

"What's wrong?" Villavaso asked. Standing inside the men's room, Hunter turned to the officer. "There's nothing cool about being indicted," he said. "We're not heroes."

Michael Hunter never wanted to climb the police ladder to stardom. He wanted to be a cop, nothing more. The officer had sent his four children, from his infant to his eight-year-old, out of town and reported to work during Katrina. His radio was promptly ruined by saltwater. His cell phone, stuck in his pocket as he patrolled the streets, was ruined too.

Each day he headed out for duty, heavily armed. When the 108 call came, Hunter raced to the driver's seat.

"He wasn't an opportunistic guy or an ass kisser," said Townsend Myers, Hunter's lawyer. "He was a quiet, solemn sort of guy. A go out there and do the police work kind of guy."

Now Hunter faced the most wrenching choice of his life. From the start, he had gone along with the cover-up. He looked himself in the mirror and admitted he hadn't had the courage to tell the truth.

But now, with FBI agents knocking on his door unannounced and word spreading that supervisors had already begun cooperating, everything had changed. "The truth had gotten out," he said. "And it was just a matter of time."

If he agreed to testify, Hunter would have to lay bare the truth of that morning, and admit that he was a criminal too. He'd also have to cross a very personal line. A Seventh District officer who worked narcotics, night watch, and other duties, he had reported to both Bowen and Gisevius as his supervisors.

His lawyer, Myers, had represented New Orleans police officers before Hunter and was close with other lawyers signing up for other NOPD officers on the bridge.

The officer and lawyer put those personal issues aside, Hunter working through the "internal conflict and demons he had to deal with," his lawyer said. What was the smartest legal step he could take, for himself and his family?

Hunter agreed to cooperate, and the stories he told were harrowing. He told the federal team how Bowen shot at citizens as they lay defenseless on one end of the bridge, and he described how his former supervisor stomped on a wheezing, dying Ronald Madison on the other. Hunter was guilty too, of aiming fire at innocents on the bridge and taking part in the cover-up. And, he told agents another crucial fact they did not know. Hunter himself was the first officer to fire that morning.

Soon enough Michael Hunter's stories would become central not only to prosecutors but also to defense attorneys for his former brothers on the force. They would describe him as a liar looking to save his own skin. Hunter braced for what would come.

Now that he had agreed to plead guilty, two other officers soon followed, the police dominos tumbling under federal pressure. Robert Barrios agreed to cooperate and, like Hunter, had to cross the blue line of police brotherhood—and deceive his former partner, Villavaso. The two were so close they were "like bread and butter," Barrios said. Now he was agreeing to tape-record his former partner as they met in the French Quarter.

"Vil, there were no guns out there, bro," Barrios told his partner repeatedly, trying to lure him into admitting guilt. He reminded Villavaso they were the outsiders—black officers from District Five, in an investigation led mostly by white supervisors from the Seventh.

"Me and you are the odd ones out in the 5th District," Barrios said. Villavaso did not break, and would not become a witness.

Barrios used raw language in another talk with Hunter, not knowing the conversation was being taped. Referring to the District Seven supervisors, Barrios again cast himself as an outsider. "Whatever them bitches did, they wasn't going to involve me because, you know, they didn't know me," he said.

Police reports said Barrios was part of the pack of officers firing at the citizens, and when Kaufman asked only those officers who fired their weapons to sit down that Sunday morning, Barrios was among them. But the officer, gripping a Remington 870 shotgun that Sunday morning, later contended he never pulled his trigger. When the Justice Department announced its one-count charge against Barrios on April 16, 2010, it accused him only of obstruction of justice in the cover-up, not of shooting at victims. The DOJ "charges that Barrios and other officers discussed the stories that they would tell about what happened on the bridge and that, on Jan. 25, 2006, before the officers gave formal, audiotaped statements about the incident, they gathered with supervisors in an abandoned and gutted out building, where they again went over the stories they would tell on tape."

With the storm looming, the officer's family had fled New Orleans. Barrios stayed behind, and then did "extraordinary work in the aftermath of Hurricane Katrina, rescuing people and doing that around the clock," said his lawyer, Robert Glass. Now he was admitting to the cover-up.

His admission did not come without drama. After Barrios entered his guilty plea in court, his wife stood up as a New Orleans federal prosecutor gave a press conference and blurted out that her husband had been forced to plead guilty. Emotions, Barrios would say, had overwhelmed her.

Officer Ignatius Hills also agreed to cooperate with the Justice Department. Hills, who had lied to protect himself, decided to lie no more.

By the summer of 2010, three officers and two supervisors pleaded guilty, cutting their cumulative potential prison time by decades by agreeing to turn over evidence and testify against their own. Lohman was the first to go, retiring in the beginning of February 2010 and, little more than three weeks later, pleading guilty in federal court to obstruction of justice. He admitted encouraging underlings to provide false stories about the events leading up to the shootings and encouraging "the involved sergeants to come up with a story justifying the shooting."

The same day Lohman pled guilty, February 24, 2010, Bowen, Gisevius, Villavaso, Hunter, Hills, and Barrios were administratively reassigned by the force, assigned to desk duties amid the mushrooming federal probe. Once again, they could no longer wear the NOPD uniform and could not drive police vehicles.

Two weeks later Lehrmann pleaded guilty to a federal charge of failing to report the cover-up.

And then, in April, the shrapnel began to fell the officers themselves. Hunter, who fired the first shots from the Budget truck while steering with one hand and shooting with the other, pleaded guilty to obstruction of justice. He now admitted that the police aimed their weapons at unarmed victims. Sergeant Bowen, Hunter said, fired his assault rifle "in a sweeping motion" toward civilians trying to shield themselves behind a concrete barrier on the bridge.

Nine days later Officer Barrios resigned, and federal charges followed. Then in May, it was Officer Hills's turn: another resignation by an officer on the bridge, and another federal obstruction charge. Marion David Ryder, the phony cop whose distress call helped set the catastrophic events in motion that Sunday morning, pleaded guilty to lying to FBI agents.

The police brotherhood, bonded by Katrina, was now tearing apart.

Finally the lies broke open like the levees.

For the federal government, and the victims who pressed for answers for nearly five years, the guilty pleas signaled a ringing rebuttal to the police line. In piercing the police department's wall of lies, the federal team convinced some of the guilty to come clean, and ugly truths washed forth. In turn, those cooperating witnesses shaved years, or even decades, from their prison terms. In the world of criminal prosecution, plea deals spin the wheels of justice. Yet in the federal courthouse of New Orleans, myriad judges would soon view the deals cut with the Danziger officers as being too sweet on the guilty.

Soon enough, the prosecution would be on the defense.

Yet for now the resignations and plea deals presaged the most significant turn to come: a string of federal grand jury indictments naming every officer who fired his weapon and the supervisors who scrubbed the truth.

CHAPTER 17

USA V. BOWEN, GISEVIUS, FAULCON, VILLAVASO, KAUFMAN AND DUGUE

ON JULY 12, 2010, in the US District Court of the Eastern District of Louisiana, the federal government's Civil Rights Division filed one of the most significant cases in its history.

"Indictment for Deprivation of Rights Under Color of Law, Use of a Weapon During Commission of a Crime of Violence, Conspiracy, Obstruction of Justice, and False Statements," read the opening summation of the thirty-two-page federal grand jury indictment.

Indicted were Sergeants Kenneth Bowen and Robert Gisevius Jr. and Officers Robert Faulcon and Anthony Villavaso, four of the shooters on the bridge; and homicide investigators Sergeants Arthur "Archie" Kaufman and Gerard Dugue, who coauthored the fifty-four-page incident report in May 2006 that concluded the Danziger Bridge case was considered solved.

The federal charges documented a damning indictment of the shooting and cover-up and described how innocent victims had been snared in the NOPD crossfire and whitewash. Nearly five years after the shootings on the bridge, the unvarnished story had come to light in New Orleans. In plain language, the twenty-seven-count indictment charged that

- Bowen, Gisevius, Faulcon, and Villavaso shot James Brissette Jr. on the bridge, killing him in a civil rights violation.
- Faulcon shot Ronald Madison, killing him in a civil rights violation.
- Bowen, Gisevius, Faulcon, and Villavaso shot Susan Bartholomew, "willfully depriving her of the right, secured and protected by the

Constitution and laws of the United States, to be free from the use of unreasonable force by a law enforcement officer."

- Bowen, Gisevius, Faulcon, and Villavaso shot Leonard Bartholomew III, Lesha Bartholomew, and Jose Holmes Jr., causing bodily harm to each due to unreasonable use of police force.
- Bowen used unlawful force against Ronald Madison. "While acting under color of law," the indictment said, Bowen "kicked and stomped Ronald Madison while Madison was on the ground, alive but mortally wounded."

The indictment detailed the battery of weapons the officers unleashed on the bridge: two AK-47 assault rifles, a .40 caliber Glock 22 semiautomatic pistol, an M4 assault rifle, and a Mossberg shotgun. It said all six defendants engaged in a cover-up, conspiring with Lieutenant Michael Lohman, Detective Jeffrey Lehrmann, and others.

The facts behind the conspiracy count stretched for nine pages in the indictment, exposing the clumsy police fraud and cover-up. Immediately after the shootings, "Kaufman and Bowen specifically discussed using Hurricane Katrina to excuse failures in the investigation, and thereby to help make any inquiry into the shooting go away."

The NOPD investigators, led by Kaufman and Lohman, failed to collect evidence, dismissed potential witnesses without questioning them, and invented stories justifying the shooting. Kaufman planted a gun, lied under oath during Lance Madison's bond hearing that Lance had a gun, and lied again when he said he found the revolver in the grassy area aside the bridge a day after the shootings. Kaufman, Bowen, and Gisevius, working with Lohman and Lehrmann, "repeatedly discussed the false statement that defendant Bowen would give to justify the shootings on the Danziger Bridge."

Bowen lied under oath during his January 25, 2006, audiotaped statement, the indictment said, and Kaufman and Dugue "failed to question or challenge statements they knew to be false." Before that statement, Kaufman and Dugue huddled with Bowen, Gisevius, and Villavaso in the NOPD Seventh District police station to get their stories straight.

"Defendant Bowen then took the lead in explaining the false story that he would tell to justify the shooting, and the other officers discussed the false stories they would tell in order to remain consistent with Bowen's story."

Gisevius lied when he said he saw Lance Madison fire a gun, and omitted, under oath, that he had repeatedly fired a rifle on the bridge.

Faulcon, who had retired from the force, was not among those gathered in the gutted police building to compare notes and get their stories on the same page, but provided an audiotaped statement in June, five months later. Faulcon perpetuated the whitewash, the indictment said, right after the shooting and in his subsequent sworn statement. "Faulcon, after being given advice about how to make his shootings appear justified, provided or approved of a false and misleading statement in which he falsely claimed that the civilians on the bridge, both male and female, were armed and fired at police, and that Faulcon shot Ronald Madison because Madison noted a police presence and quickly turned, reaching for an object in his right waistband."

The indictment detailed the ever-shifting police reports, from the thirty-two-page report to the seventeen-page version to the seven-pager and, ultimately, the fifty-four-page report that listed "Lakeisha Smith" and "James Youngman" as firsthand witnesses. The same report said Susan and Leonard Bartholomew told police Jose Holmes fired first. Another lie, exposed.

And, the indictment charged Kaufman for the stories he shared during his friendly chat with federal agents on January 22, 2009. It called out Dugue for telling agents "he had no concerns about the veracity of the officers' statements or the correctness of their actions. In fact, he had many 'red flags' and 'question marks' about the officers' stories, but he reported the questionable information as fact." Kaufman obstructed justice by his phony notation in police logs claiming he found Lance Madison's gun a day after the shootings, and he and Dugue lied in the fifty-four-page report by claiming the gun was Madison's.

All the defendants conspired to violate the civil rights of Jose Holmes by falsely prosecuting him, and Bowen, Gisevius, Kaufman, and Dugue committed the same crime against Lance Madison. Bowen made up a series of misleading statements to obscure what had really happened, falsely claiming the Bartholomew family fired guns at the officers and that "after the shooting, he saw two guns on a walkway near the dead and injured civilians; that he kicked the guns off of the bridge; and that he saw Lance Madison throw a gun into the Industrial Canal." Officer Villavaso lied too, saying that civilians fired guns, and claiming that after the Budget truck came to a stop, officers yelled, "Police! Show me your hands!"

The indictment included "Special Findings" that had deep resonance for the families of the men killed that morning.

Kenneth Bowen, Robert Gisevius Jr., Robert Faulcon Jr., and Anthony Villavaso II "killed James Brissette intentionally" and "intentionally killed or attempted to kill more than one person in a single criminal episode."

Robert Faulcon "killed Ronald Madison intentionally; intentionally inflicted serious bodily injury that resulted in the death of Ronald Madison."

Those four officers now faced the prospect of life in prison, or possibly the death penalty, for taking the lives of Ronald Madison and JJ Brissette.

With the indictment unsealed, federal authorities issued strong words about the police actions and cover-up that had, for five years, buried the truth.

Jim Letten, the US attorney based in New Orleans, said the indictment would bring to justice the officers who abused their badge and send a message to the community of law enforcement officers "who do serve the people and honor the badge." Most of all, the indictment should help "make certain that no one should ever have to fear those whose job it is to protect them."

Attorneys for the accused officers said the indictment told just part of the story. To them, the charges symbolically whitewashed the larger saga of what the police officers encountered post-Katrina. The officers responded to a life-or-death call, amid a time of unprecedented chaos, and now were painted as criminals for hopping into the Budget truck and racing to the scene of a reported gun battle.

"It was a tragedy. It wasn't an intentional act of murder that the government is trying to portray it as," attorney Eric Hessler, representing Robert Gisevius Jr., told a local reporter. "The government has ignored the circumstances and conditions under which these officers were operating. For them to say that these officers intentionally went out and shot and killed unarmed civilians, knowing that they were unarmed and posed no threat, is certainly the wrong conclusion."

Faulcon was arrested in Texas, and the three indicted officers with him in the Budget rental truck turned themselves into FBI headquarters in New Orleans. Bowen, Gisevius, and Villavaso arrived together, sending a signal that the officers would stand side by side. All four were held in federal detention, with no chance for bond. Unlike in state court, the federal charges guaranteed they would not be set free while awaiting trial and would not return to NOPD desk duty. Their police careers appeared to be over. Dugue and Kaufman, accused of the cover-up but not the shootings, were freed on bond; Dugue, fighting the charges, later took legal steps for his case to be tried separately from the other five defendants.

At the New Orleans Police Department, the unquestioned defense of the troops appeared to ebb, at least for a moment, as the federal case was unsealed. Police superintendent Warren Riley suspended without pay the three officers still on the force. Bowen, Gisevius, and Villavaso were unable to sign their "Notice of Suspension" paperwork because they were locked up without bond.

Four months later, on November 8, 2010, Riley reversed himself. He cancelled the suspensions of Sergeants Bowen and Gisevius and Officer Villavaso. The Danziger shooters remained behind bars. At the NOPD, they remained part of the family.

CHAPTER 18

JUDGMENT TIME, JUDICIAL QUESTIONS—AND AN OFFICER'S SHAME

WITH THE POLICE SHOOTERS now off the streets and plotting their defenses to the indictment, the next wave of justice began to be administered in the federal courthouse. This wave targeted the officers turned federal witnesses, who stood in the US federal courthouse in New Orleans to face their own sentences. As they did, prosecutors appeared to stand under judicial scrutiny along with them.

On September 22, 2010, former detective Jeffrey Lehrmann stood first for sentencing. The first to cooperate and not among the shooters on the bridge, Lehrmann hoped for probation. US district judge Lance M. Africk handed Lehrmann the maximum he could receive for the felony conviction he pleaded guilty to in his deal with prosecutors: three years in prison. Africk was sending a message that would echo in other courtrooms of other defendants now cooperating with the government.

A year later, federal prosecutors sought to cut Lehrmann's sentence in half, to eighteen months from thirty-six. Not only was Lehrmann the first officer to cross the blue line of police brotherhood, "Mr. Lehrmann cooperated fully with the government, providing substantial assistance throughout the government's investigation and prosecution," prosecutor Bobbi Bernstein wrote, arguing for a reduced sentence.

Lehrmann was living in Arizona when the government first reached out to him, and he "flew to New Orleans at his own expense in order to set the record straight." Once he turned, he did so fully, wearing a wire, including a several-hour-long session with Gisevius, the government said.

In that session, Gisevius acknowledged the larger cover-up, a powerful piece of evidence for the federal government. Lehrmann would later take the stand as a government witness once the other officers stood trial.

"The government has discussed this recommendation with the victims in this case, who share the government's belief that the ultimate sentence meted out should achieve a careful balance between deterrence of wrongdoing and encouragement of truthful cooperation," Bernstein wrote in the motion coauthored by Theodore Carter, an assistant US attorney based in New Orleans, and Department of Justice civil rights prosecutor Cindy K. Chung.

It took two days for Judge Africk to deny the request. The judge used strong language to describe Lehrmann's crimes, including his role in creating the name Lakeisha Smith as a witness fabricating the police line that Lance and Ronald Madison were armed.

"It is particularly abhorrent that as a result of material false statements made by you and other officers, Ronald Madison, the young man shot to death on the Danziger Bridge, and Lance Madison, who was unlawfully detained, were characterized as common criminals," the judge said. "You, being oblivious to the emotional turmoil already sustained by the Madison family, compounded and magnified it by characterizing them as such."

The judge hammered away at the litany of lies and fabrications Lehrmann had taken part in, from going along to retrieve the "ham sandwich" from his buddy Kaufman's garage, to helping create the other invented witness, James Youngman.

"As you knew," the judge said, "James Youngman did not exist."

Africk, a former state and federal prosecutor who once served as chief of the Criminal Division for the US attorney in New Orleans, added another admonition. "Those particular actions, while troublesome enough when committed by non-law enforcement witnesses, are even more troubling and disturbing to this court when committed by a law enforcement officer," he said.

Lehrmann waited four years before beginning to speak the truth, Judge Africk noted.

"It was only after Mr. Lehrmann heard the footsteps of an expansive federal investigation that he came forward," the judge said in his courtroom. "Apparently, Mr. Lehrmann's conscience waited approximately four years to reveal itself."

Had the police officers told the truth from the start, Lance Madison would not have lost his freedom to phony charges. The cover-up Lehrmann took part in was "a disgrace of immense proportion" that would hurt those wearing the badge who set out to do the right thing. "As a result of such conduct, other law enforcement officers must now continually respond to public skepticism related to the manner in which they perform their duties."

Lehrmann had already been rewarded enough with three years, the judge said. And though he may have faced tough decisions over whether to tell the truth from the start, implicating his fellow officers in the process, "his situation was not nearly as difficult as that faced by the victims and their families."

"This court cannot in good conscience support the government's view that any reward in addition to that already provided by the government is appropriate," Africk closed. Motion denied.

HUNTER GOT EIGHT YEARS in prison at sentencing in December 2010. He too received the stiffest possible sentence, considering the crimes he pleaded guilty to. Two weeks after prosecutors tried, and failed, to reduce Lehrmann's prison term, they tried the same tack with Hunter in September 2011. As in Lehrmann's case, prosecutors sought to reduce Hunter's prison term after he had taken the stand as a government witness when his former comrades stood trial.

"Mr. Hunter was the first and only officer to provide eyewitness testimony about the shootings of six civilians on the bridge," prosecutors Bernstein, Chung, and Carter wrote. "Mr. Hunter's horrific account of the shooting—in which he described police officers opening fire without cause on unarmed civilians—was consistent with the victims' accounts and with the physical evidence. . . . Mr. Hunter's account connected the other evidence in the case, and provided the key to proving that the shootings on the bridge constituted criminal acts."

Once he agreed to cooperate, Hunter, a onetime Marine with a youthful face, "provided an unflinchingly honest account of the incident on the bridge, even admitting personal wrongdoing about which federal investigators previously had no knowledge."

For one, he admitted he had been the first officer to fire his weapon. He was the officer-turned-witness who described how "Bowen stomped on a mortally-wounded civilian as the civilian lay dying in the street," the prosecutors wrote.

"Mr. Hunter continued to honor his promise to provide truthful testimony, despite the personal risk involved in cooperating against other law enforcement officers in what amounted to the functional equivalent of a murder case."

The DOJ prosecutors asked the judge to cut Hunter's prison term to five years from eight. To the prosecution, such a reduction would "send a message to other officers that it is in their personal interest to cooperate with authorities investigating police misconduct."

Bernstein pressed the issue before US district judge Sarah S. Vance in a hearing November 5, 2011. As with other officers turned witnesses, the government struggled as it sought a sentence for Hunter that punished his crime but rewarded his cooperation. "This is an unusual case and an extremely important case, with a lot of really powerful considerations, some of which work directly at odds with one another," she told the judge.

Hunter helped reveal the truth, she said, as the only police eyewitness to the shootings on the east side of the bridge, where the Bartholomew family and James Brissette were fired upon.

"From that very beginning, he stopped us right away and he said . . . Ken Bowen did not fire the first shot, I did," Bernstein said. Once he talked, Hunter never played games with the investigators, she said.

Bernstein told the judge that Lance Madison, his sister, and mother were in the courtroom that morning. "Lance was shot at for no reason. He watched his brother get shot and killed. He was falsely arrested. He was framed. He was put in jail. This family lost their brother, their son," she said. "And they have every right to be sitting here angry and demanding justice. And yet, they're here today supporting the government's request for some sort of break for Mr. Hunter."

Judge Vance heard Hunter's bid for a lower term and shot it down. Hunter, serving time in a federal prison in Bastrop, Texas, was staying there. "Mr. Hunter got the benefit of his bargain upfront under a highly generous plea agreement and it would be injustice for me to reward him any more," the judge ruled.

She questioned the extent of Hunter's truthfulness. The officer had admitted firing in the direction of the Madison brothers as they raced up the bridge, but said he aimed over their heads.

From the bench, Judge Vance called that assertion "preposterous," and she noted Hunter had fired shots toward the Bartholomew family as well. "I find it very telling that he's going to try to minimize his own behavior when he's testifying about when he's doing his own shooting."

Prosecutors said Hunter's bullets hit no victims—a "critical distinction" between his actions and that of other officers. "Mike did not shoot anybody on the bridge," Bernstein said. "And that might be the luck of him being a bad shot, but he did not shoot anybody on the bridge."

The judge was not swayed. "I understand he's important to you," she told Bernstein. "I understand you need people like this. I truly do. But I've got to take into account what he did, the justice system and society at large. And, you know, you gave him a deal upfront. He got the benefit of his bargain."

OFFICER IGNATIUS HILLS STOOD for sentencing October 5, 2011, after taking the stand in the federal prosecution of his fellow officers. Once more the government's plea deal was in the spotlight.

In a federal court courtroom again filled with members of the Madison family, Hills shared his shame for the shooting and cover-up. He apologized to the families touched by his actions.

"It was very devastating," Hills told US district judge Martin L. C. Feldman. "I'm ashamed to be a part of something so terrible in the history of New Orleans. I just wanted to offer my deepest apologies, and I keep you guys in my prayers every day."

Bernstein said the government struggled with its recommended sentence for Hills too.

"When we started this investigation, we didn't know what happened, and the truth would never have come out if it hadn't been for the deals we made with cooperators and for cooperators coming forward and telling the truth about horrible things that happened on the bridge," Bernstein told the judge. "But they are the ones that got us to the point we can stand here today and say everybody knows what happened on the bridge."

The judge hearing her plea was a Reagan appointee. A year earlier Judge Feldman attracted public criticism for blocking a government six-month moratorium on deep-water drilling projects following the massive Deepwater Horizon explosion and oil spill. The judge said the moratorium would hurt the economy.

Now, he had questions for the prosecution. Should the witnesses get a "gold star" for cooperating, he wondered, once they knew the investigation was in full bloom? "Does the government give any consideration to the—well, to be polite, to the patently abusive nature of the crimes that were committed?" Judge Feldman asked.

Absolutely, Bernstein said. "I'm a civil rights prosecutor. This is what I do. I have dedicated three years of my life to this case because I am outraged by the conduct on the bridge and because it was incredibly important to me personally, as I realize it was to this entire community, to see justice done for what happened on the bridge," she said.

"But justice for what happened on the bridge necessarily has to entail justice—it has to entail—the officers who stood at a barrier and fired into a mass of humanity cowered on the ground, justice has to include them being held accountable. The only way we could ever have made that happen, for them to be held accountable, was to have cooperation from officers."

Jacquelyn Madison Brown, sister to Lance and Ronald, stood up at the sentencing hearing.

"As a family, we will never recover from the death of our brother Ronald," she told the judge. "It has been over six years since Ronald was killed and it is still difficult to speak about. Ronald was the light of our lives. Although he was forty years old, he had the mental capacity of a five- to six-year-old child. He was a loving, sweet, shy person who filled our lives with joy and playfulness."

The loss of their brother, and the lies told about him to justify the killing, had taken a heartbreaking toll on the entire family, Jacquelyn Brown said. The pain for Lance, his brother's protector, was unspeakable. "Lance, who was with him at the time and who was unable, despite his best efforts, to protect Ronald from deadly harm from these police officers who had taken the law into their own hands," she said.

"The decision to frame Lance and to try to take Lance's life away from him was especially cruel and still fills us with horror," the sister said. "If the truth had not come out, Lance could have been wrongfully convicted and sent to prison for the rest of his life."

Officer Hills, she said, "stood by and said nothing to prevent this injustice from taking place. Instead, in an effort to cover up his own wrongdoing and that of his fellow officers, he made a conscious decision to participate in an effort to frame Lance on false charges."

But now, she said, the Madison family was thankful Hills came forward and helped puncture the police code of silence.

"We truly believe that the voice of a single individual telling the truth could have made a difference." It wouldn't have brought Ronald back, "but it might have prevented my brother Lance from being thrown in prison," she said. "It would certainly have cast a cloud upon the false-hoods and lies that the other officers were telling about our brothers and the victims on the bridge. Perhaps had any of these officers spoke out, it would not have taken so many years for the truth to be known and for justice to prevail."

The judge was sympathetic to the family's suffering and plea, but not to Hills, who shot toward a teenager's back as the boy ran away. "Hills has patently received leniency from the government by virtue of the generous charge to which he was permitted to plead guilty," Judge Feldman said from the bench. Prosecutors sought a four-year sentence. The judge gave Hills the maximum, six and a half years.

THE OTHER OFFICERS WHO pleaded guilty were now behind bars too. Officer Barrios got five years in prison. Michael Lohman, the college-educated lieutenant who made a choice to stick with a cover-up he instantly knew was "bullshit," was given a four-year prison sentence in November 2011. The Madison family, including Lance, Romell, and Jacquelyn Madison Brown, attended that sentencing, as they had for the other officers. They were there for brother Ronald. Sherrel Johnson was there, too, for JJ.

A few months before Lohman's prison term was set, as the most significant civil rights case on the Department of Justice's national docket readied to unfold inside the federal courthouse in New Orleans, another police domino tumbled. Sergeant Kaufman, who told Lohman "Everything's cool, babe" after his chat with prosecutors and FBI agents, retired from the force the first day of June 2011.

Three weeks after he left the NOPD, Kaufman would join Bowen, Faulcon, Villavaso, and Gisevius at the defendants' table for the federal trial for their crimes.

As that date loomed, a central question hovered. What legal fate awaited the band of brothers who refused to cooperate with the federal government, who continued to insist they were guilty of nothing more than responding to a call for help in time of unprecedented tragedy? In the six-story Hale Boggs federal courthouse downtown, a jury of their peers, soon to be impaneled, would consider their defense. In the summer of 2011, the events of September 4, 2005, would air for the first time; the victims, families, police, and city finally absorbing the full recounting of the shots on the bridge.

CHAPTER 19

IN THE COURTROOM

ON JUNE 27, 2011, day one of the trial for five of the six defendants who refused to plea, prosecutor Bobbi Bernstein rose and, in trademark fashion, spoke for more than an hour without a single note.

"Shoot first and ask questions later, that's how this whole case got started," Bernstein said, jumping instantly to the core of the government's case. "These five defendants sitting here are current and former NOPD officers, four of whom gunned down, not one, not two, not three, but six innocent people on the Danziger Bridge.

"These defendants, Sergeant Ken Bowen, Sergeant Rob Gisevius, Officer Robert Faulcon, and Officer Anthony Villavaso, drove onto the Danziger Bridge and they opened fire. Without warning, without so much as yelling, 'Police,' they opened fire with assault rifles and a shotgun, mowing down an unarmed family as that family huddled behind a concrete barrier, wounded and confused, trying desperately to avoid the shots.

"And then that man, Officer Faulcon, traveled more than half a mile clear to the other side of the bridge, where he raised his shotgun one more time and he shot one more innocent person through the back. When all was said and done, two innocent people lay dead on the Danziger Bridge, four others seriously wounded.

"And as soon as the shooting stopped, these four defendants, guided by the fifth defendant back there, Sergeant Archie Kaufman, started lying to cover it up. They lied because they knew they had committed a crime, because they knew that officers are not allowed to shoot first and ask questions later."

"Meanwhile, seventy-five miles away in Baton Rouge, Andrea Celestine tried every day to hold on to hope. She had evacuated before the

143

storm, but she had been separated from her mother and her little brother, seventeen-year-old James, JJ, Brissette. And every day she hoped would be the day she'd get word from her mom and her brother."

She continued, "When that shooting finally stopped, young JJ Brissette was lying face down on a pedestrian walkway on the bridge. He had bullets in his feet, in his knee, in his legs, in his arms, and in the back of his head. JJ was dead, and Andrea would never see her brother again.

"When that shooting finally stopped, Susan Bartholomew was lying on the same walkway unable to move her right arm, which had been blasted apart by an assault rifle.

"As Susan laid there wondering what had just happened, she heard the cries of her husband, her daughter, and her nephew, all of whom had been shot around her. When that shooting finally stopped, Ronald Madison was lying in a pool of blood, blasted through the back with a shotgun. As Ronald laid there and died in the street, his older brother Lance, his protector, was arrested and taken to jail. For twenty-five days, Lance Madison would sit in jail accused of something he didn't do, wondering whether he would ever be free again.

"And when that shooting finally stopped, these four men had a very big problem," Bernstein said. "And you're going to hear that they decided to make it go away, and that's where the fifth defendant, Sergeant Kaufman, comes in."

The prosecution team backed up Bernstein's precise words with more than three hundred trial exhibits, from the assault rifles, shotguns, and pistols the officers fired to the shotgun shells and pellets later discovered splayed atop the bridge. The prosecution submitted the NOPD course manual on "Use of Force" to describe how severely off course the police had veered that morning.

The federal exhibits portrayed the human toll of the police shootout. A picture of Jose Holmes, on the surgical table as his life lay in the balance, was entered into evidence. Prosecutors introduced a bullet, held in a plastic jar, recovered from Holmes's temple and X-rays and photographs depicting the shredded limbs and bloodied skin of Leonard Bartholomew III, Lesha Bartholomew, and Susan Bartholomew.

The sole photograph Sherrel Johnson had to hold onto of JJ, taken when he was nine years old, was another trial exhibit. Another photo showed the young man's dead body on a walkway. X-rays introduced at trial revealed bullets in JJ's feet, pelvis, chest, shoulders, knees, elbow, and skull.

Photos of Ronald Madison with one of his dogs, at home in his living room, beaming at graduation, and with brother Lance before Hurricane Katrina were contrasted against photographs taken after the shootout: of Lance in police custody and of Ronald's limp body, slumped on the ground at the Friendly Inn.

The defense cast an entirely different light on the events of that morning. New Orleans was under water, literally and figuratively, after Katrina, and the officers who stayed behind did so for all the right reasons. When they raced to the bridge, the officers did so thinking a fellow officer was, once again, being gunned down by the enemy.

They knew they would face fire and stood ready to respond.

"These men are not guilty. They are not guilty," Paul Fleming Jr., Faulcon's lawyer, said the moment federal prosecutor Bernstein sat down. Speaking directly to jurors, Fleming told them they had to be convinced, beyond a reasonable doubt, that the police officers were guilty, and to come to that conclusion while considering their actions "in the context of the worst domestic disaster in the history of this country, Hurricane Katrina."

"The other lawyers are going to tell you the personal stories of these five men, but I want you to remember that these five have one thing in common: They stayed. They stayed here and they did their jobs, and they did their jobs the best they could under these horrible, horrible circumstances. They didn't desert, they didn't go work other jobs," Fleming continued.

"They rescued people. They pulled people off of rooftops, pulled people out of their attics. In fact, you're going to learn that some of these men were rescued themselves; one off his own rooftop. And right after that, they jump right in and they get to work. They do their jobs. They go out and rescue people. And they do the best they could. They do the best they could without adequate leadership, without adequate food, without adequate shelter, without adequate clothing, without adequate rest, without adequate supplies, and without adequate support. These are the guys that stayed.

"These are the guys that did their job," the lawyer said, hammering the point that the men sitting at the defendants' table were, in fact, public servants.

"And that brings us to September 4th, 2005," Fleming said. "That morning they're out at the Crystal Palace getting ready to go do some more rescue runs and a call comes over the radio, and it's the worst call any police officer can ever hear, a 108. And what do they hear? 108, officer needs assistance. 108, shots fired. 108, two officers down."

In normal times, a 108 call would send the cavalry out—nearly every officer in New Orleans, from every corner possible, would race out to help their fellow officers. But this call came after Katrina, with never-ending duty calling and a patchwork assemblage of officers struggling to make do.

"Two officers dead is what everyone thought. Two officers dead or dying is what these men had in their minds when they raced out there and all piled into the rental truck," the lawyer said. "Michael Hunter's driving; Kenny Bowen's in the passenger seat; Rob Gisevius, Robert Faulcon, Tony Villavaso and others jump into the back. And in the back of the truck, they cannot see what's going on; in the back of the truck, they don't know what's going on."

The officers had two wishes as the truck raced to the bridge, he said. That the officers under distress were still alive. "And they're hoping at the end of all of this, they'll still be alive" too.

Fleming noted that officer Hunter, not among the defendants on trial, was first to fire, from the front driver's seat. With the gunfire unleashed, the officers packed inside the truck instantly assumed a gunfight was underway. Some officers in back stayed in the truck. But not the defendants, and not his client. They spilled out believing other officers were under fire.

"And they get out of that truck slap dead into the middle of a gunfight. Several people are shot; and some, no doubt, at least some are in the wrong place at the wrong time, and that's unfortunate. And two people are killed that day, and that's always unfortunate. No matter what the circumstances, that's unfortunate."

Fleming's opening statement was compelling but, prosecutors would note, only part of the truth. There was a gunfight, yes. But atop the Danziger Bridge, only the police were armed.

Frank DeSalvo, Bowen's attorney, stood next. He said prosecutor Bernstein's statement that morning sounded "more fitted to a novel."

Eric Hessler, the lawyer for Robert Gisevius Jr., painted a personal portrait of the sergeant. Gisevius reported for duty with Katrina coming, sending to safety his five-year-old child and seven-month baby boy. "He left his family behind to protect the citizens of this city," Hessler told jurors.

Some of Gisevius's relatives bemoan that decision, but say it was just like "Robbie." "Time and again I ask God why Robbie didn't flee the city with his family as so many other officers did," his cousin said. "But I know that his loyalty to New Orleans and its citizens would have made that impossible for him to do." When a former police academy member took a government job in Afghanistan, Gisevius would send messages seeing what he could do for his family. Gisevius acted like a big brother to a high school classmate, making sure "boys that I dated had the utmost respect for me." The classmate went on to become a high school theology teacher.

After Hurricane Katrina, the officer was trapped in a hotel by the floodwaters. Gisevius swam out of the building to retrieve a boat that had neither a running motor nor oars.

"So they broke some fence boards down, used those for paddles, and went and rescued other officers so they, too, could procure more boats, and began rescuing citizens. And that's how this began, with a boat and a piece of wood, and not a whole lot more. And it grew," Hessler told the courtroom. "This went on for some six days, sunup and sundown. They woke up with the sun and began rescuing people up until the sun went down."

Sometimes, it was too dangerous to go out. "Gunshots, obstructions in the water that they couldn't see. You name it, they faced it," he continued. "There was no electricity in the city, no air conditioning, no place to sleep that provided any level of comfort, very little food, very little water. He stayed through it. A lot of people couldn't. A lot of people couldn't handle it."

Then police heard of rapes in the Superdome, murder in the streets, armed gangs running around. Later, some of the wildest tales, particularly those coming from the Superdome, were proven to be invented stories, spread through hyperbole and fear. "At that time, was it believable? Yeah.

Was it believable when the mayor was saying it? Yeah. The chief of police? Yeah," his lawyer said.

Gisevius learned of a colleague officer's suicide and another officer who had taken his life.

"Who do you have to lean on? Nobody. Nobody," Hessler said. "You don't have anything to distract you. You have other people in the same situation. You have not a whole lot of anything but yourself, the darkness, and your mind. And he wakes up the next day and he goes and saves more people."

The stresses in the streets became so intense, Hessler said, police began handing out assault rifles to officers.

"And they issued them to anybody that had two hands. You didn't have to be qualified, you didn't have to know what you were doing, you just had to, I guess, be either concerned, scared enough, or ordered to pick it up and patrol the streets," the lawyer said, building a portrait of how the devastation changed the rules, even for police officers. "Now, in normal days, especially in America in New Orleans, we don't see policemen walking around with automatic weapons. And these weren't normal days, and you saw plenty of police officers walking around with automatic weapons. And that was condoned and encouraged by the NOPD."

That morning, September 4, Gisevius had just returned from another rescue mission when the urgent call went out. He could have kept rescuing people, played it safe. He stepped into the Budget truck and raced to the bridge. He sat in the back, his vision partially obstructed by the officers around him, "traveling to the worst call he could ever get."

There's no time to ask questions. The gunfire had begun. Gisevius spilled from the truck, firearm at the ready.

"What he does is what his training, what his experience, and what human instinct tells you to do," Hessler said. "You know, cops aren't perfect. And just because you become a cop doesn't mean you're a tactical expert, or you've got some higher sense of danger, or some higher ability to deal with a life-threatening, just scared-to-death situation. They become scared. Cops are human."

Gisevius saw a man running up the bridge—it was one of the Madisons—and he heard gunfire around him. "If you perceive a guy on the top of the bridge with a rifle, and you perceive him firing, what are you going to do? You're going to fire back," the lawyer explained.

Timothy Meche, attorney for Anthony Villavaso II, stood next and addressed jurors. "The government said he fired nine times. We don't dispute that. That's what happened. We all agree to that," Meche said.

More important, he said, was what was in Villavaso's mind as he, like Gisevius, sat in the back of the truck racing to what police believed was a shootout.

Villavaso, born in New Orleans and raised in the Catholic faith, was an only child who surprised his parents by finding a connection with the alto saxophone. He became the first in his family to turn to police work. Some relatives were horrified, but Villavaso felt the call to duty, and joined a unit that searched for criminals in a city that often suffered the highest murder rate in the United States. His hair cut short, Villavaso favored a thin moustache that reached down to his beard, giving a Fu Manchu appearance. He became a father of two who told his children to chase their dreams. Before Hurricane Katrina, his police file was bereft of abuse complaints but included only dismissed cases over his failure to attend court hearings for some of his arrests. The department cleared him in those two instances. Trapped by Katrina, he floated to safety with a stranger on a bed mattress— rescuing an elderly woman stuck on a roof before finding harbor himself, his lawyer said. Then came September 4 and the adrenaline-pumping race to the bridge.

"Things are happening so fast. It's not a video game. It's not a slow motion movie," Meche told the courtroom.

"Things are happening so fast, if you take the time to go out and assess the situation, you could quite likely get your head blown off, or somebody else could get their head blown off," Villavaso's lawyer said. "When he got out of the truck and fired his gun, it's because he thought people were firing back. In his mind, he saw people shooting back at him."

The issue, the lawyer told jurors, is "not whether or not they did have guns, the issue is whether these officers reasonably believed they had guns."

Inside the federal courtroom, Meche would contend, the legal decks were stacked against the officers. Media coverage after Katrina cited cases of police wrongdoing, and attendees at trial had to pass through three sets of security to get in. "It was a poisonous atmosphere in that courtroom," the lawyer later said. "It gave the impression to the jury that these were some really dangerous guys." Villavaso was a good officer two years out of the academy, who grew up in New Orleans and attended an African American high school, he said. Villavaso was not an orchestrator of any cover-up, Meche said, and the lawyer maintains his client's shots did not strike any victims. He fired from the adrenaline of the moment. "He just got caught up in that," Meche said.

In court another lawyer for Faulcon stood and, for the defense, had the last word. "Ladies and gentlemen, this is a tragedy for everyone involved: Police officers, victims, everyone involved," said the lawyer, Lindsay Larson III. "It is a horribly regrettable mistake, but it's not a federal crime."

THE FIRST WITNESS CALLED to testify was Susan Bartholomew. The bailiff asked her to raise her right arm, put her left hand on the Bible, and swear to tell the truth. Bartholomew, wearing a shawl over her clothes, didn't respond as requested, and the bailiff asked again. Finally she whispered to the court officer. She had no right arm to raise. It had been shot off on the bridge.

Bartholomew raised her left hand, and then told jurors, the bow-tied federal judge Kurt D. Engelhardt, and a full courtroom of the terror she and her family suffered that striking Sunday morning.

"Before you heard shots, did you ever hear anyone yell?" Cindy Chung, another civil rights prosecutor on the case, asked her.

"No," she told the jurors.

"Did anyone ever identify themselves to you?"

"No."

"Did you ever hear anyone give you any commands?"

"No."

Once the shooting began, Bartholomew said, "It seemed like forever." In the New Orleans Police reports, Big Leonard was quoted as saying nephew Jose had been shooting at helicopters. Prosecutor Chung read the report aloud for jurors to hear. Lies, Susan Bartholomew said. They were all lies.

Pacing toward the defendants' table, the prosecutor turned to her witness and asked, "Mrs. Bartholomew, looking at this side of the room, have you ever pointed a gun at any of these people on this side of the room?"

"No."

"Have you ever fired a gun at any of these people?"

"No."

"Have you ever pointed a weapon or fired a weapon in your life?"

"No," she answered.

The battery of defense attorneys had few questions to ask Bartholomew. One even apologized for her suffering. The defense had nowhere to go with this first witness, nothing to impeach. Instead, the team would save its fire for some of the police officers who cut deals, challenging their motives, credibility, and truthfulness.

Others took the stand for the prosecution. Taj Magee, the officer desperate to find evidence that his colleagues had cause to fire upon residents, testified, as did Jennifer Dupree, the officer who first responded and whose call helped set the events in motion. Dupree told jurors about a curious phone call she received at 1:00 a.m. one morning, as the district attorney was investigating the shootings. The call came from Archie Kaufman, who stirred her from sleep, and asked her to meet him and a lawyer at a bar. She told him no, hung up, then went back to sleep. She didn't recall the lawyer's name, just that it wasn't Steven London, Kaufman's counsel at the trial. Dupree then told Bernstein several of the statements Kaufman attributed to her in one report were false.

Morrell Johnson, the witness whose name Lance Madison told himself to remember, was called to the stand too, as was Robert Rickman, the Friendly Inn maintenance man and security guard who snapped photos of Ronald Madison, still sprawled out on the pavement hours after the gunfire. Now those photos were being introduced as evidence, and Rickman spoke of the nightmares that had haunted his dreams since that morning.

Lance Madison, Jose Holmes, Little Leonard, and Lesha Bartholomew took turns recounting the shooting, recreating that morning in short, direct language.

On the stand, Lance answered questions from Theodore Carter, another of the federal prosecutors litigating the Danziger case. He said the Madisons were a praying family where everyone looked after another. When Ronald refused to leave his dogs, with Katrina on the horizon, Lance naturally stayed back to look over him.

After the hurricane and flooding, the brothers spent two days atop Lance's roof. Lance said his brother's mental development put him at between six and seven years old.

"How was he handling all of this, the water, the flood?" the prosecutor asked.

"He was very frightened, scared. I tried to calm him down. We prayed. And I just tried to talk to him and keep him comforted."

On Sunday September 4, he told the jurors, they set out from brother Romell's office intending to make it to the family homestead on Lafon Drive. Why to your mother's house? Carter asked. "To retrieve some bicycles to ride to get as far as we can," Lance said. "We couldn't get back there, the water was real high. So we turned back around and came back."

That led them back over the bridge, and into the frenzied gunfire.

"We got about half way up the bridge, and that's when I heard a whole lot of gunshots, lots of gunshots. And I turned back around. When I turned around, I saw a truck pulled up to the bridge and had people that was coming out [of] the truck and was already out of the truck, shooting at the people that was behind me. And, next thing I know, they was shooting at us."

He looked up and saw blood spurting out of Ronald's shoulder. Lance tried to whisk his brother to safety, still utterly confused by who was shooting and why. He was instantly, fully in survival mode.

"We started running again, and I was trying to comfort Ronald. He was bleeding very badly," Lance said. "I grabbed him, put his—got under his shoulder and grabbed him and tried to run with him. He stopped me for a second and told me—And he told me to tell my mother and my brother and sisters that he loved us. And he shook my hand. And I told him, Ronald, I said: We got to go, because these guys, you know, are coming after us. And we started running. I met another guy coming [from] the opposite direction, and I told him turn around. I said: These people are shooting at us."

That was Morrell Johnson, the security guard who glimpsed the shooting on the west end of the bridge.

"When we got down to the bottom of the bridge, I told Ronald: Ronald, I'm going to go get some help. I said: Just be quiet, because you're hurt real bad. And I'm just trying to calm him down. So, when I took off to try to get some help, that's where somebody came behind and started shooting again," Lance said, holding the courtroom in silence.

"I just dove in the water and stayed in the water until I got to the back of the hotel."

He recounted how he eventually reached the state police and was quickly surrounded by NOPD officers. "I ran up to them. Next thing I know, they had arrested me," he said. "That's when I was found out it was the police shooting at me."

On cross-examination, the defense team pressed Lance Madison about his initial statements just after the shooting, when he thought he saw an object in the hands of the teens—and assumed they had guns. On the stand he said he never knew what it was that he saw. "I just saw an object, and I couldn't describe it." He now knew the truth. Only police were armed.

"I wanted to see them have justice where they never would be able to do this again," he said. "They killed innocent people out there."

Jose Holmes told jurors how he pieced his life together after the shootings, moving to Georgia, raising a five-month-old son, Jose Holmes III, and landing a job with Kroger grocery store. A year after the shooting, he returned to the West Jefferson Medical Center to visit the doctors and nurses who treated him. "I wanted to thank everybody for helping me get better and to let them see that I was doing better," he said.

Turning back to September 4, 2005, prosecutor Bernstein had Holmes stand before the jurors. He lifted his shirt to reveal his stomach scars. He raised his left arm to show another scar, held up his damaged thumb, and raised his right elbow, also scarred.

"How about your jaw, do you have any scars up there?" Bernstein asked. Holmes jutted his jaw for jurors to see.

"I heard my auntie and my cousin Lesha, I heard them screaming. I heard my Uncle Leonard, he was screaming too," Holmes said, recounting those tortuous minutes. "They were screaming out in pain."

"What were you thinking at that moment?" Bernstein asked.

"I was just hoping that we could make it."

He described how he tried to lay still, posing no threat. "I kind of figured that if they saw us lying on the ground they wouldn't shoot us."

The officers and supervisors turned government witnesses also appeared: Hunter, Hills, Barrios, Lehrmann, and Lohman. These officers publicly unveiled the fraud that had, for six years, hidden the brutal truth. Barrios was called by the defense, not the prosecution, and told jurors that, after leaving the department, he supported himself by landing part-time work as a banquet waiter at a Marriott Hotel and full-time work driving an eighteen-wheeler truck. He said he was a follower, not a leader, of the cover-up, but admitted to Bernstein, "I was guilty. I lied."

The other NOPD witnesses described how the officers who fired guns that day took part in writing the police reports about the shootings, all huddling around a supervisor's laptop to make sure the stories held tight. They described how when Sergeant Kaufman, the supervisor on trial, went out to the scene to investigate, he failed to collect a single piece of evidence and instantly decided the police shootings would be ruled justified. Lehrmann recounted that meeting, of shooters and supervisors, at the gutted-out police quarters.

"And what the meeting was, it was, basically, 'Okay, this is the story, everybody read the report, everybody know what you're going to say, so we can put it on tape and take the statements,'" he told jurors.

"Tell us about collection of evidence that day at the scene," prosecutor Chung asked him.

"There was none."

"How was that going to be explained?"

"Hurricane."

"Who decided that?"

"Archie."

In its bid to craft a believable cover-up, Lehrmann said, the department changed its story so often he lost count.

"It happened all the time," he said. "I mean, the lies changed whenever we needed to change them."

"Did it matter what really happened?" Chung asked.

"No, ma'am," Lehrmann said.

"Why not?"

"Because from the outset, we were going to cover up to make sure the officers were okay," he replied.

Defense attorneys grilled these witnesses. Timothy Meche, representing accused officer Villavaso, drilled into an early police report on the shootings listing only black officers, including his client, as striking victims with bullets.

"Officer Faulcon is gone. He is in Houston. Officers Villavaso and Barrios are from the 5th District. So here, isn't what you're doing, you're blaming it on the other guys, the outsiders?" Meche asked Lehrmann.

"Archie wrote that section. You gotta ask him," the witness said.

"That's not my question. Isn't what's going on here you're blaming it on the outsiders?"

"I can't speak to that. I didn't write that."

HUNTER, THE OFFICER TOTING his own personal AK-47 in the days after Katrina, took the stand. Prosecutor Bernstein had Hunter step out of the witness box and demonstrate for the judge, jury, and courtroom how Bowen stomped on a wheezing Ronald Madison after the gunfire. Hunter stepped outside the box, looked down at the courtroom floor, and raised his right leg. He stomped down hard with his heel. Bernstein showed jurors a picture of Ronald Madison, lifeless, a boot print on his back.

Bernstein asked Hunter about the rally, organized by the police union, days after the officers were charged with murder in state court. Supporters hoisted signs that day. "Heroes," they said.

"Were you a hero, Mr. Hunter?" Bernstein asked.

"No," he replied.

"Why are you not a hero?"

"There's nothing heroic about shooting unarmed people that are running away."

Prosecutor Carter asked Officer Ignatius Hills the same question. Were you a hero? "No," the officer said. Why not? "There wasn't anything heroic about what transpired on the bridge that day to be declared a hero," he told the courtroom.

FBI agent Bezak contributed the back story of the federal inquiry— describing how the government, at just the right moment, wanted it known the investigation was in full bloom. Bezak rarely telephoned the subjects in his sights, choosing instead to show up at their homes unannounced.

"So by popping in they can't avoid you, they're forced to talk to you. And also, if they did have something to hide, I thought by popping in it wouldn't give them the chance to talk to anybody else to try and get their stories straight," he said.

"Pressure is a good thing."

A firearms specialist with the Louisiana State Police Crime Laboratory in Baton Rouge told jurors that, after comparing the cache of weapons used by officers on the bridge with spent casings and shotgun shells, he was able to link bullets to specific weapons. Nine casings matched Villavaso's AK-47. Another nine matched the AK-47 Bowen used, and two other casings matched Bowen's Glock pistol. Four shotgun shells matched the Mossberg shotgun Faulcon used, forensic scientist Patrick Lane concluded. Another five casings could have come from an M4, the type of weapon Gisevius used that morning—but never turned in to NOPD investigators who collected guns. At least three weapons matched bullets lodged into James Brissette's body: Bowen's AK-47, a shotgun like the one used by Faulcon, and an M4 assault rifle, Lane testified.

Prosecutors brought the courtroom behind the scenes of their investigation, playing a series of conversations that had been secretly tape-recorded in 2009 between Lehrmann and Gisevius, including snippets from the three-hour session at Lucy's Retired Surfers Bar & Restaurant in downtown New Orleans.

Someone's talking, Gisevius told the detective, wearing a wire.

"Who the fuck do you think the leak is?" Gisevius asked.

Lehrmann suggested it could be Kaufman. Gisevius wasn't buying it. "He would not sink his own ship," he said, in a statement now played for all, including Kaufman, to hear.

On July 21, 2011, three weeks into trial, the government called its last witness, Lesha Bartholomew. Like their nephew Jose Holmes, the Bartholomew family fled New Orleans after the shootings on the bridge and moved to Georgia.

As they lay on the ground cowering, Lesha could see her mother's right arm being held together by skin. "And you moved closer to protect her?"

"Yes."

"With your body?"

"Yes."

"To prevent her from being shot again?"

"Yes."

"What happened as you laid there trying to protect your mother?"

"I kept hearing shots. I felt a shot in my butt."

"Did anyone say, 'Police'?"

"No."

"Did anyone say, 'Show me your hands'?"

"No."

Reading another police report justifying the shootings, a prosecutor asked Lesha whether it was the truth. "It's a lie," she said.

With those words, Bernstein turned toward the judge. "Your Honor, at this point the government rests."

On July 26, 2011, a month into the trial, jurors stepped out of the courtroom for a visit to the crime scene, the Danziger Bridge, walking over the ground that six years earlier had been covered with bullets, bodies, and bloodshed. State police and federal officials closed off the bridge from traffic, allowing jurors to walk up and over the overpass, retracing the steps of the police pursuit and the residents under fire. One juror stood at the base of the bridge, where Little Leonard Bartholomew had sprinted to escape the gunfire, and peered up to the overpass. Prosecutors Bobbi Bernstein and Cindy Chung watched the jurors retrace those steps, taking mental notes as defense attorneys also took in the scene. Judge Engelhardt stood back from the fray, watching the scene unfold, donning sunglasses, a beige summer jacket, a powder blue shirt, and his trademark bow tie instead of his judicial robes.

The defendants sat in the courtroom, day after day, and heard their crimes recounted in precise detail. Only one would take the stand.

Instead, the defense zeroed in on the police turned witnesses, particularly Hunter. Defense attorneys seized on his record of police insubordination, his early discharge from the marines, and his history of lying—even to his bosses—to protect himself. The NOPD had twice suspended him, police files show, once for a lack of "truthfulness."

"There was a time that I would have lied to just about anybody," Hunter admitted under drilling by attorneys for the defense.

"That's apparent," defense attorney Hessler shot back.

Other strategies crumbled on the stand. As part of their defense, attorneys hired a private investigator who, indeed, found a Lakeisha Smith who lived just near the bridge in 2005. The PI even took the stand and showed a copy of Lakeisha's driver's license. Bernstein ripped the theory to shreds, putting the woman on the stand. Yes, her name was

Lakeisha Smith. But, no, she was not in New Orleans during Katrina—and she never spoke to a police officer about the shootings. She was in Mississippi at the time. The fictitious eye witness remained just that.

Finally Faulcon took the witness stand, presenting the morning through his own eyes over several hours of testimony.

"It's a call that you never want to hear," he said of the 108 dispatch that sent them barreling to the bridge.

Racing to the Danziger, he said he heard gunshots being fired even before the truck came to a halt. And, he swore under oath, he saw two men up ahead with guns. He never named them, but the figures he described were Jose Holmes and JJ Brissette.

"I'm human, I have feelings too. So my heart goes out to the people that were hurt. My heart goes out to the families of the victims," he told his lawyer from the stand. "But at that time when I saw guns, I just thought my actions were justified based on what I saw in that split second. I feel horrible because of the fact, you know, in that split second when I saw guns, I might have been right or I might have been wrong; but if I had known that those civilians were unarmed, I would have never fired my weapon at unarmed civilians."

Under Bernstein's questioning, Faulcon acknowledged many of the statements attributed to him were not, in fact, the truth.

"Do you agree that all of these reports are false?" the prosecutor asked.

"Based on what I read pertaining to my actions, yes."

"Do you agree that there was a cover-up in this case?"

"Based on what I learned now, yes."

From the witness box, Faulcon was forced to admit he shot a weaponless Ronald Madison in the back as the man ran away.

"You also agree that you shot and killed that innocent man?" Bernstein asked.

"Yes," Faulcon answered. "At the point when I felt that I was threatened for my life, when I felt he was a threat."

"You agree that you shot him in the back?" Bernstein came back.

"Yes. Again, when I felt, at that point, where my life was in danger, and I presumed him to be a threat."

"You agree that you never saw Ronald Madison with a gun?"

"Yes."

"You agree that you never saw Lance Madison with a gun?"

"Yes."

"Do you agree that you can only use deadly force if you perceive that your life or the life of another person is in imminent danger?"

"Yes."

A few moments later, she asked, "Every time you fire your weapon you have to have a reason to fire, correct?"

"Yeah," Faulcon replied. "I mean, your life would have to be in danger, correct?"

"So you agree that you cannot fire your weapon simply because you presume there is a threat?"

"Well, no, not presume. But if I believe that that is a threat and it's imminent, you know, my life is in danger or others, and given the totality of the circumstances, also, has a lot to take into consideration."

Bernstein shifted from the Madison shootings to the initial shots Faulcon fired from the other side of the bridge, where the Bartholomew family cowered for their lives.

"And then you pumped that shotgun, correct?"

"Yes."

"And you fired again?"

"Yes."

"And you pumped it?"

"Yes, sir."

"And you fired again?"

"Yes."

"And you pumped it?"

"Uh-huh."

"And you fired again?"

"Yes. Now, I don't know how many times I fired. I'm just—I didn't know at that time."

The prosecutor then asked Faulcon if he had talked to the other shooters also standing trial—Bowen, Villavaso, and Gisevius—from the time of the shootings until nine months later, when Faulcon gave a statement to Kaufman.

"No, I don't think I did," Faulcon said. "I didn't even have their telephone numbers."

Bernstein promptly unfurled phone records showing that Faulcon spoke to Bowen eight times on a single day a month after the shootings. They talked for more than half an hour a month later. The same month, he talked to Villavaso for eight minutes, and then he spoke to Bowen twice more in December and January. He talked to Gisevius that December as well.

On January 25, 2006, the day many officers provided formal statements about the shootings, Bernstein's records showed that Faulcon spoke to Bowen and Villavaso, and that he had a follow up conversation with Villavaso a day later.

Faulcon had taken the stand to save himself, but in the end, he cemented the very issues the government aimed to drive home. Officers had no legal basis to fire on the families on the bridge, and they engaged in a whitewash to conceal the truth.

On August 2, 2011, with the testimony finished, prosecutors and defense attorneys provided dueling arguments about the law and the events of that morning.

"The government's case is built on the accomplices," Eric Hessler, the attorney for Gisevius, told jurors. "Lohman, Lehrmann, Hills, Hunter, Barrios. Sounds like a law firm."

Defense attorney Frank DeSalvo ripped into Hunter's testimony recounting the horrors he attributed to DeSalvo's client, Bowen. They were lies, DeSalvo said.

"Michael Hunter came in and said all those bad things about Sergeant Bowen. And they went for that bait like a trout, and swallowed it hook, line and sinker, because that's what they wanted to hear," he said of the prosecution team. "But the facts and the physical evidence tell you another story. And he was an outlier because he saw things that no one else saw, both on the east side of the bridge and on the west side, where Ronald Madison lay dead. He was the only one who said that Kenneth Bowen leaned over that barrier and fired at those people as they lay on that walkway. He was the only one that said Kenneth Bowen went up and started stomping Ronald Madison."

The mark on Madison's back was not from a boot, DeSalvo told jurors, but was a smudge mark from the fender of a nearby Chevy van he must have brushed up against as he fell to the ground. The lawyer said physical evidence contradicted Hunter's contention that Bowen sprayed gunfire at residents.

As DeSalvo sat down, Bernstein rose from her seat and turned toward jurors. "Everything Bowen says is a lie," she said. The sergeant, she said, fired repeatedly at "unarmed defenseless people on the walkway." The officers "assumed that everybody out on that bridge was going to be a bad guy, when in fact it was two good families," she said. "Two good families, minding their own business." Bernstein's final words returned jurors' attention to the two families on the bridge. "All of those victims who told you what happened to them that day. Remember them, remember what they said."

On August 3, 2011, following more than five weeks of trial testimony, jurors stepped out of the federal courtroom and began deliberating the evidence they had absorbed. At 2:00 p.m. the next afternoon, jurors were clearly debating the most serious question—whether the officers, in particular Faulcon in his shooting of Ronald Madison, committed murder. "Could the judge please come in and explain 'murder' to the jury. We are having difficulty in understanding the definition," the jury foreman asked, pointing to the charge specifically against Faulcon. Judge Engelhardt referred jurors to his legal instructions, already provided.

JUST BEFORE NOON ON AUGUST 5, 2011, six years to the month after Katrina recast the history of New Orleans, jurors returned with a verdict.

Guilty, guilty, guilty, guilty, guilty. The officers were convicted of violating the civil rights of every victim on the bridge, including the two men killed and the two men falsely charged; of unlawfully unloading their weapons; of making false statements in their reports; and of obstruction of justice by launching a cover-up to mask the truth.

The prosecutors won on most counts, but not every single one.

Bowen, Gisevius, Faulcon, and Villavaso were found guilty of violating James Brissette's civil rights, and jurors decreed that the violation resulted in the teenager's death. Yet jurors said the four "Did Not" cause the death of James Brissette—a mixed verdict that haunts JJ's mother, Sherrel Johnson.

"I just sat there frozen in my seat," she later said. "He's dead because they had weapons. He's dead because he was shot. But their actions did not cause his death? It just doesn't make sense. And if it doesn't make sense, it's not true."

"My child is dead and you're going to say your actions did not cause his death?" she continued. "You don't have to put a name on the bullet. You've got five. Pick one."

Sherrel will never recover from the loss of her son, or come to understand how the police officers could do what they did that Sunday morning. "You robbed my child of his life in broad daylight. He had nothing to hurt you with."

The jurors ruled that Robert Faulcon "Did" cause the death of Ronald Madison. But they did not agree the shooting constituted murder. That split verdict could well spare Faulcon life in prison.

On every other of the twenty-five counts brought to trial, jurors marked a big X by "Guilty." They convicted the officers for falsely prosecuting Lance Madison and Jose Holmes Jr., and jurors ruled that Kenneth Bowen violated Ronald Madison's civil rights by kicking his limp body.

For the families who had so long pushed for justice, the August verdict shone like a beam. Outside the courtroom, prosecutor Bernstein clasped her hands together in a quiet moment of reflection and put her head down, her eyes shaded with dark sunglasses. To her right, Lance Madison embraced prosecutor Cindy Chung, savoring the moment the family had worried might never arrive. Bernstein, the face and leader of the federal government's team, put both arms around Lance Madison's neck; Lance embraced the civil rights prosecutor, his eyes closed, the six years of pain washing over him and turning, finally, to relief. Romell Madison stepped into the bright August day and was instantly surrounded by friends and supporters stretching their arms to take him in.

Sherrel Johnson wiped her tears with a white handkerchief as Jim Letten, the local US attorney, spoke about the verdict just rendered. Supporters put their hands on her back, a literal support beam, as officials held a press conference to discuss the historic verdict just announced.

The Bartholomews had "laid their hearts open" during their testimony on the stand. Now, they held faith the justice system would right the wrong. "They were hopeful," said their lawyer, Edwin Shorty. "They could see or feel a light at the end of the tunnel."

One supporter, draped in dark clothing and wearing a black beret on his head, raised his right fist to the sky, signaling that cries for justice had just been answered. Other residents embraced one another at the foot of the federal courthouse, some wearing placards of police protest around their necks.

Federal jurors had, with their guilty verdicts, officially damned the shootings and the cover-up. For perhaps the first time since the gunfire, the victims and survivors could breathe relief, and savor vindication.

"Jury Gives NOPD Another Strike," the *Times-Picayune*'s front page screamed. "Prosecutors garner nearly a clean sweep on charges against 5 Danziger defendants."

For years, the NOPD's internal affairs unit, the Public Integrity Bureau (PIB), often closed cases against officers, including cases against several of those standing trial in this case, without bringing discipline. Most of the time, the PIB said evidence supporting punishment did not exist. But following the guilty verdicts, the Public Integrity Bureau would sustain a string of internal charges against Bowen, Gisevius, and Villavaso, three officers still technically on the force. The bureau said evidence existed to sustain charges against other officers who had recently resigned: Hunter, Barrios, Hills, Lohman, Kaufman, and Gerard Dugue, the sergeant who had yet to face trial.

"Clear and convincing evidence existed, based on the FBI and Department of Justice investigation, that the accused officers violated criminal and departmental polices," the office wrote in a report authored by Sergeant Omar M. Diaz. The top brass, including superintendent of police Ronal W. Serpas, tapped from the Nashville police force to replace the retiring Riley in 2010, signed off on the report.

The PIB case was not a criminal inquiry and drew scant attention, but the battery of sustained charges sent a message. The actions of the officers on the bridge was so untoward, the department itself was brandishing it with a black eye. Two months after the guilty verdicts, the Louisiana Supreme Court suspended the law license of Sergeant Kenneth Bowen.

With his own innocence reaffirmed along with the guilty verdicts for the officers, Lance Madison spoke outside the courthouse, with Bernstein, the lead prosecutor, behind him and the family's civil lawyer, Mary Howell, to his side. Dressed in coat and tie, he spoke for thirty seconds, reading from paper steadied in place atop a FedEx envelope.

"I am thankful for having some closure after six long years of struggling for justice," Lance said. "Without the support and hard work of my family, I might still be in prison for false charges and the truth about what happened on the Danziger Bridge might never have been known. We will never be completely healed because we will never have Ronald Madison back."

As he said his brother's name, Bernstein nodded her head. Then Lance caught his breath and was finished.

As Bobbi Bernstein stepped into the city's streets in the days after the trial that had consumed her for three years, more than one resident pulled her aside. Thank you, they told her.

PART IV
JUSTICE HELD UP

CHAPTER 20

THE ONLINE COMMENTATORS

AS IN ANY CITY with big news and impassioned views, the online section of the local newspaper in New Orleans is sometimes filled with angry bluster—the kind of anonymous postings that allow viewers to say what they really think, often shielded behind the online world's protective cloak of secrecy.

So it was that before, during, and after the trial of the Danziger 5, the comments section at NOLA.com, the news site of the local *Times-Picayune*, was filled with bluster and venom. Some readers ripped the prosecutors for taking on officers who stayed behind to serve their city. Others praised the Feds for doing the job the locals seemed ill equipped to handle; former DA Eddie Jordan was a steady, ready target. Yet other writers aimed their sights on the police officers and the department they served, describing how the events exposed in federal court finally let the larger world in on a dirty secret: the NOPD doesn't always shoot straight. The Danziger trial was just one of a string of police misconduct cases drawing these razor-sharp, and seemingly anonymous, critiques.

Yet some careful readers were scrutinizing these online comments and pressing to discover the identities behind the missives, the true names of the writers tapping the keyboards with swift rancor. These interested parties included lawyers for accused criminals, particularly those working for the public sector. They also included defense attorneys for the police officers convicted in court, and now behind bars in federal lockup, in the Danziger shootings. Where others saw angry but meaningless blather, the defense team suspected something more sinister at play, particularly when it was revealed that one of the most frequent scribes was an assistant United States attorney based in New Orleans named Sal Perricone.

Perricone was raised in New Orleans and built a name for himself the hard way. After high school he joined the Jefferson Parish Sheriff's Office in 1972, starting as a patrolman and rising to become a sergeant, while putting himself through college. In 1975 he became a detective for the NOPD and turned next to law school at Loyola University New Orleans College of Law. In 1986 Perricone jumped to the FBI, supervising an antidrug squad operating between LA and Seattle. Then, with his law degree in hand, in 1991 he became a prosecutor for the US Attorney's Office in his hometown. He put away dirty politicians and mobsters while working the courtroom with a focused intensity.

Even as he rose as a prosecutor, Perricone maintained a keen interest in police issues. He once put his name in the hat for the police superintendent's job, along with two FBI agents and a Drug Enforcement Administration agent. None got the job. "I never had any intent to be police superintendent," Perricone wrote me. He said he applied "to test the fairness of the selection process." He followed police department misdeeds intently and once taught a course to NOPD officers entitled "How to Not Get Indicted," outlining federal law on civil rights and use of force.

Writing on NOLA.com under multiple pseudonyms, including "Henry L. Mencken1951," Perricone seemingly chided the NOPD at every turn, in every case of police corruption then in the news. Under a variety of pen names, he targeted the force and onetime superintendent Warren Riley, calling the NOPD out as "corrupt," "a joke for a long time," and "totally dysfunctional."

Perricone was not part of the Danziger prosecuting team, and said he followed the case merely by reading the papers. But to the defense, his missives reflected directly on the US Attorney's Office that employed him and were relevant to the prosecution at hand. The online comments, the Danziger defense team would argue, were part of a larger government conspiracy to "engage in a secret public relations campaign designed to make the NOPD the household name for corruption." This conspiratorial plan was created to turn the public against the police, convicting the accused before anyone set foot in court and forcing officers to plead guilty under pressure. And, ultimately, the intent was to "prejudice the defendants during trial through online activities designed to secure their convictions," they contended.

On March 12, 2012, three weeks before the Danziger police officers would face judgment at sentencing, Perricone was exposed as the writer of rebukes of the department in the Danziger case and others. His identity was revealed in another case then in the courts, but his online persona quickly became relevant for the police officers convicted of killing innocents and covering up their crimes on the bridge.

Perricone would later admit writing under a string of pseudonyms beyond the one named after Mencken, the journalistic sage of Baltimore known for his penetrating prose. Other online names Perricone put to use included "dramatis personae," "legacyusa," and "campstblue."

His criticism began well before the Danziger Bridge prosecution. In 2008, three years before the Danziger 5 case went to trial, Perricone weighed in after a news report about an NOPD officer who was arrested after getting into a fight with a Mississippi River bridge officer.

"There is an old Italian proverb: the fish rots from the head down," he wrote on June 8, 2008.

A year later another of his online postings called for Riley's head. "The Government [Department of Justice] needs to take over the police department . . . NOW!!!!!" he wrote.

The comments went on and on, ripping the superintendent and his force. In December 2010, Perricone opined about another case of police misconduct then in the courthouse, in which white New Orleans police officers stood trial in federal court for the savage burning death of a black man shot by police after Katrina.

"This case, no matter how it turns out, has revealed the NOPD to be a collection of self-centered, self-interested, self-promoting, insular, arrogant, overweening, prevaricating, libidinous fools and that the entire agency should be re-engineered from the bottom up," he wrote. "This case has ripped the veil of respectability away from the police department. . . . Thank God for the Feds [DOJ]—can you imagine New Orleans without a federal presence?"

When that case came back with a split verdict, with the lead defendant officer convicted on some counts, Perricone wrote, "There is no Katrina defense. . . . Danziger is totally different. I am sure the attorneys will proffer this defense, but it will fail." He called out the "gang of thugs [NOPD] on the bridge that day. They bailed out the rental truck, guns ablazing."

As the Danziger guilty pleas began to mount, Perricone's online persona often contributed to the commentary section that built up, comment after comment, once stories were posted involving police controversies. On February 23, 2010, the *Times-Picayune* disclosed an early plea deal about to surface in the case, involving Lieutenant Lohman. Nine and a half minutes after the scoop, Perricone, using his "legacyusa" online persona, wrote, "Despite defense attorneys' protestations to the contrary, it would be prudent for those involved to consider the track record of the U.S. Attorney's Office. Letten's people are not to be trifled with."

At quarter until eleven that evening, another posting was aimed at Sergeant Kaufman, who had not yet faced charges. "The cover up is always worse than the crime. Archie . . . your time is up."

Two days later: "I am afraid that the NOPD has inoperable cancer. . . . Indeed, the fish has rotten from the head down." As other officers began to resign and readied to enter their own guilty pleas and cooperate, Perricone's online fingers praised them for coming forward. "The Feds never forget . . . this officer is doing the right thing . . . with the others would, then IT would be over," he wrote on May 20, 2010, as news broke of Ignatius Hills's resignation and possible plea deal.

Ten minutes before the Danziger Bridge jury selection began on June 22, 2011, at 8:19 a.m., "legacyusa" had some thoughts to share. "NONE of these guys should had have ever been given a badge. We should research how they got on the police department, who trained them, who supervised them and why were they ever promoted. You put crap in—you get crap out!!!"

After Officer Faulcon took the stand, Perricone, using his "dramatis personae" online name, targeted the police cover-up being exposed in court. "Where is Madison's gun? Come on officer, tell us," he wrote July 29, 2011.

Once his identity was unmasked, Perricone told a judge these postings were "my little secret." No one at the Department of Justice knew about it, he said. In all, Perricone had posted some twenty-six hundred comments over five years. Perricone said just a fraction of them dealt with legal matters. "ONLY .44% had anything to do with cases," he wrote. "Do the math. (99.56% had nothing to do with work.)"

A week after his cloak of online anonymity was revealed, Sal Perricone resigned from the US Attorney's Office. Perricone said he intended to retire at the end of 2012 to launch a career writing fiction, but left nine months earlier "and pursued that dream." His first novel, *Blue Steel Crucifix*, a tale of murder and corruption set in New Orleans, would be published in December 2014.

As he left the US Attorney's Office amid the glow of scrutiny, the DOJ brass said it would launch an internal inquiry. Jim Letten, the top federal prosecutor in New Orleans, called Perricone's behavior unacceptable. "Our partners in government and law enforcement and the citizens we serve must know that absolutely none of the comments, criticisms, or characterizations made were in any way reflective of my views or opinions—or those of the Department or this office or our people," Letten said in a prepared statement. "To the contrary, we resoundingly reject the caustic criticisms and sentiments expressed in these messages."

Perricone, his secret online life now exposed, hoped to retreat again to the shadows. "I just want to be left alone," he told a local reporter who reached him for comment.

Defense attorneys would not let him, or the larger DOJ team, get away so easily. Two weeks away, sentencing day loomed for the Danziger defendants, and the defense team prepared to file a battery of court motions seeking to get the verdict overturned, citing early leaks it said impaired justice—and the online postings it portrayed as part of the larger DOJ conspiracy.

Their bids for a new trial seemed like a long shot. While Perricone's dispatches appeared in the comments section at NOLA.com multitudes of times, presaging his next career turn as a fiction writer, there's no evidence a single juror saw his postings. And, no tangible evidence was produced showing that such postings impaired justice.

It was a long shot, but with the police officers facing the prospect of decades behind bars, the defense team was pushing any angle it could find. Their motions for a new trial landed on the desk of the judge who had overseen the Danziger case, US district judge Kurt D. Engelhardt.

FROM PREP SCHOOL
TO POLITICS TO DANZIGER

A Judge's Prayerful Path

BORN IN NEW ORLEANS, Kurt Damian Engelhardt donned glasses as a youth, fitting right in at summer band camp and later as a flute, piccolo, and alto sax player in the band at Brother Martin High School, an all-male, Catholic, college preparatory school in the city. As a senior, he was a drum major, proudly donning the school's crimson and gold colors, and no longer always wearing his dark-framed glasses. He had worked for the school paper, served on the student council, and earned the Golden Crusader Award.

Kurt stayed close to home for his postsecondary schooling, first attending the University of New Orleans before transferring to Louisiana State University in Baton Rouge. There, he studied history as an undergraduate and served in the Tiger Band, performing at halftime at the prized LSU football team's home games. When he graduated from LSU in 1982, Engelhardt made a choice. His older brother became a surgeon, but Kurt Engelhardt had a different career path in mind.

"My father suggested the law as a career because I liked to argue," he later told his high school newspaper for a profile it published. He enrolled in law school at LSU, earning his degree in 1985.

Out of school, Engelhardt served as a law clerk for an appeals court judge, and then became partner in a midsized law firm in Metairie, a suburb of New Orleans in Jefferson Parish. With Hailey, McNamara, Hall, Larmann & Papale, he focused on commercial transactions and litigation—handling real estate, bankruptcy, insurance defense, and contract disputes, among other issues. Also on his legal docket: personal injury litigation and white-collar criminal defense work.

He soon became active in civic and political circles, joining the Alliance for Good Government and becoming involved in Republican political campaigns. He backed Republican David Vitter's first run for the state legislature, a path that would take Vitter to the US Senate representing Louisiana. That friendship would later come to benefit Engelhardt's own ambitions.

In 1995 the Louisiana governor appointed Engelhardt to the Louisiana Judiciary Commission, a governmental body that explores allegations of misconduct against judges and makes recommendations for action to the state Supreme Court. In 1998 Engelhardt was elected the commission's chairman.

That experience piqued his interest in becoming a judge and, a year later, Engelhardt eyed a potential judicial opening in Jefferson Parish. Vitter told him to have a little patience and to wait one year. "The Governor of Texas is running for president," Vitter noted to his lawyer friend.

That governor was George W. Bush, elected to the nation's highest office in 2000. Engelhardt knew him well; he worked on the Bush for President Campaign and traveled to Washington for Bush's inauguration in January 2001. Soon Vitter put Engelhardt's name in the hopper for a federal judgeship. Engelhardt carried support from the Louisiana Congressional Delegation, including Democratic members.

Vitter's nomination led to a political whirlwind for Engelhardt, with a series of interviews and background checks in Washington. "My neighbors asked me if I was in trouble since the FBI had called on them. They even interviewed my college roommates," Engelhardt later remarked to the *Crimson Shield*, the online magazine of his high-school alma mater.

On September 4, 2001, four years to the day before the Danziger Bridge shootings, President Bush appointed Engelhardt to the federal bench. The US Senate confirmed him December 11, 2001, and Engelhardt took the oath of office two days later.

In his time on the federal bench in New Orleans, no case would come close to matching the Danziger trial for its drama, significance, and the attention it drew. And now, with the officers on trial facing sentencing in a month, in April 2012, and the judge's desk awaiting defense requests to dismiss the verdicts, Engelhardt faced his biggest judicial test. He would issue prison sentences for the five officers convicted by a jury. He'd have to approve, or deny, defense pleas for a new trial.

Though the prosecution won a huge victory at trial with the jurors' verdict, Engelhardt had subsequently handed the defense some noticeable victories. In October 2011, two months after the guilty verdicts, Engelhardt tossed one major charge from the case—the jury's conviction of Kenneth Bowen for stomping on a dying, wheezing Ronald Madison. In Engelhardt's eyes, jurors didn't hear enough evidence to convict Bowen of that charge, which was based on the eyewitness testimony of Michael Hunter, the officer who faced a battery of defense questions on the stand. With his judicial order, Engelhardt struck that charge from among the convictions agreed to by jurors.

The judge also tossed a conviction against Bowen and three others for falsely prosecuting Jose Holmes Jr.; though police planned to arrest Holmes on attempted murder charges, they never took him into custody. They couldn't. Holmes was in a hospital bed fighting for his life.

Engelhardt did leave most of the verdict intact, but his dismissing of the jurors' verdict on two important counts was a rare victory for the defense. The police attorneys hoped those dismissals would help shave at least some time off the prison sentences when their clients stood for sentencing. "Nobody is going free," said Frank DeSalvo, Bowen's lawyer. "How much it helps us at sentencing, only time will tell."

That decision would rest with a judge who admits he sometimes loses sleep during big cases. At those times, Judge Engelhardt told the reporter interviewing him for his Catholic high school profile, he strives for balance through reflection and prayer. "The morality instilled in me by my parents and my Catholic education helps me keep things in perspective. Prayer is an important part of my job. I couldn't do the job without it," he said.

Several times a week the bow-tied judge treks from the federal courthouse to the historic, hallowed St. Patrick's Roman Catholic Church in downtown New Orleans, a fifteen-minute walk that helps free his thoughts, helps clear his internal docket. There, he steps inside the building of Gothic architecture with its 185-foot-tall bell tower. Paintings above the altar depict the transfiguration of Jesus, and Jesus Christ pulling Saint Peter from the sea. In this setting the judge attends a late morning Mass.

"It's good to get away to see the big picture."

CHAPTER 22

JUDGMENT DAY

A Mother and Brother Confront the Convicted

ON A BLACK MORNING of torrential rain, April 4, 2012, the five convicted officers stepped into a packed federal courtroom in downtown New Orleans. One side of the courtroom, filled with relatives of the shooters, stood in respect. The other side, filled with families of the victims and their attorneys, stayed in their seats. Seven years after Katrina and the shots on the bridge, New Orleans remained divided, the horrific day unsettled.

Judge Engelhardt's gavel tapped, the sentencing hearing began. Lance Madison rose first, and, turning to each officer, named them by name and called them out for their crimes.

"Mr. Faulcon, when I look at you my pain becomes unbearable. It feels like I have been stabbed in my heart. When you shot down my brother, Ronald, you took the life of an angel and basically ripped my heart out. I still have nightmares about my brother being killed and myself running to get help, to no avail.

"Mr. Bowen, to this day, I am still stunned by your cowardly acts of shooting innocent, unarmed people. You shot down a whole family and I will always believe that you kicked my brother as he lay dying on the ground. In the years since you devastated my family and so many others, I wonder if you have ever thought about how you would feel if someone committed these same crimes against your own family."

He called out Robert Gisevius Jr., Anthony Villavaso, and Archie Kaufman. "Mr. Kaufman, I have to be frank and say that when I think of you, what I feel is disgust," he said. "You tried to frame me, a man who you knew was innocent, and send me to prison for the rest of my life. You tried to protect these officers, who you knew had shot and killed innocent people. I will never forget when you took the witness stand in state court and lied and told the judge that I had a gun on the bridge."

Sherrel Johnson stood next.

"If I had been there on the scene, I would have begged and crawled on my knees and asked them, 'Please don't kill my child. He is so young. Let him live. If you have to shoot someone, then let it be me,'" she said, her normally fervent diction delivered this day in a low tone. "You just shot him all up and just tore him to pieces. And then you stood there with your guns and gave him a shotgun blast to the back of his head, and there his brains lay on the concrete walk of the Danziger Bridge.

"So why should you be free and walk around?" Sherrel asked the police officers. "You just stood there, and shot round after round after round. . . . My child never got to even start his life. He will never live to be an old man. You stopped him right in his tracks. James Jr., your mama can't never get you back," she said.

The courtroom also heard the voices of Lesha Bartholomew and Jose Holmes Jr., but not directly. The two young adults each testified at trial to help bring the prosecution's case to the fore. Now at the sentencing hearing, the pair had messages to share, but asked their lawyers to read the words for them.

Lesha's words—entitled "Why Is This Happening to Us?"—were read aloud by the family's New Orleans lawyer, Edwin M. Shorty Jr. Her mother had suffered the most, Lesha said, and spent each day in pain. She could still hear her father's screams.

Jose Holmes's words, read by his attorney Gary Bizal, filled the courtroom. As the attorney read his statement, Jose buried his face in his arms.

"For you to have shot an unarmed innocent person should make you feel guilty and ashamed," he said. "I have you to blame for all of my scars, depression, and the embarrassment of having to wear a colostomy bag, the hurt and the way that I can't do things as well with my left hand. Things like playing basketball, drawing, having trouble picking things up and playing the piano.

"It hurts to see my auntie missing her arm and the pain that you caused my family," Jose added. "But when it's all said and done I'm a loving person so I have to forgive you for what you've done to me because God forbids me to have hatred in my heart. Even though I have to forgive you, no evil deed should go unpunished. It took six years for me to finally have justice for what you did to me and my family. Now everyone finally sees that I'm a terrific human being and not what you tried to make them believe.

"I'm so happy to have closure." Jose was "truly blessed to be here today," he said.

Not a single officer spoke. Instead, they let their attorneys, their families, and their fellow officers speak for them.

"I think there was a lot of fear on top of the bridge that day," said Eric Hessler, Gisevius's lawyer.

"I think the evidence is overwhelming that it was out of fear . . . not malice," said Bowen's federal public defender, Robin E. Schulberg. "And I think that makes all the difference in the world."

Schulberg, a former civil rights lawyer and "child of the sixties," wasn't thrilled when she got the assignment. "Look, I'm not the person to defend police who shot people," she said later.

Then she met Bowen and saw the issue from a new vantage point. "I began to see things a lot more from the perspective of the police officer on the street. We expect the cops to face down the most dangerous people in society, but if they make a mistake or a bad judgment call, we are going to put them in jail for the rest of their lives? That doesn't make sense to me." She believes the cover-up amounted to officers who thought they saw guns in the civilians' hands and stuck to their story.

Kenneth Bowen Sr., a former police officer who served in Internal Affairs for NOPD and then went on to practice law, said he taught his son at an early age, "You don't lie and you don't steal." Like his father, the younger Bowen attended law school by night while working as an officer by day, and, after graduating from Loyola University College of Law, received his license to practice law in October 2005, one month after the shootings. He named his own son, born four and a half months after the hurricane, Kenneth.

With Katrina barreling toward the city, the elder Bowen said, his son told him he did not want to leave. "There's too many people here that need our help," Kenneth Bowen Sr. told the court, paraphrasing his son.

And then he asked a question many other police supporters had pondered, from the moment word of the shootings on the bridge surfaced. "Why would a group of well-trained, well-educated police officers, who had been saving people day after day after day . . . all of the sudden wake up and say, 'Let's go shoot somebody,' and do it in broad daylight?"

They wouldn't, Bowen Sr. said. It was chaos, it was crazy, and the officers acted on instinct. "He had a few seconds to act . . . at a time of unprecedented—*unprecedented*—chaos and lawlessness in the city." Weeks before the sentencing hearing, Bowen's mother, Maria, wrote Engelhardt, "Despite the many dangers, the hardships and losses, the lack of manpower and lack of resources, my son stayed and he saved many lives."

Faulcon's father, the Reverend Robert L. Faulcon Sr., said his son also learned the difference between good and bad. "He hasn't been one to go looking for trouble," the father said in Judge Engelhardt's courtroom. "Bobby is one that looks to help folk, not harm folk." Faulcon's brother, Anthony, a church minister, said his brother is a man of God. "There is no book, no video, no training, military or civilian-wise, that could have prepared you or anyone else for the situation that happened during Katrina," he told the judge.

Other officers who also stayed behind described the challenge they faced once Katrina landed, sleeping with their guns at their side. Policing a city plagued by putrid water, dead bodies, and disorganized leadership, many officers found a way to surmount those horrors and save the desperate.

While not excusing the bloodletting that morning, several police officers told the court that, in such a frenzied time, what happened on the bridge could have happened to them too. "That could have been me," one said.

They pointed out that a comrade, NOPD officer Kevin Thomas, was nearly murdered after apprehending looters.

Prosecutor Bernstein agreed that the officers did not wake up that morning intending to hurt people. But their actions on the bridge, and after the shooting stopped, were unconscionable. "These defendants are not evil men," she said. "But on September Fourth 2005, that honor was nowhere to be found because every one of these defendants stood at that walkway and fired repeatedly. Over time, as seconds went by, they fired at unarmed people. Then after that, for the days and weeks and months and years that followed that shooting, honor played no role."

"They lied to preserve themselves."

THE DECISION NOW RESTED with Judge Engelhardt. Instead of rendering the sentences, the judge took a circuitous path. Just before noon, he closed the courtroom, barring anyone not already seated from coming in, and delivered a judicial sermon for more than two hours about the case he oversaw and the evidence he heard during the course of the trial.

While the five defendants were on trial and sat awaiting the precise terms of their prison sentences, Engelhardt turned his judicial gaze upon the federal prosecutors and FBI agents who broke the case. Families of the victims and relatives of the officers all sat tight, quietly, as the judge turned page after page from books and notes on his bench and held forth.

"Sentencing in this case is no longer and cannot be about sending a message because the government's plea bargaining in this case has already severely undercut any message that could possibly be sent," he told spectators.

The judge was "astonished and deeply troubled by the plea bargains," and he ticked them off, one by one, careful to detail the respective crimes of every officer who had pleaded guilty and testified for the prosecution. Some, he said, benefited from sweetheart deals.

Lieutenant Lohman, he noted, was well respected and had an almost spotless record before Katrina. But then, "as far as 'cover-ups' go, Lohman was the ring leader, the Consigliere, the Chief Executive Officer when it comes to engineering the incident we refer to as Danziger."

Lohman got four years, and now the government wanted to put Kaufman away for twenty, the judge noted.

He called Robert Barrios "the biggest winner in the plea bargain sweepstakes," describing the officer as "one who simply lies to get out of trouble. . . . He was allowed to do so." Barrios, who admitted going along with the cover story until his own guilty plea, was given five years in prison.

By cutting the deals, the judge said, the government was usurping the power of judges. Engelhardt called the plea agreements "an affront to the court and a disservice to this community."

"It is, quite frankly, shocking that the government so grossly discounted such serious and grave criminal conduct," Engelhardt said.

He cited a Tennessee Williams phrase, "air of mendacity."

"Using liars lying to convict liars is no way to pursue justice," Engelhardt said.

Suddenly, in the courtroom full of victims, it felt as though the prosecutors and FBI were on trial. The victims and relatives of those killed appeared taken aback by the judge's focus, delivered as all awaited the final judgment seven years in coming.

In hearing after hearing, the prosecution said it had to cut those deals to expose the lies. There would have been no case without those officers pleading guilty and unmasking the cover-up. Yes, they helped themselves in the process; that's how the system works, from coast to coast. More than 90 percent of criminal convictions spring from those very plea deals, the cases never going to trial. The Danziger victims supported this approach. Without it, judgment day for the convicted would never have arrived. "The only way we could ever have made that happen, for them to be held accountable, was to have cooperation from officers," Bernstein had told one federal judge.

FINALLY THE JUDGE PUT down his speech and turned to the sentences.

He gave Bowen—who unloaded the AK-47 on Jose Holmes, James Brissette, and others, and who played a pivotal role in creating the police cover-up—forty years. Gisevius, who fired at the Madisons and toward Susan Bartholomew and Brissette, also received forty years. Villavaso, who unloaded his AK-47 at least nine times, got thirty-eight years. Kaufman, the supervisor who helped concoct a fiction, got six years, far fewer than prosecutors believed his actions warranted.

Robert Faulcon Jr., age forty-eight, who had never fired his police gun before that day and whose son was a Katrina baby, landed the stiffest term. He was sentenced to prison for sixty-five years.

Those sentences finally invoked, the courtroom breathed a collective sigh of relief and sorrow, not joy. No one could find happiness in this day. Not the kin of the officers now whisked away to serve their time, not the families of the men and women hunted down atop the bridge. Yet six years and seven months after the shootings on the bridge, closure, it appeared, had finally arrived.

As prosecutors spoke of the sentences, Susan Bartholomew listened to their words, her head down and eyes closed. She placed her left hand over her right shoulder and the shawl covering her amputated arm, a quiet, poignant reminder of the suffering.

That the sentences were rendered on a dark, foreboding morning seemed fitting. The April day felt like an exhausting end to a long road toward justice. Steep, surprising curves remained in the distance.

CHAPTER 23

THE CONSENT DECREE
A History of Police Abuse, Documented

FOR THE NEW ORLEANS Police Department, the shootings on the bridge were not an isolated incident. That the victims were all black was, for the NOPD, part of a larger pattern that had begun long before the events on the Danziger Bridge, and persisted even after those events, in a city whose murder rate often ranked as the highest in the country, earning it the distinction as "Murder Capital of the United States."

In May 2010, two months before the city was jolted by news that six NOPD officers and sergeants were indicted for the killings and cover-up, the US Department of Justice's Civil Rights Division launched what would become its most significant review, ever, of a police department's practices. For months, the DOJ dug into more than thirty-six thousand pages of NOPD internal documents, reviewing written practices and protocols for police training, use of force, stop and search procedures, recruitment, and supervision. The DOJ pulled the fine print on the subjects of police arrests and the targets of its fire. It explored deep-seated community allegations of discriminatory policing—allegations laid bare over the years and decades in light of police shootings of black subjects, some of them gunned down unarmed.

That the NOPD had a black eye was a long-running, pained story for residents.

There was the well-known case of Len Davis, "Robocop," and the killing of Kim Groves in 1994. Groves had been a mother of three, with a soft face, alert eyes, and ready smile, whose only crime was to try to protect a neighborhood teen and then file a complaint that Robocop Davis abused her too. The night of the murder, Groves had sung "Happy Birthday" to daughter Jasmine, who was turning thirteen the next day.

Seventeen years after the shooting, the gunman who killed her at Robocop's command, Paul "Cool" Hardy, finally received his sentence. He got life behind bars.

Groves's son, sixteen at the time, said the murder sent him into deep despair, a life on drugs, and thoughts of suicide. "I desperately wanted to get stopped by an NOPD officer so that I could either kill one of them or force one of them to kill me. This is how angry, hurt, and confused I was after the murder of my mother," the son, by then an adult, said at the sentencing hearing for the triggerman that, because of the long grind of justice, did not come until 2011.

At the hearing, reported on by the local *Times-Picayune*, the Groves family was represented by Mary Howell, the same lawyer representing the Madison family in its civil case against the city. Howell also represented families in another police case of lore, the Algiers 7 killings in 1980, when city police responded to the death of a young white officer by gunning down four black residents.

Even with such dark episodes, police reforms amounted mostly to empty words. "We have to fix this problem," Mary Howell said when Kim Groves's killer was finally sentenced, a cry that had become all too familiar.

The Len Davis, Antoinette Frank, and Algiers 7 cases, long viewed as the NOPD's darkest hours, may have been matched by the series of police killings after Hurricane Katrina.

On September 2, 2005, two days before the bridge massacre, a thirty-one-year-old black man named Henry Glover was planning to flee the city with his brother. First, they stopped at a strip mall to gather suitcases filled with stolen merchandise left behind by friends. In the days after Katrina, that strip mall was also used as a temporary detective bureau. A rookie white police officer providing security for the office, David Warren, glimpsed Glover from a second floor lookout and, authorities said, shot him in the back as Glover, unarmed, tried to flee.

Glover's brother flagged down a passing motorist, and the Good Samaritan tried to find medical help for the bleeding Glover in the back seat. Desperate for help, they turned to another police headquarters, this one a former elementary school being used as a special operations bureau.

Police held them at gunpoint, handcuffed them, and, the Samaritan said, beat them. Then another white officer, Greg McRae, drove off in the 2000 Chevy Malibu, with Glover's dying, bloodied body in the back. He parked at a levee behind a police headquarters and, with Glover still in the back seat, set the car afire.

Just as it had with the Danziger defendants, the Department of Justice initially scored major prosecution victories in the death of Henry Glover.

Warren said he acted in self-defense, saying he thought Glover was an armed looter. In December 2010 federal jurors convicted Warren, McRae, and another white officer, Lieutenant Travis McCabe, who had submitted a false report about the death. The federal jury acquitted two other officers also on trial for the death, burning, and cover-up.

Warren was sentenced to twenty-five years and nine months in prison and ordered to pay $7,642.32 to Glover's family for funeral expenses. McRae was given seventeen years and three months in prison.

That salving of the victims' wounds did not last long.

In December 2012 a federal appeals court threw out Warren's conviction, saying his case should have been tried separately from his codefendants. A year later another jury acquitted Warren, who continued to say he acted appropriately. "I believe I took the proper action that day," Warren told reporters as he walked free from prison.

A judge later dismissed the conviction against Lieutenant McCabe and, in 2014, the US Attorney's Office announced it would not retry the case. McCabe and his family were "absolutely elated with the government's decision to dismiss the indictment against him," his lawyers said. McCabe was reinstated to the force. He got three years' back pay.

McRae, who burned Glover's body, was the only officer whose conviction stood. He sought a new trial, citing a psychologist's report that he suffered post-traumatic stress disorder brought on by Katrina. His seventeen-year sentence stuck.

For the Glover family justice remained elusive. After Warren's acquittal, the family left federal court arm in arm, praying that the state would pick up the case that faltered in federal court, praying that someone would pay for Henry Glover's death.

Their quest could be seen as a metaphor for the larger bid to reform the NOPD. Even with hard evidence of crimes, justice always appeared out of reach. In Glover's case, an unarmed black man had been shot in the back by a white police officer, another white officer set a car afire while a bleeding man was in it, and others covered up the macabre scene. Just one officer was convicted and most of the accused were freed.

Likewise, larger reforms never fully took root. Former mayor Marc Morial pushed corruption cases, but then his handpicked police chief lost in a bid for the mayor's seat in 2002, and the reform framework crumbled with a new administration.

In the years after Len Davis's cocaine-protecting, execution-ordering ways were exposed, the Department of Justice and others would urge sweeping reform of the New Orleans Police Department. Several years before the Danziger shootings, the DOJ found that city police officers could not always articulate proper legal standards for stops, searches, or arrests.

The Justice Department's suggestions to change those patterns were largely ignored. The department "still does not provide meaningful in-service training to officers on how to properly carry out stops, searches, and arrests. NOPD's failure to train officers or otherwise provide guidance on the limits and requirements of the Fourth Amendment contributes directly to the pattern of unconstitutional stops, searches, and arrests we observed," the Justice Department found in 2011, nearly a decade later.

In 2001 a report issued by a Police-Civilian Review Task Force, comprising community leaders and police officials, suggested that the department establish an independent monitor who would review brutality, excessive force, and other complaints, fill elected officials in on the department's progress, and make further suggestions for change.

It took eight years for the city to create the Office of the Independent Police Monitor. And, it took the monitor more than a year to start getting the information from police to assess those questions.

AND THEN, AS THAT independent monitor position was just being put in place, nearly a decade after the community called for it, the DOJ issued a damning rebuke of the police department's practices in a report entitled "Investigation of the New Orleans Police Department," released on March 16, 2011.

The New Orleans police was so focused on statistics, the Department of Justice review found, that officers routinely pushed the limits of the law to make numbers goals.

"The NOPD has long been a troubled agency. Basic elements of effective policing—clear policies, training, accountability, and confidence of the citizenry—have been absent for years. Far too often officers show a lack of respect for the civil rights and dignity of the people of New Orleans," said the 158-page report.

The civil inquiry called upon the expertise of a dozen police training experts and included onsite visits to the department and meetings with church and community groups. Because the Danziger investigation was active at the time, the inquiry excluded that case, focusing instead on police actions not then on trial. The review did not include any of the post-Katrina cases of misconduct—including the death and burning of Henry Glover, whose killing was explored in a PBS *Frontline* report, "Law and Disorder," produced with ProPublica and the *Times-Picayune*.

Even with those cases excluded, the Justice Department's findings were starkly damning. "We find reasonable cause to believe that NOPD engages in patterns of misconduct that violate the Constitution and federal law," the Justice Department concluded.

"NOPD's statistics-driven approach to policing appears to contribute to the strong community perception of bias in stops, arrests, and other encounters. Individuals we spoke with, particularly youth, African Americans, ethnic minorities, and members of the LGBT community, told of frequent stops and of being targeted, booked, and arrested for minor infractions. They consistently described how these tactics serve to drive a wedge between the police and the public, antagonizing and alienating members of the community."

The facts supporting this conclusion touched nearly every component of the police department's practices, from the way officers were trained to how and when they stopped suspects, how and when they decided to fire their weapons, even how they put police dogs into use. Police officers often fired without cause, but the department rarely punished its own, the Justice Department found.

"Our review of officer-involved shootings within just the last two years revealed many instances in which NOPD officers used deadly force contrary to NOPD policy or law. Despite the clear policy violations we observed, NOPD has not found that an officer-involved shooting violated policy in at least six years, and NOPD officials we spoke with could recall only one out-of-policy finding even before that time."

The department had long re-assigned officers involved in a shooting to the city's Homicide Section temporarily as the case played out. There, any statements the officer made to internal investigators were adjudged as being "compelled," meaning the statements could not be later used against them should a criminal case arise. "It is difficult to interpret this practice as anything other than a deliberate attempt to make it more difficult to criminally prosecute any officer in these cases," the Justice Department concluded.

The DOJ saw cases where poor training alone could not explain the investigative missteps. Cases where the force failed to lift fingerprints from a handgun found on the scene of shooting or misrepresented witness statements to make it appear they acknowledged having guns. The department's canines were often uncontrollable, attacking their own handlers and suspects. Officers roughed up subjects in handcuffs.

"Even the most serious uses of force, such as officer-involved shootings and in-custody deaths, are investigated inadequately or not at all. NOPD's mishandling of officer-involved shooting investigations was so blatant and egregious that it appeared intentional in some respects."

The most startling findings involved the subjects of officers' fire and aggression. As one Orleans Parish judge told the DOJ, "If you are a black teenager and grew up in New Orleans, I guarantee you have had a bad incident with the police."

In a report filled with sobering findings, the statistical evidence affixed hard numbers upon longstanding complaints of racial profiling, including the following:

- In 2009 NOPD officers arrested five hundred African American males under age seventeen for serious offenses, ranging from homicide to larceny over fifty dollars. In the same time, they arrested eight white males in this age group.
- The department arrested sixty-five African American females, but just one white female in the same period.

Adjusting for population, the black to white arrest ratio was sixteen to one. Nationwide the ratio was three to one. "The level of disparity for youth in New Orleans is so severe and so divergent from nationally reported data that it cannot plausibly be attributed entirely to the underlying rates at which these youth commit crimes, and unquestionably warrants a searching review and a meaningful response from the Department," the 2011 civil rights investigation found.

The NOPD use of force data, examining when officers fired their weapons at subjects, was equally as stark.

- From January 2009 to May 2010 NOPD officers fired their weapons at suspects twenty-seven times. In all twenty-seven cases, the target was black.
- The Justice Department reviewed resisting-arrest charges in cases involving the police force. Of the ninety-six cases on file, eighty one, or 84 percent, involved black citizens.

"What we have found so far is strongly suggestive of differential enforcement for whites and African Americans," the Justice Department concluded. "NOPD personnel at all levels of the Department not only acknowledged that the community perceives racial and ethnic profiling as a significant problem, but some also expressed their own belief that such discriminatory conduct occurs."

New Orleans police officers say there is no targeted enforcement. "I don't necessarily think it's skewed," said Eric Hessler, the former narcotics officer now representing police as a lawyer. "I think that's the unfortunate fact of urban New Orleans. There's a violent crime problem. Violent criminals are usually armed and will do what they need to do to get away."

Hessler recounts an episode from his days on the force, after he handcuffed a young black suspect in the back of his police car. "Shorty, why are you guys always in here messing with us?" the man wanted to know. "Until the violence stops," Hessler came back, "we're going to be in here."

THE VIOLENCE SOMETIMES EBBED, but never stopped. The DOJ demanded change, entering into a formal, court-approved consent decree with the city of New Orleans that would force structural reform. In July 2012, three months after the Danziger 5 were sent away to federal prison, the Department of Justice announced that historic consent decree. "This agreement is the most widespread, wide-ranging in the department's history," Attorney General Eric Holder said, New Orleans mayor Mitch Landrieu at his side. All officers would get special training on use of force and would be barred from stopping people based on their race.

That decree required the force to institute "broad changes in policies and practices related to use of force; stops, searches and arrests; custodial interrogations; photographic line-ups; preventing discriminatory policing." And, it encouraged community engagement, stronger recruitment and training, officer assistance and support, performance evaluations and promotions, and misconduct investigations. It mandated more transparency by the New Orleans Police Department in how it operates and encouraged greater civil oversight.

The consent decree required that a court-appointed monitoring team be established and that the team submit regular reports assessing the department's status in embracing change. The pact would remain in effect, essentially, until the department proved it had systematically changed its ways.

Jim Letten, the local US attorney, called the consent decree a blueprint for moving forward. "This groundbreaking agreement represents a critical milestone in the recovery of New Orleans and a victory for our city, its police department and most of all its citizens," Letten said.

Inside the Big Easy the idea of having the federal government come in drew a mixed response. Some looked at the millions spent probing into every fiber of the force and said the money should be spent elsewhere.

Hessler, the police lawyer, saw potential positive results for the officers on the street. The federal government's watchful eye could ensure the department does a better job of recruiting officers and pays them more. He said NOPD officers, earning $37,000 fresh from the academy, earn less than officers in neighboring departments, anywhere from 6 to 28 percent less. A pay and hiring freeze depleted the ranks of hundreds of officers. "How do you recruit when ninety-five percent of what you read about the New Orleans Police Department across the country is bad?" he asks. The consent decree, done right, could change those perceptions.

The Justice Department lauded the city for cooperating during the review. "We will continue our partnership with Mayor Landrieu, the police department and the community to ensure that the critical reforms are achieved," said Thomas E. Perez, the Civil Rights Division's assistant attorney general, who would later become President Obama's secretary of labor.

That July day Mayor Landrieu ushered Attorney General Holder into the press conference to announce the decree in Gallier Hall, the historic Greek Revival building that once served as city hall.

In January 2013 US district judge Susie Morgan signed the decree.

Within a month, the city was having second thoughts.

Landrieu went to court to try to undo the pact, citing the unexpected costs of administering the decree while upgrading the Orleans Parish Prison, another mandate forced upon the city. The mayor also cited the string of online comments by former federal prosecutor Sal Perricone. Those comments, the mayor argued in court papers, tainted the pact and should serve as a way out.

In September 2013 federal appeals court judges refused to let the city back out. The city knew what it was getting into, the judges ruled. Perricone's comments had no bearing on the consent decree.

That legal tussle aside, the NOPD's top boss was telling the public he advocated reform.

Superintendent Ronal Serpas had launched his police career in New Orleans, working as a top underling to Richard Pennington during the Morial administration when the city cracked down on scofflaws. Next Serpas made reform waves in Nashville, Tennessee, before returning home as the NOPD chief in May 2010. As superintendent, Serpas touted a sixty-five-point reform plan, cited cases like Danziger as a black eye not a rallying point, and said he was working with, not against, the Department of Justice. NOPD had "zero tolerance for untruthfulness," the superintendent said.

"Since May of 2010, Chief Serpas has worked closely with the United States Department of Justice Civil Rights Team to investigate allegations of patterns and practices of unconstitutional policing by the NOPD in the wake of Hurricane Katrina and the years that followed, which has also resulted in the conviction in Federal Court of numerous officers for crimes that resulted in the death of citizens and subsequent cover-up by NOPD officers and supervisors," the superintendent's website said.

In September 2013 Serpas told the community his office was taking concrete steps to build trust. Officers would start wearing body cameras so that each time an allegation of abuse arose, the public could see what really happened. "Imagine a day in the city of New Orleans . . . where every single time we pull over a car, we ask somebody who they are or what they're doing, that the entire incident is audiotaped and videotaped," he said.

The reality proved less noble than the promise. When a Justice Department monitoring team reviewed how often officers turned those body cameras on during use of force events, the results were sobering. Nearly 60 percent of the time no video had been shot or preserved. Jarvis DeBerry, a *Times-Picayune* columnist with an interest in police conduct, wrote a column headlined "What Good Are Body Cameras If NOPD Won't Turn Them On?"

Then in August 2014 Serpas abruptly announced his resignation, leaving on the same day to take a job in academia. Once more the NOPD was looking for a leader to right the ship.

EVEN WITH THE REVOLVING door of the superintendent's office spinning again, the appeals court ruling affirming the consent decree appeared as yet another success in the federal government's quest to quash police corruption in New Orleans. Those victories had not gone unnoticed by the Department of Justice.

Earlier, the DOJ had honored its Danziger team with the Attorney General's Award for Exceptional Service for its successful prosecution of one of the largest police misconduct cases ever brought by the federal government. Cited were deputy chief Bobbi Bernstein, FBI agent William Bezak, special litigation counsel Forrest Christian, trial attorney Cindy K. Chung, and paralegal specialist Steven D. Harrell. Five years earlier prosecutor Bernstein had won the same award for putting away Latino gang members in Los Angeles who targeted blacks.

The police shooters were behind bars. The consent decree was moving forward. Victims were breathing, finally, in relief that the truth was revealed. Even the prosecution team was bestowed with honors.

Still, in one corner of New Orleans, one man remained intently focused on the Danziger Bridge case. As much as anyone—along with, perhaps, the defense attorneys representing the convicted police officers—this man was deeply troubled by the online comments, some posted years earlier, deriding the police actions. As the DOJ was honoring its prosecutors and investigators, this man was busily, quietly putting his own view of those same actions on paper.

By the time he was done, justice would be unsettled once more over the gunfire and bloodshed atop the Danziger Bridge.

CHAPTER 24

"THE INTEREST OF JUSTICE"
The Reversal

ON SEPTEMBER 17, 2013, US district judge Kurt Damian Engelhardt shook the foundation of the case, and the peace of the Danziger families, with a ruling that overturned the federal jury convictions of Robert Faulcon Jr., Kenneth Bowen, Robert Gisevius Jr., Anthony Villavaso II, and Arthur Kaufman. Two years after the victims rejoiced over the jury convictions outside the federal courthouse and in the streets of New Orleans, Engelhardt buried that sense of calm. His 129-page ruling read like a diatribe against the federal team that secured the convictions. Engelhardt's ruling didn't challenge the core of the case: that officers stormed the bridge, firing their mass of weapons at unarmed victims with machine-gun relentlessness, and then covered up their crimes by planting a gun, inventing witnesses, and lying through their collective teeth. None of those hard facts were in dispute.

Instead, in an adjective-filled ruling in which the judge cast himself as the vehicle to safeguard the integrity of the federal jury trial process, Engelhardt dismissed the jurors' convictions largely because of anonymous online comments that had been posted at NOLA.com by staffers employed by the Department of Justice, and because of the prosecutorial "misconduct" he had railed against during the sentencing hearing for the officers, including his view that prosecutors cut sweetheart deals with cooperators.

For the Madison family, which had led the fight to shine a light on the police conduct, it now felt as though Ronald's killing had never been avenged, that Lance had never been truly exonerated for the phony murder charges. Eight years after Katrina the Madison family and the other families of victims were symbolically back atop the Danziger Bridge.

"It was very disappointing for the whole family," said Romell Madison, trying to absorb the judge's ruling. "What we once thought was justice was reversed."

There's no evidence a single juror saw any of the anonymous comments that filled the core of Engelhardt's order or, for that matter, that anyone knew the comments—tacked on to the bottom of stories on the *Times-Picayune* website—had been crafted by DOJ employees. And legally, the judge's criticism of the federal investigative tactics and plea deals was something of a broken record. Those were issues that had already played out in court.

In his ruling Engelhardt said this "carnival type atmosphere" was enough to unfairly prejudice the defense and was the basis for ordering a new trial and erasing the most significant police corruption convictions in the city's history. "Re-trying this case is a very small price to pay in order to protect the validity of the verdict in this case, the institutional integrity of this Court, and the criminal justice system as a whole," Engelhardt wrote on page 127. "In an abundance of caution, the motion must be granted."

His ruling was filled with language rarely used in a judicial document—"shock and dismay," the judge wrote, describing his discoveries of the prosecutorial actions, and "shock and dismay" again.

To the judge the online postings by Sal Perricone and others whom a court-appointed monitor discovered—including a DOJ prosecutor based in Washington who did behind-the-scenes work on the Danziger Bridge case—coupled with what the judge described as "shockingly coercive tactics" by the investigative team were abuses grievous enough to invalidate the jury verdict.

On May 18, 2012, a month after the officers were sentenced to prison for the killing and cover-ups, and two months after Perricone had been exposed as the habitual online poster at NOLA.com, the defense lawyers for the convicted officers filed a motion seeking a new trial. Their bases: an early leak about the pending plea deal with Lieutenant Lohman coupled with the spate of online comments created an unfair environment for the clients. The government "engaged in a secret public relations campaign" designed to sully not only the department but also the officers on trial, aiming to make NOPD the household name for corruption, the defense team argued. This campaign, they said, created an atmosphere that essentially convicted the accused before anyone set foot in the New Orleans federal courtroom.

The motion had seemed a long shot to overturn the case. In an early court hearing, the judge said so himself.

But then the judge, as he described the process in his ruling, began "slowing peeling layers of an onion." Engelhardt did not like what he smelled. His targets were not the police killers but the prosecution team and anyone with DOJ who anonymously posted a comment on the newspaper's website.

In June 2012, little less than a month after the defense lawyers sought to overturn the convictions, Engelhardt ordered the DOJ to investigate the source of the leak that led to news coverage of Lohman's pending plea deal two years earlier; the defense was arguing the leak was part of the larger DOJ campaign to prejudice the trial. A month later the judge directed the Justice Department to produce documents revealing the identities of any staffers who posted online comments over a two-year period. A New Orleans federal prosecutor named Jan Mann was assigned to handle both tasks—the federal government's inquiry of reported internal leaks in the case and the review of any online posting by DOJ staff members during the Danziger case.

That October Judge Engelhardt questioned Perricone in court, and the disgraced prosecutor said the comments were "my little secret." In short, that they were his alone and the Danziger prosecuting team had no role in them and no knowledge he was the habitual critic of the NOPD.

Then, a month later, a lawsuit in another case contended that Jan Mann, the same first assistant US attorney investigating the leak and online postings, had been an online writer herself, using the moniker "eweman." Again the DOJ team, led by prosecutor Bobbi Bernstein, said it was unaware of these anonymous postings.

Engelhardt, troubled by the news and believing the DOJ was too slow in adhering to his order for openness, again directed the department to investigate the leak and postings. This was November 26, 2012, six months after the defense motions. A week later a federal prosecutor from Georgia, John Horn, was assigned as special attorney to the attorney general to head up a deeper review of these issues. Horn would report directly to the federal judge Engelhardt.

Then, suddenly, Justice Department casualties began mounting.

Jim Letten, the lead federal prosecutor in New Orleans, a Republican who remained the longest serving US attorney in the country under Democratic President Obama, resigned December 6, 2012. His resignation came as the online scandal bloomed in the courthouse, touching on cases beyond just the Danziger prosecution, and just as the special prosecutor, Horn, was assigned the review. Then Mann and her husband, another federal prosecutor, retired that same month.

Horn's review included fresh discoveries. In January 2013 he filed a report to the federal judge saying another DOJ attorney, using the online name "Dispos," had filed six postings on the NOLA.com site over four days of the trial. These postings were not the screeds of Perricone, ripping the department. Instead, they were written by a federal attorney based in Washington, DC, asking other online commenters to keep her apprised of the trial developments unfolding in New Orleans. "You are performing a valuable public service!" Dispos wrote to one writer filing online updates. Another time she asked if a frequent commenter would "cover the closings"—the closing arguments at the trial—with updates.

Horn's report did not include the identity behind Dispos, just that the writer was an employee of the Civil Rights Division in Washington. He described the postings as not "inflammatory, critical or prejudicial" and not revealing any grand jury or other nonpublic information.

The judge wanted to know more.

Over the coming months Engelhardt greeted each of Horn's updates with thanks and a directive for more information. He wanted the names behind the identities, particularly that of "Dispos." A month after Horn's first report that January, the judge sent him thirteen follow-up questions to answer. What duties did "Dispos" handle for the DOJ, and who were this person's superiors? What inquiries have been made into other online postings, beyond the NOLA.com site?

Horn came back in March with more answers. The judge was not satisfied.

"The March 29, 2013 First Supplemental Report still conspicuously did not name the Civil Rights Division employee who posted as 'Dispos,' an omission the Court found truly odd, and which further peaked its curiosity," he wrote.

A month later the judge chatted with Horn, pressing for more answers. That day he sent Horn an e-mail with eight more questions to pursue, including "The full name and title of (a) Civil Rights Division employee . . . and (b) the direct supervisor referenced."

The judge soon sent along ten more questions. He wanted to know if anyone at DOJ was editing Horn's reports, suggesting that the reports "expressed advocation in the form of arguably debatable mitigating commentary." He was questioning whether the reports had been edited to advocate for the Department of Justice.

"Please provide the names and title of all persons, as well as a short description of their respective roles, participating in the preparation, including drafting, editing, approving, and/or supervising, of your reports and submissions to the Court," he wrote. Engelhardt wanted names.

Horn assured him he and a colleague were writing the reports and the conclusions were theirs. Yet it was clear the judge remained suspicious of the Department of Justice.

"While accepting Mr. Horn's assertion, the Court nonetheless again expressed its concern and objection to anyone editing his reports to either change or delete facts that have been found, or changing accurate information that was originally included, or adding verbiage in the nature of advocacy to mitigate what findings had been made," he wrote.

The judge's focus could not be clearer. He was on a mission to uproot misconduct by the Feds.

On May 15, 2013, Engelhardt got what he was after: the identity of "Dispos," the writer from DC who had sought updates on the case.

"To the Court's shock and dismay, 'Dispos' eventually was identified . . . as Karla Dobinski, a trial attorney in the Criminal Section of DOJ's Civil Rights Division," his ruling said. Six pages later, Engelhardt again expressed "shock and dismay" that the online poster was an attorney who had a behind-the-scenes role in the Danziger case. Dobinski's task was to ensure that the trial prosecutors did not introduce constitutionally protected evidence or testimony at trial.

There's no evidence jurors ever saw her few postings. And no evidence that those postings influenced the justice delivered in the courtroom. The judge was deeply unsettled by the news.

Her online postings, checking on the case from DC, represented a "wanton reckless course of action," Engelhardt concluded.

The judge wanted more information, sending seven more questions to Horn and a colleague to answer in June, and then, after they did, two more requests that month.

By the end of Engelhardt's judicial inquiry, July 31, 2013, Horn would file five reports to the judge.

This information "had clearly blossomed into a series of newly discovered facts and admissions, unanswered questions, additional apostasies, and a fetor extending far beyond the simple disconcerting notion of a single rogue prosecutor," he concluded.

The "carnival type atmosphere," the judge made clear, had made him deeply rethink the defendants' motion to void the case.

Beyond his ire at the online postings, the judge reiterated his displeasure with the prosecution's deals with the officers-turned-witnesses: Hunter, Hills, Barrios, Lohman, and Lehrmann. In his 129-page order, Engelhardt again chided the government's handling of these plea agreements. He criticized FBI agent Bezak's "frank trial testimony" describing the team's aggressive ways of pushing for evidence. The judge was unsettled by the agency's aggressive approach.

"Pressure is a good thing," Bezak said at trial, "because in my experience, to flip a subject, to get a subject to admit that they've committed a crime, it's not like the movies where you go into a room and three hours later you come out with a confession. In my experience, the only time I've been able to get somebody to admit what they've done is to back them into a corner; to have, you know, a case that is so strong that they have nowhere to go except to admit the truth."

To practiced investigators Bezak's description was no surprise. You press to get the truth, pushing the witnesses as far as you can. The DOJ had honored Bezak's work in doing just that to help uncover the massive cover-up.

To Engelhardt the tactics were further evidence of a federal prosecution that upset the decorum of the justice system.

Likewise, the plea deals Engelhardt and other judges had derided were, law enforcement experts know, part of the process. The deal's fine print is fair game for scrutiny, but that they occur is hardly a secret in the criminal justice system. Sometimes the guilty help save themselves by telling on others. In a case as high stakes as Danziger, with the police blue line as deeply entrenched as the Mississippi River, it took cracking these officers—Hunter, Hills, Barrios, Lohman, and Lehrmann—to unearth the lies.

"A cavalier attitude toward the truth cannot be indulged at any juncture or level," Judge Engelhardt wrote on page 101 of his ruling, speaking specifically about police who pleaded guilty to help save their own skin and to shave time off their prison terms. Some of those officers, Engelhardt believed, fudged the truth on the stand, further tainting the justice in his courtroom.

The judge so deeply questioned Hunter's credibility, for instance, he had voided the jury's guilty verdict that Bowen stomped on Ronald Madison. "In granting Bowen's motion directed to Count X, the Court noted that Hunter's credibility was so grievously called into question at trial that the Court had taken the unprecedented (for the undersigned) step of ordering the production of FBI Agent Bezak's handwritten notes of interviews he conducted with Hunter," Judge Engelhardt wrote.

Hills was given a deal after firing "his side arm twice at the fleeing teenager," fourteen-year-old Leonard Bartholomew, "albeit missing both times." Another officer who pleaded guilty and testified, Robert Barrios, "had been forced to admit guilt and to cooperate despite the fact that he was innocent," the judge wrote, citing the statements of Barrios's wife, who had interrupted a federal press conference to say he had been forced to plead guilty. To the judge, this was another sign of undue prosecutorial pressure, and he noted that Barrios was not called to the stand by prosecutors but by the defense. On the stand, however, Barrios said he made the choice to plead guilty. His wife's outburst was born of the intensity of the moment. "It was just emotions," he said. "It was at the heat of the moment, that it happened in front of her and she just blew up."

Finally, the judge blasted the plea deal handed to Lehrmann, the detective who blurted out the name "Lakeisha," helping to invent a phony police witness, calling the government's handling of this witness just as disturbing. Engelhardt expressed derision that Lehrmann went to work for the federal government, as an agent with the Immigration and Customs Enforcement division in 2006. Lehrmann joined ICE two years before the federal government officially took over the case, and four years before he pleaded guilty to taking part on the cover-up. The judge was not pleased by those developments, noting that Lehrmann remained on the ICE payroll for three months after his guilty plea.

"It was with some astonishment that the Court learned at trial that Lehrmann, having falsified official police records and attempted to frame an innocent man, matriculated into federal law enforcement, seemingly the worst place to put a man guilty of such transgressions so offensive to the administration of justice."

The judge devoted six pages of his ruling to dissecting the prosecution's deals and handling of witnesses.

Yet a simple question loomed. Why? The plea deals had been signed, sealed, and already undergone judicial scrutiny. Those deals, legally, had nothing to do with the appeal at hand. To Engelhardt, they were part of a larger "carnival" atmosphere he felt he had to legally reprimand.

The judge's order devoted thousands of words to online postings jurors may never have seen and to the prosecution deals already hashed out by other federal judges. Very few words of the 129 pages mentioned the police killing of unarmed residents.

"With a history of unprecedented events and acts, consideration of the defendants' motion has taken the Court on a legal odyssey unlike any other," the judge wrote, ". . . to the Court's knowledge, there is no case similar, in nature or scope, to this bizarre and appalling turn of events."

The prosecutorial abuses he saw were "astonishing," Engelhardt concluded.

"This case started as one featuring allegations of brazen abuse of authority, violation of the law, and corruption of the criminal justice system; unfortunately, though the focus has switched from the accused to the accusers, it has continued to be about those very issues. After much reflection, the Court cannot journey as far as it has in this case only to ironically accept grotesque prosecutorial misconduct in the end."

Prosecutors, fighting the defense motion, had said the anonymous postings were "remarkably low profile musings of an unrecognizable citizen."

For the judge, the balance had tipped. A judge can dismiss even the significance of a jury's guilty verdict "if the interest of justice so requires," he wrote. His role, he said, was "safeguarding the integrity of the jury trial."

"This testimony and other recited information illustrate the diseased root that unfortunately casts an ineradicable taint on these convictions," he opined. "The government's actions, and initial lack of candor and credibility thereafter, is like scar tissue that will long evidence infidelity to the principles of ethics, professionalism, and basic fairness and common sense necessary to every criminal prosecution, wherever it should occur in this country."

The judge made a choice. The interest of justice called for a new trial. The totality of the circumstances, Judge Kurt Engelhardt concluded, "is more than this Court can bear."

His ruling elated the defense team and officers, emboldened scores of other defendants then facing prosecution by the Department of Justice, and stunned the relatives of the two residents killed on the bridge that morning.

Sherrel Johnson had sat through each day of the trial, unable to leave the courtroom and needing to hear every word of how and why her child was taken from her. With the ruling, it felt as though JJ was being taken from her again. "Is my son going to get a new lease on life?" she asked, when an Associated Press reporter called her following the judge's ruling. "Is he coming back? What about the mental anguish that these people put us through?"

Engelhardt's sledgehammer against the prosecution triggered immediate, tangible action. A string of criminal defendants filed motions in the federal courthouse, seeking to block evidence or overturn convictions based on online postings in their cases.

One of them was former mayor Ray Nagin, who led the city's response during Hurricane Katrina but was later indicted, and ultimately convicted, for exchanging city business for a string of personal perks, including trips to Jamaica, work-free consulting jobs, and shipments of granite for his countertop company. The former mayor, who took office with no political experience and appointed a populist insider to run the police department, was sentenced to ten years in prison. That sentence earned Nagin distinction as the first mayor in city history imprisoned for corruption.

Four days after the ruling, the *Times-Picayune* reported this swell of events:

When U.S. District Judge Kurt Engelhardt last week granted a new trial for five former police officers convicted in the Danziger Bridge shootings post-Katrina, observers wondered how long it would take for the implications of the order to manifest across the federal courthouse.

The answer came only a couple of days later, as high-profile defendants facing unrelated corruption charges began scrambling to leverage the blistering decision, and the government misconduct it revealed, to help their own cases. The list so far includes . . . Ray Nagin and Stacey Jackson, who headed the Nagin administration's botched effort to fix homes after the storm.

More are expected to come. An attorney for Renee Gill Pratt, the former state representative and New Orleans City Council member convicted of corruption, is already considering a motion for a new trial.

That's only part of the fallout, experts said, from a 129-page order that's forced the Justice Department into a defensive stance across several fronts . . .

Sergeant Archie Kaufman, who helped concoct the script casting police as superheroes and the victims as thugs, he of the "Everything's cool, babe" slogan, was set free from prison while the case awaited a potential retrial.

Lance Madison now worried that the officers who shot his brother and framed him would be free too. "Lance's real concern was, Are they going to get out of jail?" said Shannon Fay, the Baton Rouge attorney who had helped free Lance.

Those defendants were not freed, at least not yet. Because they fired their weapons at the residents, the other four convicted officers, Faulcon, Bowen, Villavaso, and Gisevius, remained behind bars while prosecutors, the defendants, and the families braced for the next legal turn.

The federal government challenged Engelhardt's ruling on appeal. His decision was not grounded in the law, the Justice Department said, arguing that the judge was not objective and should be removed from the case.

Instantly, some in the community of defense lawyers hailed Engelhardt.

"Move over, Emmet Sullivan and Carmac Carney. Add Kurt D. Engelhardt to the Honor Roll roster of federal district judges willing to speak truth to the U.S. Department of Justice. Willing to speak truth and to do something about it," one defense lawyer wrote on a white-collar-defense crime blog. "Judge Engelhardt's opinion is lengthy, but one that should be required reading for every criminal defense attorney who practices in federal court and every DOJ prosecutor throughout the land."

Yet in other legal circles Judge Engelhardt's view failed to gain traction. Other New Orleans officials facing public corruption cases failed in their attempts to latch on to Engelhardt's ruling. Nagin's bid to delay his sentencing, citing the ruling and online comments, was rejected. Another judge dismissed former New Orleans City Council member Renee Gill Pratt's bid for a new trial, ordering her to serve her four-year corruption sentence. Housing official Stacey Jackson failed to parlay the online comments into her own legal gain.

From his office at the National Urban League in New York, former mayor Marc Morial was taken aback by Engelhardt's ruling. Morial was troubled by the online conduct of federal prosecutors in the New Orleans US Attorney's Office. They should be punished, and severely. But revoking the verdict altogether because of anonymous banter posted on the bottom of stories, comments few people saw? "I think the judge overstepped. I think those prosecutors should have been disciplined but by throwing out the case, I think the judge overreached. I think it went too far."

For prosecutors Engelhardt's ruling raised further complicating factors. Detective Lehrmann, the first to cooperate, has served his three-year sentence. Would Lehrmann take the stand again? "Jeff's already worked out his deal. There's nothing over his head," said his lawyer, Davidson Ehle. "What incentive would Jeffrey Lehrmann have to expose himself to those kinds of attacks again?"

Other defendants who pleaded guilty, including Lohman and Barrios, would have served their sentences within two or three years after the judge's ruling. If the appeals dragged on for years, they too would potentially have no reason to testify.

Ehle is among those questioning Engelhardt's ruling. Sure, the prosecutors were "idiots" for engaging in the online ramblings. But he questions the connection between those musings and the trial itself. "I was very surprised by his reasoning," the lawyer said. "I just think it took contorting to arrive at the end result he did. . . . I can tell you there are a lot of folks still scratching their heads."

The judge's ruling continues to delay any action in the civil lawsuits brought by the Madisons, the Bartholomews, Sherrel Johnson, and Jose

Holmes Jr. against the city and police. Once criminal charges were filed those civil cases were put on hold until the criminal case resolved. Engelhardt's order means the families must continue to wait for their day in civil court.

"It's a setback, but I don't know if you can say they expect a whole lot of justice to be served," said the Bartholomew family's lawyer, Edwin Shorty. "I mean, how much justice do you expect when you've been shot by a police officer?"

More than a year after Engelhardt's ruling, the city had taken no affirmative steps to settle their civil case, the lawyer said, raising the question: Will this family have to testify again, once more reliving that morning—both in a potential retrial, and again in a civil case? "Nobody wants to see them testify again," he said.

Also awaiting his day in court is former sergeant Gerard Dugue, who separated his case from the other Danziger defendants and is challenging the government's charges. At Dugue's first trial, Engelhardt declared a mistrial, citing a prosecutorial error in court. No second trial date has been set, and the judge's order vacating the string of guilty verdicts against the other New Orleans officers means Dugue's case continues to be on hold.

Judge Engelhardt did not want to discuss his ruling. "The judge does not give out interviews, especially on that matter," his office said. Perricone, the online commentator whose words factored so heavily into the judge's order, also declined to comment while the case coursed through the appeals court. "I will not have any comment, until that court rules, if ever," he wrote me. "I hope you understand."

Four days after Engelhardt's order the *Washington Post* editorial page weighed in. The newspaper took no issue with criticism of the online comments, calling them "egregious, unjustifiable, unprofessional abuses of authority."

"However, his conclusion that the online postings created a 'prejudicial, poisonous atmosphere' that justified throwing out the convictions is a huge stretch. By that logic, overturning the convictions might also be justified by the TV show 'Treme,' which began airing on HBO 14 months before the officers' trial and depicts the New Orleans police as corrupt, brutal and violent. It's a safe bet that more New Orleanians have seen 'Treme' than the prosecutors' online postings."

The judge acknowledged "there is no evidence that members of the jury saw the online postings in question or any online postings about the case," the paper noted.

"In the howling wind of pre-trial publicity about the case—in print, online, on television and in social media—it is far-fetched to believe that the online rants of the prosecutors, while blatantly improper, were anything more than a speck of dust," the Post continued.

"Judge Engelhardt's emotional 129-page ruling is unconvincing in the extreme. It gives the impression that he is so exasperated and infuriated with prosecutors, for a host of reasons not confined to the online postings that he has thrown out the officers' convictions in a fit of pique."

The editorial closed with a sentiment shared by many in the Bayou city and renewed with the judge's order: "The result is to restore what many people in New Orleans surely wished had receded along with Katrina's floodwaters: an abiding sense that justice has not been done."

AS A NATIONAL CIVIL RIGHTS MOVEMENT STIRS, JUSTICE IS ON HOLD IN NEW ORLEANS

THE MUDDY IMAGES WERE captured by a bystander's cell phone on April 4, 2015. A black man in a bright short-sleeved shirt sprinted for his life, as a white police officer in a dark uniform stood firm, his pistol raised shoulder high and steadied by two hands. *Pop, pop, pop, pop, pop, pop, pop, pop.* Eight shots rang out, each one aimed at Walter L. Scott, a fifty-year-old forklift operator pulled over minutes earlier for a faulty tail light. Scott had jumped out of his car after the traffic stop and, following a tussle with the officer, sought to escape. Officer Michael T. Slager raised his weapon. On his eighth shot, Scott crumpled to the ground, his knees buckling mid-step. Moments later, with Scott's face crushed into a patch of grass and his lifeless arms locked by handcuffs, Slager tossed his Taser near the body, appearing to plant evidence to justify his actions. The world awoke the next day to reports detailing yet another instance of an unarmed black man dying at the hands of a white police officer, this time in North Charleston, South Carolina, a city of some 100,000 that once was home to slave plantations.

In Staten Island, New York, nine months earlier, on July 17, 2014, police accused Eric Garner, forty-three, of illegally selling single cigarettes, a small-time crime. One officer put Garner in a chokehold for fifteen seconds. "I can't breathe," the 350-pound Garner said eleven times, before taking his final breath. Less than a month later, on August 9, 2014, in Ferguson, Missouri, Michael Brown, eighteen, was killed by a gunshot from a twenty-eight-year-old police officer, the traumatic event set in motion all because the teenager had earlier snatched cigarillos from a convenience store. The teenager's death brought national attention to the killing of black residents at the hands of officers in blue.

During the latter months that I researched the shootings on a small bridge in New Orleans six days after Hurricane Katrina, the specter of black victims killed by police stirred outrage across the country—and sparked a new civil rights movement. Protestors marched in the streets, praying for change and sometimes pushing back against police with violence. They carried signs with the message *Black Lives Matter*.

The signs were carried again, this time in Baltimore, as masses shouted those words and raised their fists skyward after another suspicious death of a black man, that of Freddie Gray, who died Sunday, April 19, 2015, a week after suffering a severed spinal cord while in police custody. When he was initially taken in, Gray, twenty-five, winced in pain as police surrounded him. He was then forced into a van for transport to a police station. Forty-five minutes after its initial contact with Gray, the Baltimore PD called for a medic unit to treat his "serious medical distress." Gray's death, and the mystery over how he suffered three broken vertebrae, stoked decades of mistrust between residents and police in the predominantly black city. Suddenly looters were setting police vans afire, hurling rocks toward officers, burning buildings and shattering glass, and shutting down swaths of the city. As the National Guard came to town, the Baltimore Orioles played a baseball game closed to spectators, the empty Camden Yards a surreal consequence of the city's rapid descent.

"Riots Erupt," the *Baltimore Sun* front page declared April 28, twenty-three days after images of Walter Scott's final steps had splashed across newspapers. The *Sun* front page carried three stories that morning, encapsulating the loss and chaos: "Funeral," "Violence," "State of Emergency." Voices, from former Baltimore Ravens superstar Ray Lewis to renowned Baltimore crime chronicler David Simon, urged peace in the streets and a deeper look at police misconduct. President Obama decried the rioters as "criminals and thugs" but said Gray's death warranted a searching review of police and race.

As those events played out, I kept thinking back to the two families hunted on the Danziger Bridge on September 4, 2005, following a police distress call that had nothing to do with these eight residents, each of them black and unarmed. Ten years later, justice for these families remained an open question, a development both sobering and telling.

On April 29, 2015, three weeks after absorbing the front-page images of a tumbling Walter Scott and one day after studying pictures of burning police cars in Baltimore, I returned to New Orleans to hear legal arguments over whether the five police officers convicted at trial in the Danziger Bridge case would receive a new trial. The evidence of their guilt was compelling, detailed in court by other officers who pled guilty and unmasked the truth of that morning, and by the victims who survived the bloodshed. Yet those convictions were put into question by a legal red herring involving online comments written on the local newspaper's website by federal prosecutors.

This April morning, lawyers for the government and the officers made their case before three judges sitting as the US Court of Appeals, Fifth Circuit. The Madison family and Sherrel Johnson sat in the spectators' front row, while prosecutor Bobbi Bernstein and civil lawyer Mary Howell sat one row behind them. They likely were not encouraged by what they heard.

The judges peppered Justice Department lawyer Elizabeth Collery with questions about the online postings of former New Orleans prosecutors Sal Perricone and Jan Mann and Washington DOJ staffer Karla Dobinski, several times interrupting Collery with more questions. The DOJ lawyer agreed the online commentary was out of bounds, with Perricone and Mann using pseudonyms in filling the local newspaper's website with derisive barbs aimed at police in New Orleans in the Danziger case and others. The DOJ's internal watchdog, the Office of Professional Responsibility, concluded those actions damaged the office's integrity. "What Mr. Perricone did was misconduct, and it was reprehensible," Collery said, adding that Mann also had committed "misconduct." Both had been forbidden to practice law in the circuit, and Dobinski, whose comments were far less frequent and much more benign, had become the subject of an internal DOJ review. But, Collery argued, their comments had no bearing on the jurors' verdict, a decision the government said should be reinstated. "Your honor, none of that has anything to do with the jury's verdict in this case," Collery said. "The blogging never affected the trial in the first place."

The appeals court jurists—charged with deciding whether to order a new trial or reinstate the verdict—did not seem convinced. "It still seems a little sleazy, doesn't it?" one judge asked, citing Judge Engelhardt's finding of prosecutorial misconduct in his 129-page order. Billy Gibbens, an appeals attorney for former sergeant Arthur Kaufman, said the cover-up that had occurred was one perpetrated by prosecutors in withholding information from the trial judge, who had to press to get the full story about the online commenting. The appeals court judges did not interrupt Gibbens as they had DOJ's Collery. They did not rule right away, but their behavior left the impression that the events of that Sunday morning on the Danziger Bridge could replay in a second trial.

Ten years after the shootings on the bridge, the victims left court this April morning without resolution in one of the most egregious police civil rights abuses of our lifetime, waiting for the next legal ruling. What does the Danziger case tell us about the similar cases now playing out before a captivated nation? With renewed attention focused on police killings in the nation's cities, I kept returning in my mind to an insight Marc Morial, the former New Orleans mayor and current president of the National Urban League, shared as I interviewed him about the Danziger Bridge case in the summer of 2014.

"In order to convict a police officer, you don't have to convict him beyond a reasonable doubt," Morial said. "You have to convict him beyond all doubt."

I also recalled the words of Edwin Shorty, the Bartholomew family lawyer, as the press for legal closure remained in limbo: "How much justice do you expect when you've been shot by a police officer?"

In other words, when police are the suspects, the barriers to achieving justice are that much higher. Police proponents would argue with that assessment, I am sure. But exploring the shootings on the bridge, and the long, bumpy road to justice that followed, I could come to no other conclusion. Police gunned down innocent victims and built a paper trail of lies to cover their crimes. They were paraded as heroes in the city's streets, beat back state charges, and, following their convictions in federal court, won an appeal on issues having nothing to do with the events of September 4, 2005.

Would the newer wave of police killings level the legal field? In 2014, police officers went uncharged in the deaths of Eric Garner and Michael

Brown. Yet by 2015, a legal tide seemed to shift. Officer Slager faced a murder charge for Walter Scott's death. In Baltimore, a passionate young prosecutor, Marilyn J. Mosby, announced criminal charges against six police officers, three white and three black, in Freddie Gray's death. The police union chastised what it called a rush to judgment and, even as many residents rejoiced in Baltimore's streets, some worried that the state attorney's quest to bring justice had been pushed too quickly. A riveted nation braced for what would come.

The Baltimore charges represented a potential shift in the larger struggle to hold police officers accountable. Mosby made her announcement just eleven days after Freddie Gray's death. In New Orleans, it took state prosecutors more than fifteen months to file charges over the bridge shootings, charges that came only after the families filed a series of lawsuits documenting the horrors. In May 2015, the DOJ announced it would open a civil rights investigation into the Baltimore Police Department, just as it had with the NOPD following the abuses after Hurricane Katrina.

In New Orleans, the families of the victims continue to pray.

Sherrel Johnson awakes each morning to a home without her son, JJ, the seventeen-year-old killed on the bridge. "It's never going to go away," Sherrel told me recently. "I loved him to death and I loved the ground he walked on.

"I wonder what he would be. I wonder 'what if.' My whole life," she said, "is spent wondering."

ACKNOWLEDGMENTS

Shots on the Bridge was constructed with support from many voices. Helene Atwan, director of Beacon Press, saw promise in my proposal and encouraged me to do justice to the events of September 4, 2005. Helene's careful read helped propel these pages, and I thank the entire Beacon Press team for its support. I am indebted to my literary agent, Esmond Harmsworth, of Zachary Shuster Harmsworth, who answered my every query with sage advice.

I owe a debt of gratitude to my fellow writers in the Johns Hopkins University graduate writing program, where I obtained a master's degree while researching this book. Colleagues read early sections and responded with rich feedback. The Hopkins teaching community helped me hone my words and ideas: Cathy Alter, David Everett, Margaret Guroff, and Robert Wilson.

Many people took time to field my questions, sharing recollections or, in some cases, photographs. I thank Romell Madison and the Madison family, Sherrel Johnson, Shannon Fay, Nathan Fisher, Eric Hessler, Marc Morial, Mary Howell, Timothy Meche, Davidson Ehle III, Robin E. Schulberg, Raymond Bigelow, Gary Bizal, Jose Holmes Jr., Townsend Myers, Dylan Utley, Robert Glass, Edwin Shorty Jr., Rafael Goyeneche, Sal Perricone, and Daniel Abel.

Finally, a special thanks to four journalists. Joe Mozingo, a skilled *Los Angeles Times* writer, read my manuscript and offered astute feedback. Michael Sallah, a *Miami Herald* investigative journalist, fielded my calls for advice with one message: keep reporting. Juliet Linderman, my AP colleague who covered portions of the Danziger legal twists while with the *Times-Picayune*, kindly read a draft of these pages and offered feedback. And, I thank my wife and fellow journalist, Beth Reinhard, who is at once my staunchest supporter and sharpest-eyed critic. Beth read my working draft and returned pages blanketed with notes. All of her suggestions came down to one point: let the story tell itself.

ABOUT THE RESEARCH

My research for *Shots on the Bridge* is built from tens of thousands of pages of public documents, interviews with key voices in Louisiana and beyond, and multiple visits to New Orleans, where I strove to recreate the steps of the men and women who found themselves atop the Danziger Bridge the first Sunday after Hurricane Katrina. I explored a trove of sources to better understand these events and the people affected by them. Chief among them is the nearly six thousand pages of trial transcripts in the Department of Justice criminal prosecution of five New Orleans Police Department officers in 2011, *United States of America v. Kenneth Bowen, Robert Gisevius, Robert Faulcon, Anthony Villavaso and Arthur Kaufman*. I obtained this trial transcript, which includes the most detailed description, from the witnesses themselves, of the police shootings on the bridge and the subsequent police cover-up. The transcripts include opening and closing statements from prosecutors and defense attorneys, opening a window into the perspective of each side in this seminal civil rights trial.

Beyond the transcripts, I examined other documents in the *USA v. Bowen et al.* federal case file that, as of March 2015, included more than 1,300 separate filings. These include everything from the initial indictment to the jury verdict, and multiple filings in between and since the case went on appeal. As the defendants faced sentencing, for instance, several family members, friends, and former employers filed letters attesting to their backgrounds; those files helped flesh out some of the profile material of officers. And, the case file included Judge Kurt Engelhardt's 129-page ruling overturning the conviction and ordering a new trial.

Separately, I reviewed filings on the federal prosecution of officers who entered plea deals and agreed to cooperate with the Justice Department. Multiple other public records aided my research. The Madison family, Bartholomew family, Jose Holmes Jr., and Sherrel Johnson all filed civil lawsuits against the city over the harm inflicted on their families; I reviewed the case files, which include narratives fleshing out the events of Sunday, September 4, 2005. I examined the fifty-four page NOPD report, *Attempted Murder of a Police Officer*, New Orleans Police Department case number J-05934-05, filed May 2006, to justify the shootings on the bridge; explored After Action Reports filed by police supervisors detailing the department's readiness for Hurricane Katrina; and filed public records requests to obtain police disciplinary files of the officers accused in the Danziger shootings and cover-up. In response, the city attorney's office in July and September 2013 provided me indexes of Public Integrity Bureau cases involving the officers, which included the disposition of each case. But the city said some of the case-file narratives I sought "could not be located and are presumed destroyed in the 2005 flooding of the Public Integrity Bureau headquarters following Hurricane Katrina." Among other records, I reviewed the 737-page Senate report produced in 2006, *Hurricane Katrina: A Nation Still Unprepared*, and the Justice Department Civil Rights Division report *Investigation of the New Orleans Police Department*, published March 16, 2011.

Paper documents alone cannot tell the story of September 4, 2005, as officers raced to the bridge after a distress call six days after Hurricane Katrina devastated their city. I made five reporting trips to Louisiana, starting in April 2012, when I traveled to New Orleans to attend the sentencing of five officers who stood trial and were convicted by a jury. The federal courtroom downtown was packed—with supporters of the officers filling one side and supporters of the victims the other. Before the judge issued sentences, police officers, family, and friends of the officers addressed the court; relatives of the two citizens killed and four wounded spoke too. This hearing enhanced my understanding of the case and, while in New Orleans, I made contact with key participants. In that trip and four subsequent visits to Louisiana in 2013, 2014, and 2015, I retraced the path the officers and citizens took that morning to reach the Danziger Bridge. I reached out to the family victims and their attorneys and to the attorneys or families of the officers convicted of the shooting and cover-up. My research was enriched by interviews with people affected by the shootings on the bridge—from a mother whose son was killed that morning to a former mayor who urged federal authorities to launch a civil rights review, to a former judge who dismissed an earlier state case against police, to a former NOPD narcotics officer turned lawyer for police, to the brother of another victim killed on the bridge.

The case posed reporting challenges, particularly after Judge Engelhardt, in September 2013, vacated the jury verdict, essentially putting justice on hold and raising the specter of a second trial. Citing the judge's ruling, several story subjects said they could not discuss the case while it remained on appeal. I sought interviews with the officers convicted in federal court, both the group of five who entered guilty pleas and the separate group of five who stood trial in New Orleans. Their attorneys, without exception, said their clients would not discuss the case while it remained pending. Likewise, officials with the FBI and US Attorney's Office declined multiple interview requests. Those hurdles made my reporting trips to Louisiana all the more important. I spent hours retracing the steps officers and residents took that Sunday morning to reach the Danziger Bridge, following the respective paths as they were brought together by nature and fate. I researched the backgrounds of victims and police officers through multiple sources, obtaining autopsies, a death certificate, and funeral brochure for some victims; and letters family and friends wrote on behalf of officers, along with internal police investigative files. This research, coupled with thousands of documents from the trial and other interviews, allowed me to recreate the narrative produced here.

I was first drawn to this case in August 2011 when I happened to read an Associated Press account of the federal jury conviction of the officers. Reading the story that afternoon in my newsroom in Washington, DC, I knew instantly these events were worthy of a book. Over the next three-plus years, as I learned more about the events that morning, the lives ensnared atop the bridge, and the circuitous path of justice that followed, my initial instinct evolved into a firm conviction. My retelling of those events benefited from media coverage of the Danziger Bridge case, starting with that first AP story along with coverage of prior police corruption trials involving the NOPD, often in the New Orleans *Times-Picayune*.

Here, chapter by chapter, I will describe the sources of my research for *Shots on the Bridge*.

PROLOGUE

I relied on multiple, disparate sources to create this opening section of the book, which begins with officers awaiting their call at the Crystal Palace six days after Hurricane Katrina and ends with victims on the bridge, the cover-up in bloom, and families seeking justice.

My visits to New Orleans allowed me to describe both the seven-lane Danziger Bridge and the Crystal Palace, and I reviewed an online brochure describing the banquet hall. Details describing Hurricane Katrina come from myriad sources. The description of the levee collapse and 911 emergency calls come from *Hurricane Katrina: A Nation Still Unprepared* (2006), the report the US Senate issued a year after the hurricane. Images of families trying to survive the hurricane come from photographs taken by the Associated Press and other media. The quote "This whole place is going under water!" comes from a YouTube video of a storm chaser navigating New Orleans the morning of Katrina, *Katrina New Orleans Sunrise*, August 29, 2005, https://www.youtube.com/watch?v=QpTlukPbHnY.

The Senate report is the source for the section describing how unprepared New Orleans was for Katrina. The quote beginning, "There were no rules in place . . ." comes from an interview with Eric Hessler, a former New Orleans Police Department officer who now is a lawyer for police, on September 12, 2014.

The description of the police arsenal that morning comes from court documents in the criminal case, *USA v. Bowen et al.*, 2010, and testimony from officers called to the stand. Information involving past disciplinary cases involving officers comes from the Public Integrity Bureau files I obtained from the city of New Orleans under a public records request.

Newspaper and other material are sources for prior police corruption cases including the case against "Robocop," the Kim Anh restaurant shooting, and the Algiers 7. Notable among them was a November 11, 2010, story retracing the Algiers 7 brutality case by Brendan McCarthy in the *Times-Picayune*. A 1998 Human Rights Watch report, *Shielded from Justice: Police Brutality and Accountability in the United States*, included a recounting of the case involving Robocop.

Information on the department's prior civil rights record comes largely from the Justice Department's *Investigation of the New Orleans Police Department*, published in March 2011 by the DOJ's Civil Rights Division.

The quote in the paragraph about the police brotherhood, describing how the officers served without adequate food, leadership, or shelter, comes from defense lawyer Paul Fleming Jr.'s opening statement June 27, 2011, at the trial of Officer Robert Faulcon Jr. and other officers, *USA v. Bowen et al.* The quotes in the paragraph to follow, citing the traumatic days of patrolling after Katrina, come from the sentencing hearing for the police officers in that same case on April 2012, which I attended. The description of the scene atop the bridge and the shooting of citizens comes from testimony at the trial of the officers in *USA v. Bowen et al.* The quote about the cover-up—"I knew this was a bullshit story"—also came out during the trial. The racial divide exposed in early police reports was gleaned from an interview on September 10, 2014, with Timothy Meche, the lawyer for officer Anthony Villavaso, and explored in cross-examination of a police witness at trial.

CHAPTER 1 *A Family's Bond, a Threatening Storm*

I relied on interviews and research to describe the Madison family. Part of the family profile information comes from Romell Madison, the oldest of the Madison children, who was kind enough to sit down with me in between treating patients at his dental office during one of my visits to New Orleans in 2013. Dr. Madison later fielded some of my follow-up calls, including one shortly after the federal judge overturned the jury convictions.

Other material about the family comes from myriad sources. I obtained "A Celebration of Life" booklets produced for the funerals of Ronald Curtis Madison in 2005 and family patriarch James Madison in 2002. These tributes included information on the histories of Ronald, his father, and the Madison family. They also included photographs that helped me describe this stalwart New Orleans family.

I visited the Madison family neighborhood in the Academy Park section of New Orleans, allowing me to describe the community and put its location in context of the events that would later unfold on the bridge. Information from the Zillow website helped me further describe the family home and the price of residences in this quiet community. Likewise, I was able to describe Romell Madison's office after a personal visit there. Other family history was gathered from a biographical interview with Romell by writer Tina Gianoulis in 2004.

Trial testimony provided further information about Ronald Madison and how his brothers and sisters watched over him as he rode his bike around the block. Interviews with Romell and paperwork in the family's civil lawsuit against the city of New Orleans explained the family's decision to leave Ronald behind with his brother Lance and the family dogs. Jacquelyn Madison Brown's description of her brother Ronald came during her testimony at trial July 7, 2011. Trial testimony in the criminal case against police also provided some of the profile information about Lance Madison. I researched his listing on the roster of the NFL Kansas City Chiefs.

CHAPTER 2 *A Mother's Last Chance*

This chapter is built largely from a two-hour interview with Sherrel Johnson, the mother of James Brissette Jr., on April 5, 2012, the day after officers were sentenced for their crimes. Sherrel, desperate for answers, followed every step of the case against the officers. She was eager to speak of her son, and I have strived to capture the essence of a teen on the cusp of adulthood.

JJ's sister, Andrea Celestine, testified at trial in the federal prosecution of officers on July 6, 2011, and that testimony enriched this chapter, including the Spic and Span anecdote and the username for his first e-mail address. This chapter also benefited from the profile "Mother of Danziger Victim Still Seeking Justice," by Edmund W. Lewis in the *Louisiana Weekly*, August 29, 2011.

CHAPTER 3 *Eleven People, One Van, a Second-Floor Apartment*

This chapter, focusing on the Bartholomew family and their nephew Jose Holmes Jr., is built largely from trial testimony by family members in the prosecution of officers in *USA v. Bowen et al.* in New Orleans federal court. Susan Bartholomew was the first to testify, on June 27, 2011, and other family members testified over the following weeks of trial, with daughter Lesha testifying last, on July 21, 2011. Lawsuits against the city by the Bartholomew family, *Bartholomew v. The City of New Orleans et al.*, 2006, and separately by Jose Holmes Jr., *Holmes v. City of New Orleans et al.*, 2006, provide further details.

CHAPTER 4 *An Officer, a Baby Due, a Choice*

Of the five officers prosecuted at trial, only Robert Faulcon Jr. took the stand. His testimony in *USA v. Bowen et al.* on July 27, 2011—describing his personal career arc, the challenges of patrolling New Orleans, and the unprecedented turmoil in the days after Hurricane Katrina—form the framework of this chapter. Other sources flesh out the profile material. One is a letter on Faulcon's behalf by his wife, Stacey Scineaux, written to the sentencing judge on November 20, 2011. At Faulcon's sentencing on April 4, 2012, his father addressed the court, and his words likewise helped describe the officer. At trial one of Faulcon's defense attorneys sketched a family history in opening remarks June 27, 2011, and that information is also cited here.

I obtained information about the commendations Faulcon earned while on duty, including when he responded after a citizen pulled a gun on a mail carrier on June 4, 2003, from the statements written on his behalf before sentencing. Separately, I obtained Public Integrity Bureau disciplinary files from the city of New Orleans.

CHAPTER 5 *A City Under Water*

Descriptions of how the families and Officer Faulcon navigated the first days after the storm come in part from testimony in the criminal trial, *USA v. Bowen et al.*, such as Lance Madison's testimony describing how he and brother Ronald made their way from Lance's condo to their brother's dental office. During a trip to New Orleans, I retraced the path from Lance's condo to the dental office. My visit to the dental office helped me describe its setting. Other information about the brothers' ordeal comes from the Madisons' civil lawsuit against police, *Madison v. City of New Orleans et al.*, 2006, and from research and interviews with Lance Madison's criminal attorneys Nathan Fisher and Shannon Fay. I first spoke with Nathan Fisher on October 21, 2013, interviewed Shannon Fay in Louisiana on November 12, 2013, and interviewed Fisher and Fay again on September 5, 2014. Four months later, Nathan S. Fisher died, at age 72, after a long battle with cancer.

Information about Sherrel and JJ comes from my interview with Sherrel Johnson in April 2012. Descriptions of the Bartholomew family's days after Katrina come from testimony at trial by Susan Bartholomew and other members of the family, including nephew Jose Holmes Jr.'s testimony in *USA v. Bowen et al.*, on June 29, 2011.

Officer Faulcon's testimony described his days after the hurricane flooded the city and the steps he took to survive. The conversation with his father is cited in a letter Robert Faulcon Sr. wrote the court on August 23, 2010. I obtained other information to describe the police tension in those tortuous days, including the August 30, 2005, police report on the shooting of Officer Kevin Thomas a day after Hurricane Katrina's landfall. *Times-Picayune* coverage of the Thomas case provided other details. Police officers who served during Katrina spoke at the sentencing for officers on April 4, 2012, which I attended, and some of their quotes are reflected here.

Information about Katrina's destruction on New Orleans, and how even the local Homeland Security director was largely helpless to aid victims, comes from the US Senate report *Hurricane Katrina: A Nation Still Unprepared*. Other information describing Katrina's landfall comes from sources including a hurricane timeline compiled in *Wikipedia* and multiple media reports at the time of the storm's arrival, including coverage by the New Orleans *Times-Picayune*, CBS News, Reuters, and the *Los Angeles Times*.

CHAPTER 6 *108*

Jennifer Dupree, the officer who placed the initial 108 distress call over the police radio, testified at trial on June 29, 2011, in the case of *USA v. Bowen et al.*; that testimony forms the framework for part of this chapter. I reviewed a New Orleans Police Department district map to help me describe the boundaries of police districts. Testimony from other trial witnesses, including officers Robert Faulcon Jr., Robert Barrios, and Michael Hunter, provided further information about the police pursuit after the 108 call. The section describing officer Kenneth Bowen's second degree murder case is built from *Times-Picayune* coverage of that shooting, and from Public Integrity Bureau records I obtained from the city of New Orleans law department. Trial testimony from Susan Bartholomew and Lance Madison describe the respective families' paths to the bridge that morning.

CHAPTER 7 *The Shots on the Bridge*

This chapter is built largely from documents in the federal prosecution against five officers and from trial testimony, including from Michael

Hunter on July 6, 7, and 27, 2011, in the case of *USA v. Bowen et al.*
It is also built from testimony from multiple other witnesses, including
Lance Madison on July 8, 2011, along with Susan Bartholomew, her children Lesha and Little Leonard, and nephew Jose Holmes Jr. Other trial
testimony in *USA v. Bowen et al.* comes from officers on the scene that
morning: Kevin Bryan, Robert Barrios, Ignatius Hills, and Taj Magee,
citizen witnesses Morrell Johnson and Robert Rickman, paramedic Stanton Doyle Arnold, and Louisiana State Police sergeant Michael Christopher Baron.

The description of the shootings on the bridge is also built from the
opening statement on June 27, 2011, by prosecutor Barbara "Bobbi"
Bernstein in the federal trial, including details on which officers fired
at which victims. Bernstein's narrative includes details described in the
federal government's indictment of the officers in *USA v. Bowen et al.*
and information from the fifty-four page police report, *Attempted Murder of a Police Officer*, New Orleans Police Department case number
J-05934-05, justifying the shootings, such as the description of victims
shot on the bridge.

CHAPTER 8   *Triage*

This chapter is built from the courtroom testimony of Craig Robert
Thompson, the surgeon who was living at the West Jefferson Medical
Center after Katrina destroyed his home, and who treated the four shooting victims and helped save their lives. Thompson testified on July 12,
2011, in the case of *USA v. Bowen et al.*

CHAPTER 9   *NOPD Triage*

Weeks after the hurricane's landfall, New Orleans Police Department
supervisors filed reports describing how ill-prepared the city was for
Katrina. I reviewed these memos, filed in October 2005 and titled
"Hurricane Katrina After Action Reports," along with testimony Captain Timothy P. Bayard made to the US Senate Committee on Homeland Security and Governmental Affairs on January 30, 2006. Bayard's

testimony described the hazards New Orleans police encountered in the days after Katrina.

CHAPTER 10 *The Cover-Up*

Lieutenant Michael Lohman was the lead supervisor on hand when the 108 call went out. A well-regarded officer, Lohman arrived at the bridge and was immediately troubled by what he saw: victims bloodied on the ground, but unarmed. Lohman's description of the cover-up, outlined in his testimony at the *USA v. Bowen et al.* trial on June 28 and 29, 2011, after he agreed to cooperate with authorities, is one key source for this chapter. Another officer who took part in the cover-up but later entered a plea agreement and testified is Detective Jeffrey Lehrmann. His testimony at trial July 11, 2011, further describing the cover-up, is also cited here. Trial testimony on July 5, 2011, from another officer on the bridge, Kevin Bryan, who did not fire his gun and was not charged, provides further detail explaining how the cover-up played out at NOPD. Testimony on July 6 and 7, 2011, from a cooperating witness who did fire, Michael Hunter, describes how the police story took form. Hunter was also called to the stand by the defense on July 27, 2011.

Public documents enhance this chapter. Information describing the lack of investigative zeal that morning comes from the federal indictment of officers filed by the US Department of Justice in July 2010 in the case of *USA v. Bowen et al.* The fullest description of the official police account comes from the fifty-four-page report the department filed to explain the shootings *Attempted Murder of a Police Officer*, New Orleans Police Department case number J-05934-05; the report detailed the questioning of officers by fellow NOPD officers. I also obtained a two-page press release issued one month after the shooting, dated October 4, 2005, and headlined "Update Information on Two Suspects Fatally Wounded and Four Others Wounded," describing the citizens as criminals and the police as victims. Other details of the cover-up were presented in court during prosecutor Bernstein's opening statement.

Details of Robert Faulcon's decision to leave the force and go to trucking school come from his courtroom testimony on July 27, 2011, in the case of *USA v. Bowen et al.*

CHAPTER 11 *Shock, Funerals, Police Visits—and a Family's Quest for Answers*

Information about the Madison family comes from multiple sources, including an interview with Romell Madison on July 12, 2013, in New Orleans. Quotes from sister Jacquelyn were made during her trial testimony July 7, 2011, in the case of *USA v. Bowen et al.* During my research, I discovered a piece of writing Jacquelyn's daughter, Brittney Brown, compiled for a Xavier University five-year commemoration of Hurricane Katrina, *Hurricane Katrina 5 Years Later: Reflections from the Xavier Family.* Her powerful passage included details of the family's escape from New Orleans and of the dreams that haunted her mother in the days before the storm. Officer Ignatius Hills had been a patient of Doctor Madison as a child, a fact gleaned from Hills's testimony on June 30, 2011, in *USA v. Bowen et al.*

I interviewed Nathan Fisher and Shannon Fay, the Baton Rouge lawyers who represented Lance Madison after he was charged with attempted murder and who helped set him free, in 2013 and 2014. Fisher and Fay generously shared their experience working this case, which came when Fay was still in law school. Lance's testimony on July 8, 2011, in the case of *USA v. Bowen et al.* detailed his experience moving from facility to facility after his arrest.

I reviewed the transcript of the bond court hearing held September 28, 2005, at the Hunt Correctional Facility following Lance's arrest and incarceration, including sworn testimony by Sergeant Arthur Kaufman. In that hearing magistrate judge Gerard Hansen expressed doubt that Lance fired at anyone. I researched Hansen's background as a judge, including a profile that aired October 20, 2013, by WWLTV-4 in New Orleans upon his retirement. In September 2014, I visited the family Sno-Bliz stand in New Orleans where he had worked as a child. I also obtained a one-page police report, called a Gist Sheet, that came under question at the bond hearing after Lance's lawyers noticed two sets of police handwriting on the single page. The Gist Sheet, dated September 4, 2005, is New Orleans Police Department Item Number I-0003-05.

Details about Ronald Madison's funeral come from the booklet "A Celebration of Life" on November 2, 2005. Also obtained were Ronald's death certificate, prepared by the State of Louisiana in November 2005, and the autopsy conducted by the Orleans Parish coroner on September 14, 2005.

The section describing the Bartholomew family's ordeal after the shooting comes from trial testimony by mother Susan Bartholomew and nephew Jose Holmes Jr. The scene describing Leonard Bartholomew IV's reunion with his family is built from his testimony in the federal court case on July 5, 2011, and that of cousin Jose.

Multiple sources helped me describe what happened to Sherrel Johnson and her family in the months after Hurricane Katrina. Details about her son-in-law Lawrence Celestine's death come from a Louisiana Fourth Circuit Court of Appeals ruling in Andrea Celestine's lawsuit against the city, *Celestine v. City of New Orleans*, 2010, and from media accounts including a *Times-Picayune* editorial published November 17, 2010, "Probing the Death of New Orleans Police Officer Lawrence Celestine." Researching Sherrel Johnson's quest to find her son JJ, I explored a state of Louisiana Department of Public Health program meant to connect missing loved ones after Katrina, including a press release, "Identification of Katrina Victims Continues," published December 30, 2005. My understanding of that public health program was enriched by a *New York Times* article by Shaila Dewan, "Storm's Missing: Lives Not Lost but Disconnected," published March 1, 2006. I also reviewed the autopsy report performed on James Brissette Jr. on September 14, 2005, by the Orleans Parish Coroner's Office, with Brissette initially described as "unknown black male."

Other information about JJ came from an interview with Sherrel in April 2012, the *Louisiana Weekly* profile in 2011 that included the fact that she enrolled her son in school in Tennessee, and daughter Andrea's court testimony in *USA v. Bowen et al.*

CHAPTER 12 *Victims Shine a Legal Light*

Before the district attorney filed charges against the officers on the bridge, the families made the first public accusations that the police killed unarmed residents and concocted a cover-up. Those contentions were made in a series of lawsuits filed against the city, Mayor Ray Nagin, police superintendent Edwin P. Compass III, and others. I reviewed those lawsuits, which frame a key portion of this chapter. Also obtained was the fifty-four-page police report defending the shootings in May 2006. The quote from former superintendent Compass—"Give me some love!"—came from "Deluged," a January 9, 2006, *New Yorker* article by writer Dan Baum.

This chapter benefited from interviews with Shannon Fay and Nathan Fisher, the defense team for Lance Madison, and talks with Mary Howell, the Madison family's civil attorney, who has a decades-long history of representing citizens abused by police in New Orleans and who shared some of that history with me. I began reaching out to Howell in November 2011 and met the lawyer at her New Orleans law office September 4, 2014.

I obtained a statement Lesha Bartholomew wrote after the shootings on the bridge and quote from it here. Edwin Shorty Jr., the lawyer for the Bartholomew family, had read Lesha's statement in court during the sentencing for officers in the *USA v. Bowen et al.* case on April 4, 2012, a hearing I attended. Shorty shared Lesha's statement with me in September 2013, and later answered my questions during an interview October 1, 2014.

During my research, I obtained a letter from a Winn-Dixie regional vice president to Lance Madison, returning his fifty-dollar check from September 18, 2006.

The section on the city's colorful history of district attorneys benefited from a *New York* magazine profile of one of the state's most colorful politicians, headlined "Edwin Edwards Will Live Forever," written by Mark Jacobson in July 2014.

CHAPTER 13 *The District Attorney Brings Charges—and the Police Brotherhood Fights Back*

Three days after Christmas 2006, the office of Orleans Parish district attorney Eddie Jordan brought murder and attempted murder charges against seven New Orleans Police Department officers who exited the Budget truck with weapons drawn. Those charges—filed December 28, 2006, in the case *State of Louisiana v. Robert Barrios, Kenneth Bowen, Robert Faulcon, Robert Gisevius, Ignatius Hills, Michael Hunter, and Anthony Villavaso*—open this chapter, along with details from the DA's decision to formally drop charges against Lance Madison. I obtained those files detailing charges brought by the state grand jury.

Interviews with Madison's defense team helped describe how the family pushed the DA to find the truth, and this section benefited from reports in the *Times-Picayune* and Associated Press describing the various reactions in New Orleans to this significant legal turn.

During my research, I gathered information describing the police response to the charges, including messages written on Signal 26, an online message board "by and for the NOPD." I reviewed dispatches written by Mike Glasser, the president of the Police Association of New Orleans, including one sent December 30, 2006, urging police supporters to rally around the troops as they faced their booking on the charges days after New Year 2007.

I recreated the scene of the accused officers walking to their booking surrounded by swarms of supporters from viewing Associated Press and *Times-Picayune* photographs taken that day.

CHAPTER 14 *From Narcotics Cop to Police Attorney*

Eric Hessler served seventeen years as an NOPD officer and then became a lawyer representing the police union and Sergeant Robert Gisevius Jr., one of the accused officers. His perspective, as a former street officer who served under multiple police bosses, and current defense attorney in the Danziger Bridge case, was relevant. I interviewed Hessler at length September 12, 2014, and conducted a follow-up interview January 13, 2015. His views frame this chapter. They are coupled with court information I researched on cases when Hessler served the force, including a Louisiana Fourth Circuit Court of Appeal ruling in a civil lawsuit brought over his 2000 police shooting incident, *Robertson et al. v. Hessler and the New Orleans Police Department*, filed March 19, 2000.

CHAPTER 15 *Judicial Ties, Prosecutorial Error, and the NOPD Walks Free*

Researching the state case brought against the seven officers, I reviewed a report filed January 5, 2007 by Judge Raymond Bigelow shortly after the case landed on his docket in which he disclosed ties between his office and the defense team. On September 3, 2014, I interviewed Bigelow about those ties and his decision to grant bond for the officers accused of murder. Bigelow's view—that he disclosed the connections and bond and would have stepped aside if the DA raised an issue—is reflected in this chapter. The DA did not immediately seek to remove him, and Bigelow stayed on the case. I made five attempts to interview former DA Eddie Jordan from July 30 to September 4, 2014; he never responded. Likewise, I contacted the assistant DA who handled the case, Dustin Davis, on November 27, 2013. By then a federal prosecutor in Miami, Davis said he could not discuss an active case.

Even as the state case moved ahead, some voices, notably the Madison family, were pressing for a federal civil rights investigation. They didn't believe the case would resolve locally and urged the Justice Department to step in. One voice pushing for federal intervention was former New Orleans mayor Marc Morial, whom I interviewed at length two times in 2014, on August 27 and September 5. His views, as a former mayor who advocated police reform and now as president of the National Urban League, were insightful.

I had earlier obtained Morial's letter to the Congressional Black Caucus written on February 20, 2007, urging action and obtained similar letters written in early 2007 by sources ranging from the National Dental Association to a group called Safe Streets/Strong Communities. Assessing the police department's history of abuses, I contacted Rafael Goyeneche III, president of the nonprofit Metropolitan Crime Commission, located in New Orleans, which works to root out corruption, and interviewed him on August 27, 2014. I reached former police superintendent Edwin P. Compass III and interviewed him briefly September 4, 2014. Statistics about the racial makeup of the police force and the city in 2007 come from research conducted for me by my colleague at the Associated Press Jack Gillum. It was built from public documents, including a racial breakdown of the force and city.

Ultimately, in August 2008, Judge Bigelow dismissed the charges against the officers, citing prosecutorial error. The Justice Department, indeed, stepped in. My research was aided by *Times-Picayune* coverage of the judicial turns in 2008.

CHAPTER 16 *Conspiracy Cracks Under Federal Glare*

By late 2008 the Justice Department and FBI were officially on the case. The chapter describing their pursuit is built in part from testimony from an FBI agent who helped crack open the cover-up, William Be-zak. Bezak testified over three days of trial in the case of *USA v. Bowen et al.*, on July 18, 19, and 21, 2011. I researched the background of the lead federal civil rights prosecutor, Bobbi Bernstein, examining cases she brought against Los Angeles gang members and hate crime purvey-ors in Illinois. Those cases were detailed in Department of Justice court filings and press releases involving the Illinois hate crime prosecution in 2008, and the Los Angeles gang hate crime prosecuted in 2006. Ber-nstein described her view of the significance of the Danziger Bridge case during a sentencing hearing for Officer Michael Hunter on No-vember 5, 2011, another transcript I reviewed during the research. This section, explaining federal involvement in a case formally dismissed in state court, included interviews with Lance Madison's defense team and court testimony from another FBI official, Kelly Bryson, then based in New Orleans. Bryson testified in the *USA v. Bowen et al.* federal prose-cution on July 12, 2011.

I interviewed Davidson Ehle III, the attorney for the first officer to cooperate with the federal government, Detective Jeffrey Lehrmann, on September 19, 2014. I interviewed Townsend Myers, the lawyer for Hunter, who became the first shooter to agree to cooperate with the Jus-tice Department investigation, on December 3, 2014, and learned more about Hunter's decision through his courtroom testimony in 2011. Also, I interviewed Robert Glass, the lawyer for patrolman Robert Barrios, an-other officer to enter a plea, on October 6, 2014. Barrios's testimony in 2011 in *USA v. Bowen et al.* provided further insight into how his case unfolded. A July 18, 2011, *Times-Picayune* story, "Danziger Bridge Jury Hears Cops' Profanity-Laced, Secretly Taped Conversation," included excerpts from the secret tape-recording of Sergeant Gisevius.

CHAPTER 17 *USA v. Bowen, Gisevius, Faulcon, Villavaso, Kaufman and Dugue*

In July 2010, nearly five years after the shots on the bridge, the Justice Department secured indictments against four shooters and two supervi-sors, building a case constructed with the help of plea deals from other officers. The thirty-two-page grand jury indictment, *USA v. Bowen et al.*, details those charges and helps frame this chapter. I reviewed press statements issued by DOJ following the indictment and comments from defense lawyers reported at the time in the local media.

I also obtained a thirty-five-page police Public Integrity Bureau file on the Danziger Bridge case, dated September 27, 2011, that included a lengthy chronology of events and the departmental status of each accused officer. I obtained the file through a 2013 public records request to the city of New Orleans. Since the inquiry occurred after the hurricane, this was one of the PIB narrative files not destroyed by the storm.

CHAPTER 18 *Judgment Time, Judicial Questions—and an Officer's Shame*

This chapter, detailing the sentences given to the officers who cooperated with the Justice Department, is built largely from federal court files on their cases, including transcripts of sentencing hearings. One of those cases involved Detective Jeffrey Lehrmann; I obtained US district judge Lance M. Africk's eight-page order, dated September 15, 2011, detailing his reasons for denying the government's motion to reduce Lehrmann's prison sentence. A second hearing involved Officer Michael Hunter, held November 5, 2011, in the court of US district judge Sarah S. Vance; and a third concerned Officer Ignatius Hills, who expressed shame for his role in the shootings and cover-up. Hills was sentenced October 5, 2011, before US district judge Martin L. C. Feldman. The chapter includes courtroom comments from judges overseeing those cases; several took issue with the length of sentences given the cooperating witnesses. I researched biographical information on those judges on judicial and university websites, such as a Tulane University Law School profile of Judge Lance Africk, and in published reports, including coverage of Judge Martin Feldman's ruling involving the Deepwater Horizon.

CHAPTER 19 *In the Courtroom*

This chapter is built largely from the 2011 trial transcript in the case of *USA v. Bowen et al.*, including detailed opening statements by both the prosecution and the defense teams. I obtained the list of exhibits introduced at trial and in 2014 interviewed defense lawyers for several of the officers, including Eric Hessler, representing Robert Gisevius Jr., and

Timothy Meche, representing Anthony Villavaso II. I reviewed the jury verdict and described the public reaction to this significant civil rights prosecution. I interviewed Sherrel Johnson about the verdict in April 2012, examined photographs taken by the Associated Press following the verdict, and read coverage in the *Times-Picayune* and New Orleans *Independent Examiner*. On August 18, 2011, NPR aired a segment about the case, citing the reaction Bobbi Bernstein received as she walked the streets following the convictions: "Verdict in Katrina Shooting Buoys Police Reform."

Some profile information on the officers, including Sergeant Gisevius and Officer Villavaso, came from letters later filed to the court on their behalf by family and friends in late 2011 and early 2012 as the officers awaited sentencing in the federal prosecution on April 4, 2012. In addition, I cite the police department's own finding of wrongdoing by officers, spelled out in the Public Integrity Bureau files I obtained.

CHAPTER 20 *The Online Commentators*

Details about the online comments made by prosecutor Sal Perricone are documented in federal judge Kurt Engelhardt's September 17, 2013, order dismissing the jury verdicts. I sought Perricone's perspective in December 2014, and the retired prosecutor answered some questions about his background and shared information about his overall online activities. He also pointed me to his LinkedIn profile, which included further biographical information. But he said he could not discuss the Danziger case while it remained in court. This chapter also benefited from coverage of the Perricone comments in the *Times-Picayune* and a detailed *Los Angeles Times* story published September 10, 2014 by writer Timothy M. Phelps, "His Own Words Help Bring Down New Orleans Prosecutor."

CHAPTER 21 *From Prep School to Politics to Danziger*

Researching Kurt Damian Engelhardt, the judge who would make waves by dismissing the jury verdict, I found a Q&A profile of Engelhardt published in January 2013 by the *Crimson Shield*, the online magazine of Brother Martin High School. Headlined "From Band to Bench," the profile included background about the judge's political and career path and his judicial outlook.

I researched other background on the judge, including his career arc from a Metairie law firm to the bench, from sources including the New Orleans Bar Association and Federal Judicial Center, and I observed Engelhardt in action during the sentencing of officers in April 2012.

CHAPTER 22 *Judgment Day*

Early into my research the five convicted officers came up for sentencing. I flew to New Orleans to attend the sentencing, a reporting trip that formed the framework of this chapter. I also reviewed the court transcript of the April 4, 2012, hearing, which included comments from victims, lawyers, police officers, and the parents of Kenneth Bowen and Robert Faulcon Jr.

I obtained the statement Lance Madison read in court at sentencing and statements written by Lesha Bartholomew and Jose Holmes Jr., whose passages were read by their lawyers, Edwin Shorty Jr. and Gary Bizal. An AP photograph of Susan Bartholomew helped me set the scene. I interviewed Robin E. Schulberg, the federal public defender for Sergeant Kenneth Bowen, on September 19, 2014. The figure on the percent of cases that end in plea deals comes from a 2011 Bureau of Justice Assistance report, *Plea and Charge Bargaining*.

CHAPTER 23 *The Consent Decree*

This chapter is built largely from the Justice Department's March 16, 2011, report *Investigation of the New Orleans Police Department* detailing civil rights violations in the NOPD and urging reform. The material also includes reports issued by the Justice Department detailing the consent decree it later entered into with the city. They include a July 24, 2012, civil action brought by the US government against the city police department and a 124-page pact, "Consent Decree Regarding the New Orleans Police Department," approved January 11, 2003, by US district judge Susie Morgan and signed by parties including police superintendent Ronal W. Serpas and Mayor Mitchell Landrieu.

My research into prior abuse cases benefited from coverage of the Len Davis case in the *Times-Picayune*, including a December 21, 2011 story, "Hit Man Who Killed Kim Groves in 1994 Is Sentenced to Life in Prison," and in the 1998 Human Rights Watch report exploring police abuses nationwide. The section exploring the Henry Glover case was built from a review of Justice Department statements on the case and media reports, notably "Law and Disorder," a fifty-six minute broadcast on PBS *Frontline* on August 25, 2010, produced with ProPublica and the *Times-Picayune*. Newspaper clips described NOPD officer Antoinette Frank's death row case, including a May 23, 2007, story in the *Times-Picayune* headlined "Death Penalty Upheld for N.O. Ex-Cop." Lawyer Mary Howell shared insights about the history of police abuses in an interview.

I reviewed then superintendent Ronal Serpas's website maintained by the NOPD urging reform in the ranks, and I benefited from a *Times-Picayune* column September 7, 2014, by Jarvis DeBerry exploring truths behind the department's promise to wear body cameras. Preparing to visit New Orleans in September 2014, I filed an interview request with Superintendent Serpas on July 31, 2014, seeking to schedule a meeting to hear his perspective on the Danziger Bridge case and larger civil rights issues. I followed up repeatedly with police public affairs officials to set the interview, to no avail. Then on August 18, 2014, Serpas suddenly resigned. I followed up, seeking to interview his interim replacement, Lieutenant Michael Harrison. The department refused the request.

CHAPTER 24 *"The Interests of Justice"*

More than two years into my research, US district judge Kurt Engelhardt ordered an abrupt reversal in the case, overturning jurors' conviction of the five officers and ordering a new trial. Much of this chapter is built from this 129-page ruling September 17, 2013. I spoke with key players about the order, including Romell Madison, former mayor Marc Morial, Bartholomew family lawyer Edwin Shorty Jr., and Davidson Ehle III, lawyer for Detective Jeffrey Lehrmann, the first NOPD officer to cooperate. Civil lawyer Mary Howell described in a 2014 interview how defendants in other public corruption prosecutions failed to cash in on Engelhardt's ruling in their cases. The chapter includes court testimony from Officer

Robert Barrios and FBI agent William Bezak in the *USA v. Bowen et al.* federal prosecution; legal analysis on attorney blogs, including the *White Collar Crime Prof Blog*, September 18, 2013; and a *Washington Post* editorial four days after the ruling, "No Justice in New Orleans Danziger Bridge Case."

INDEX